ROVER SD1

THE FULL STORY 1976–1986

James Taylor

OTHER TITLES IN THE CROWOOD AUTOCLASSICS SERIES

ROVER SD1

THE FULL STORY 1976–1986

James Taylor

THE CROWOOD PRESS

First published in 2016 by
The Crowood Press Ltd
Ramsbury, Marlborough
Wiltshire SN8 2HR

enquiries@crowood.com

www.crowood.com

Paperback edition 2021

British Library Cataloguing-in-Publication Data
A catalogue record for this book is available from the British Library.

ISBN 978 1 78500 926 6

Disclaimer
Every reasonable effort has been made to trace and credit illustration copyright holders. If you own the copyright to an image appearing in this book and have not been credited, please contact the publisher, who will be pleased to add a credit in any future edition.

About the author
James Taylor has been writing professionally about cars since the late 1970s, and his interests embrace a wide range of older cars of all makes and nationalities, as well as classic buses, lorries and military vehicles. He has written several books about BMW cars within a portfolio that now consists of well over 130 books. Many of these have been definitive one-make or one-model titles, including a number for Crowood. He has also written for enthusiast magazines in several countries, has translated books from foreign languages, and makes sure he always has something old and interesting in the garage.

Designed and typeset by Guy Croton Publishing Services, Tonbridge, Kent
Cover design by Maggie Mellett
Printed and bound in India by Parksons Graphics Pvt. Ltd., Mumbai.

CONTENTS

INTRODUCTION AND ACKNOWLEDGEMENTS

The Rover SD1 was the new kid on the block when I first became interested in the products of the Rover Company. By that time, of course, there was no Rover Company any more, and Rover was just a name used for the car that fitted into a certain bracket within the British Leyland range hierarchy. However, the SD1 had been largely designed by the old Rover team, and was built at the old Rover factory in Solihull. So it felt like a real Rover, and I joined many others in hoping that it would become a success.

As we now know, the multiple problems that beset British Leyland in the 1970s meant that the SD1 never really fulfilled its true potential. Quality was so variable that buying one in the first five or so years of its life was a calculated risk. I have owned four of them, and one of them (a late model 2600) was a really good car. That says it all, really.

Yet the SD1 was fundamentally an excellent design. I followed its progress throughout its production life, and was lucky enough to meet and interview several people involved with it. So I owe a major debt of gratitude to Gordon Bashford, Spen King and David Bache, all of whom enlightened me about the background to the design. There were many others, too, some of them acknowledged in the narrative.

In putting this book together, I also drew on the knowledge and enthusiasm of several other people. In particular, I must single out Ian Elliott, who had the unenviable task of preparing most of the UK press releases about the car, and who saw much of the story from the inside. On the enthusiast side, thanks go to Chris Powell, historian of the Rover SD1 Club, whose research provided valuable information that was not available elsewhere. I am very grateful also to Paddy Carpenter, of the Police Vehicle Enthusiasts' Club, for providing a number of photographs relating to his specialism. Several overseas enthusiasts added their knowledge of SD1 sales outside the UK, so thanks go to Rob Turner and Tony Cope in Australia, John Miller in New Zealand, Rob Hafkamp in the Netherlands and to João Peres and José Almeida in Portugal. Others have certainly added to my knowledge over the years, and I'm sorry I can't remember and list every one of them here.

Most of the photographs and illustrations have come from my own collection. However, I must add special thanks to photographer Craig Pusey for the photographs of his Vitesse and to Lisa Stevens at the British Motor Industry Heritage Trust in Gaydon. Please note that all publicity material and photographs originally produced for or by the British Leyland Motor Corporation and British Leyland Ltd, including all its subsidiary companies, is now the copyright of the British Motor Industry Heritage Trust; anyone wishing to reuse this material should contact BMIHT for permission to do so.
Finally, in quoting VINs I have gone for additional clarity by inserting a hyphen between the prefix code and the serial number (eg SARRRWVF3AA-000803). This hyphen does not appear on the identification plates or on documents associated with the cars.

James Taylor
Oxfordshire
October 2015

The oldest-known Rover SD1. Wearing chassis number five and registration number JYF 227N, the car was built in 1975 as a pre-production model.

CHAPTER ONE

EARLY DEVELOPMENT, 1969–1972

THE ROVER STORY

Although the Rover name remained constant during the production life of the SD1, the Rover identity was in an almost constant state of change. To document those changes in detail as they occurred would unnecessarily complicate the story of the car, so they are explained here as a way of providing some context for the story that follows.

Rover began making cars in 1904, and before that had been involved in the bicycle and sewing machine industries in Coventry. However, it was not until the 1930s that the company really made its name, under the guidance of brothers Spencer Wilks as managing director and Maurice Wilks as chief engineer. Rover became makers of 'One of Britain's Fine Cars', as their publicity material put it, building discreet and elegant cars of high quality that were largely aimed at the professional middle classes.

This business continued after the Second World War when Rover moved to Solihull, to the south-east of Birmingham. The company was still guided by the Wilks brothers, and a younger generation of the Wilks family now joined as well. From 1948, car sales were supplemented by the light commercial Land Rover, which was a worldwide success and generated the profits that allowed the Rover Company to remain a viable, if small, independent car manufacturer.

Mergers – Rover within BLMC, 1967–1974

Rover's days of independence were over by the time the Rover SD1 was launched in 1976. Prompted by mergers elsewhere in the British motor industry that threatened their body supplies, in early 1967 Rover sought refuge within the Leyland bus and truck group, which already owned car maker Standard-Triumph. During 1968, Leyland then merged with the other major British car combine, the British Motor Corporation (BMC), to become the British Leyland Motor Corporation (BLMC). Although little changed in the way Rover was run for a few years, it was inevitable that belonging to a larger combine, which united several formerly rival British car makers, would have an effect.

The first effects became apparent around the turn of the decade. In 1969, Rover's planned new sports car (known as the P9 and due to be built under the Alvis name) was cancelled because of a clash with Jaguar. A further clash with Jaguar saw the new Rover P8 saloon cancelled in 1971. In 1972, Rover and Triumph were effectively merged when it became clear that their planned new executive-class saloons would compete against one another – and out of this merger came the car that would become the SD1.

Meanwhile, Rover's management was changing, too, as the Wilks family lost its hold on the remains of the company and British Leyland began to hire professional managers to run its various businesses. The enormous and varied problems that would beset British Leyland over the next two decades made the subsequent history of Rover and its identity both complex and hard to follow.

In 1972, Rover ceased to exist as a separate business and became part of the merged Rover Triumph, which was a business within the British Leyland combine that now became known as the Specialist Division. The Specialist Division was headed by Bill Davis between 1972 and 1973, although other key management figures were former Rover men: Bernard Jackman became managing director and Spen King (a nephew of the Wilks brothers) became chief engineer. Former Rover man A. B. Smith became chairman in 1973, and then in 1974 former Triumph engineer John Lloyd became chief engineer when Spen King was moved to take overall charge of car engineering for British Leyland.

Nationalization – the British Leyland and BL Years, 1975–1986

BLMC's losses had been mounting and at the end of 1974 the company turned to the British government for financial support to remain open and safeguard jobs. As a result, the company was nationalized; the last BLMC board meeting was on 24 April 1975 and the company was renamed British Leyland Ltd. Within that renamed company, the plan was for the individual car marques to be suppressed and for their operations to be united as Leyland Cars, which was run by Derek Whittaker. Within Leyland Cars, the former Rover, Triumph and Jaguar marques were to be united as the Large Cars division, which was run by Tony Thompson. This was the position when the SD1 was launched in 1976; formally, it was the new Rover from Leyland Cars, and all the publicity at the time of the launch made that very clear.

The years 1976 and 1977 saw some changes in top management, of which the most far-reaching was the appointment of Michael Edwardes (a highly competent professional manager rather than a car man) as chairman and CEO of British Leyland. Edwardes inherited a company that was once again on the verge of collapse, thanks to falling overseas sales and an epidemic of strikes within the workforce, and from July 1978 he made further changes.

British Leyland Ltd now became BL Ltd, and its Leyland Cars division became BL Cars Ltd. Jaguar Rover Triumph (JRT) was formed as a division of BL Cars, and Land Rover Ltd was created as a separate company. Head of BL Cars was Ray Horrocks, William Pratt Thompson was appointed head of JRT and Jeff Herbert became head of Rover Triumph. Jaguar was separately managed, and the plans to suppress the old marque names were abandoned. From 1980, JRT was split up yet again, and the Rover marque became part of the Light-Medium Cars division.

This arrangement lasted for two more years. Michael Edwardes, by now knighted for his achievement in keeping the company afloat, left in 1982 and a further reorganization ensued. Under Sir Austin Bide as chairman of BL Ltd, all the car marques except Jaguar and Land Rover were united as Austin Rover, with Harold Musgrove as its chairman. So it was as part of this group that the Rover name survived to the end of SD1 production in 1986. Yet, although the Rover Company had long since ceased to exist, the Rover name and what it stood for remained valuable business assets. As a result, in 1986, when there was yet another reorganization of what had begun as BLMC, the entire company was renamed the Rover Group under its new chairman, Graham Day.

FROM P10 TO SD1 VIA RD1

The chain of events that led to the introduction of the Rover SD1 in 1976 was immensely complicated, and was affected from the beginning by the twists and turns in the saga of British Leyland outlined above. Even though it carried the hugely respected name of Rover, the car was not purely a Rover design but a hybrid of Rover and Triumph design and components. Legend has it that there was a suggestion at one stage that it should not be a Rover at all but should instead carry Leyland badges.

Despite its excellent reputation for building well-made quality cars, Rover in the early 1960s was still a small independent manufacturer. Profits from booming Land Rover sales had enabled the company to move at the end of the 1950s from a single model range (coded P4) to two model ranges (P4 and P5), and then in 1963 to replace the older of those ranges with a very advanced new design (P6). However, this left the company with the problem of replacing both the P5 and the P6 ranges in the first half of the 1970s. Design and engineering resources were finite, so Rover planned to replace both model ranges with a single design. Work on what was known internally as the P8 began in 1964, making use of design and engineering resources freed up after the P6 had entered production in 1963.

However, the Rover plans were disrupted by corporate changes in the middle of the decade. Early in 1967, Rover merged with the Leyland truck and bus combine, which already owned Standard-Triumph and now planned to enlarge its car interests to rival the large BMC group, which owned Austin and Morris. BMC had also acquired Jaguar in 1966, and Leyland now planned to use Rover to counter the big Jaguar saloons.

One result of this was that Leyland instructed Rover to abandon work on the smaller-engined versions of the P8 and to focus on it as a large car that would compete with the Jaguars. This move left Rover with no replacement in prospect for its P6 range, so the company aimed to begin work on such a car as soon as designers and engineers could be spared from the P8 project.

As things were to turn out, the P8 never became a production model. After the Leyland-BMC merger that created BLMC in 1968, Rover found itself part of the same group as Jaguar. Belatedly recognizing the danger of competition between the two marques, the British Leyland board gave priority to Jaguar as a maker of large luxury saloons, and the

ROVER CAR PROJECTS, 1945–1976

The P code appears in Rover documents for the first time in 1945. There is no documented evidence for its significance, but a strong possibility is that it stood for Post-war.

- P Model P was a series of mock-ups designed to modernize the appearance of the pre-war Rovers for post-war use. It was abandoned.
- P2 The P2 name has been applied to the revived pre-war models produced between December 1945 and early 1948.
- P3 An interim model, using pre-war styling on a new chassis with a new engine. It lasted in production from 1948 to 1949.
- P4 A completely restyled car, introduced in 1949 and built until 1964. Its chassis and engine were both developments of the P3 type.
- P5 Built alongside the P4 from 1958, this car was Rover's first monocoque design and sold at a higher price. From 1967, it was re-engined with the ex-Buick V8 to become P5B, and remained in production until 1973.
- P6 Built from 1963 to 1977, P6 was an advanced design that replaced P4 as the 'junior' Rover. From 1968, the V8-engined 3500 became available alongside the original 4-cylinder car.
- P7 Originally planned as a re-engined P6, P7 became a series of development prototypes that fed into both P8 and P10 projects.
- P8 Planned as the replacement for the P5B with a 1971 start to production, P8 was cancelled at the last minute because of a feared clash with the Jaguar XJ6; the makers of both cars were by this stage united under British Leyland.
- P9 This was a short-lived plan to productionize the BS (also known as P6BS), an experimental mid-engined sports coupé designed within Rover. It was swiftly cancelled because of a feared clash with the Jaguar E-type.
- P10 The last of the P-series Rover projects, P10 was intended as the replacement for the 'junior' Rover, the P6. It later became RT1 and then SD1 soon afterwards.

P8 project was cancelled in 1971, a matter of weeks before the first pre-production cars were to be built.

The Rover people were not to know that back in 1969, by which time the bulk of the design and development had been completed on P8, and resources began to free up again. So they turned to the next new project, which was to design the replacement for the smaller Rover, the P6.

Preliminary Ideas

The replacement for the P6 gained the internal code name P10. Several of the Rover designers had already had some informal preliminary thoughts about such a car, including Gordon Bashford, whose responsibility was chassis design and overall packaging, and David Bache, who ran the styling studio. However, the first formal briefing about P10 was not held until March 1969.

For the next twelve months, as P8 progressed towards production and work associated with aspects of its design diminished, the key players at Rover developed their preliminary ideas about P10. Then, in March 1970, the scope of the programme was formally outlined. P10 was to have two basic models, one being a four-door saloon with seating for four or five people, the other being a two-door sports

A full-size buck of the gull-wing body centre section was built from wood in the styling studio, and some work was done on interior layout as well. This photograph was taken in January 1971.

Not all the early sketches for P10 showed gull-wing designs; this one is clearly a four-door saloon, but it does have the fastback design that Bache wanted. Although undated, this sketch certainly existed by mid-1970.

Rover's David Bache was keen from the start to make the new Rover saloon a hatchback design. He was also keen on the idea of gull-wing doors. Both ideas are incorporated in this early sketch by Ian Beech, a member of the Rover styling studio.

saloon that used the same mechanical elements and the same structural elements as far as possible.

The project now began to gather pace. In June 1970, Gordon Bashford's package drawings, which provided the basic dimensions for the car, were passed to David Bache's styling studios so that work on the car's shape could begin. That same month, Rover's chief engine designer, Jack Swaine, was asked to begin work on the engines for the new car. At the top of the range would be the existing 3.5-litre V8 type, below which would be a 4-cylinder based on the existing P6 engine and available in two different states of tune; some later handwritten notes by Gordon Bashford show that a 2.8-litre version of the V8 engine (known as the Redcap type, but never built) was also under consideration as the companion engine to the 4-cylinders. According to the minutes of the Rover board meeting held on 1 June 1970, P10 was expected to replace P6 in autumn 1974.

Gordon Bashford remembered that his team was attracted to the idea of front-wheel drive in the early stages of P10. Rex Marvin, who then ran development at Rover, told Karen Pender (*Rover SD1: The Complete Story*) that some feasibility work was done on braking for such a design, using a front-wheel-drive BMC 1800 car. However, the designers reasoned that the space-saving advantages in a car of P10's size were minimal and a poor trade-off against the known handling qualities of a rear-wheel-drive layout. So rear-wheel drive was chosen.

There were also discussions in the second half of 1970 about the actual construction of P10. Rover had used base-unit construction for the P6, where unstressed outer panels were hung on a stressed inner structure. This brought the advantage that a facelift could be achieved relatively cheaply – although no major change was in fact ever made to the P6 panels during the car's production life. Discussions with Pressed Steel Fisher at Cowley, who were Rover's existing body suppliers, showed that a monocoque would be more expensive than a base unit; the actual figures were £6 per unit more on a production of 600 bodies per week. This issue seems not to have been resolved before the P10 project moved into its next phase during 1971.

By December 1970, the most promising of the initial P10 design themes had been turned into a number of 3/10 scale models. This one had different treatments of the theme on each side.

These pictures show the other side of the 3/10 scale model. A first reaction from today's perspective is that the shape resembles a Citroën CX – although that car would not reach the market until five years later and cannot have been an inspiration. The 'flying buttress' shape at the rear gives the appearance of a fastback, although the design is actually for a three-box saloon!

Dated October 1970, this was an early P10 interior mock-up. It was clear that the dashboard was always going to be very different from earlier Rover designs.

THE SKELETAL ROVER BADGE

The design for a new Rover badge, with a skeletal style replacing the traditional Viking ship image, seems to have entered the picture towards the end of 1969. It was in evidence on the full-size P8 saloon mock-up photographed in early December that year and appeared again on the full-size mock-up for the P9 sports car photographed in March 1970.

The original design was done by Ian Beech in the styling department and it was approved and promoted by David Bache. It seems to have been unaltered when it was adopted for the production SD1 in 1976. However, traditionalists regretted the loss of the familiar Viking ship emblem and from 1979 Rover reinstated a version of this on the nose of the SD1.

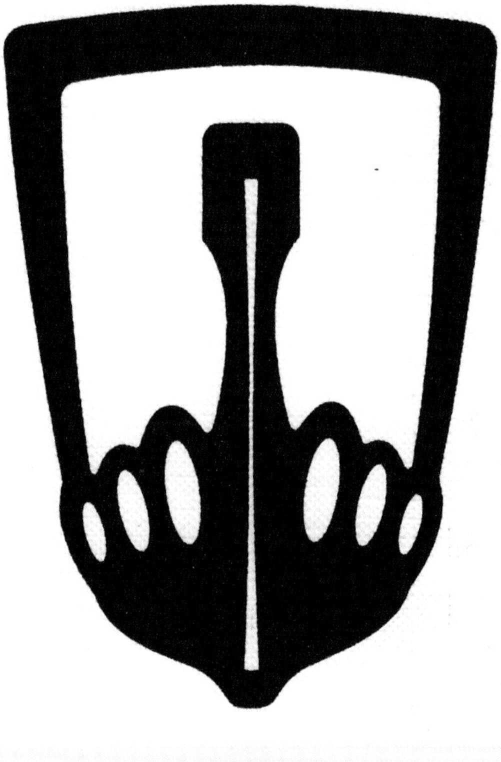

The infamous 'skeletal' Rover badge pre-dated the SD1 by several years but never appeared on any other production Rover.

Meanwhile, David Bache was coming up with his first ideas for the new car. He had been keen for some time on the idea of a large hatchback design, inspired no doubt by the practicality of cars such as the Renault 16 and the Austin Maxi, the latter to be released during 1969. So his first thoughts were of fastback designs, and early design sketches showed how he wanted to combine these with smooth, flowing lines. By the standards of the late 1960s, they were remarkably advanced shapes.

Bache was also keen on the idea of gull-wing doors, which were hinged in the roof panel and opened upwards. Theoretically these offered greater ease of access than conventional side-hinged doors, and such doors could be fully opened in tight parking spaces where a conventional door can not. It was also true that gull-wing doors still brought the wow factor to a design, thanks mainly to their pioneering use on the legendary Mercedes-Benz 300SL coupé of 1954. Bache was so convinced of the idea's merits that he had a full-size gull-wing buck built in the styling studio. Combining these doors with a hatchback on a saloon car such as the P10 was to be would certainly have given the car an image of advanced design, and that fitted well with the image of Rover at the time.

The Engine that Never Was – Rover's dohc Slant-4

Rover's plan for P10 was to have three models, with the existing 3.5-litre V8 engine in the top model and the two cheaper models having a new 4-cylinder engine in two different states of tune. This new engine was to be a twin-cam, 16-valve derivative of the 4-cylinder ohc used in the Rover 2000. Work began on it in June 1970, when Jack Swaine entrusted the project to Dave Wall. At that stage, engine production for sales was scheduled to start in May 1974.

Dave Wall reflected on the design of the engine in a 1987 interview with the author, which was subsequently published in the February 1988 issue of *Thoroughbred & Classic Cars* magazine.

Working with Wall were Ray Cobley, who was responsible for the detail design of the cylinder block, and Jack Read, who dealt with the cylinder head. There was a tight design brief, which included using the existing P6 2000 engine transfer line tooling in order to save costs and ensuring that the engine would meet the known and likely future requirements of exhaust emissions control regulations, particularly in the USA.

With the basic parameters of the cylinder block already defined by the need to use P6 tooling, Wall decided to go for more power by using a twin-ohc cylinder head with 4 valves per cylinder. The 16-valve head was also expected to convey an image of high performance and technical sophistication at a time when the 4-valve configuration was still largely exclusive to racing engines. Although the requirement was for 145bhp in the more powerful version of the engine (and 120bhp in the entry-level version), Wall's team aimed for 170bhp in the prototypes in order to give an adequate margin for further development and, of course, for losses caused by changes to meet future exhaust emissions regulations.

Although the 16-valve head was clearly going to be the key feature of the new engine, some significant alterations were also made to the block. The bore was enlarged from 85.7mm to 90.5mm, partly as a way of making room for more valve area in the combustion chambers, and this took the capacity up to 2204cc from the original 1978cc. This was the origin of the enlarged bore adopted when the 2000 engine was uprated for the P6 2200 models in 1973, which had that same 2204cc capacity.

The block was also redeveloped in conjunction with the Wolverhampton-based C & B Smith Foundry, using thin-wall castings to save weight and solid sides in place of the leak-prone side cover plates of the P6 engine. The P10 was being planned with a low bonnet line, so the engine was designed to be installed with a slant of 35 degrees to the vertical, which in turn demanded a new sump design.

Around £10,000 was invested in pattern equipment to manufacture the revised block, which was both lighter and more rigid than the original. However, the open sides of the P6 block had allowed the water jacket to be cast into a design without core holes, and the new solid-side design required another way to achieve this. So Wall's team redesigned the block to use wet liners, so that the water jacket could be supported during casting through the top of the block; the liners would then be inserted later. The plan was to hold them in position with Loctite, a feature that was tested on a number of modified Land Rover engines and proved very effective.

A chain drive was chosen for the camshafts because of the need to keep as close as possible to the original P6 engine design. The camshafts themselves ran directly in cast housings, which had cast weirs to ensure adequate cam lubrication on start-up. One great advantage of the new engine was that it was possible to change both inlet and exhaust timing by simply rotating the camshafts relative to one another, which gave great flexibility in tuning for control of exhaust emissions.

Taper-seat spark plugs were positioned centrally in the classic twin-cam tradition and the inlet ports were completely separated, while the exhausts were siamesed just before the outlet facing and a phased exhaust manifold was designed. Rover sought advice on gas flow from Walter Hassan and Harry Mundy at Jaguar (who were of course colleagues under British Leyland), and the inlet tract shape incorporated on the prototype engines derived from Mundy's suggestions.

The valves themselves had an included angle of 44 degrees and single, high-rate springs. Actuation was through bucket tappets with shim adjustment, similar to the P6 design. Tappet clearance adjustment was simpler than on the parent engine, however, because the camshafts on the dohc engine could be removed without undoing the head bolts. The light weight of the valve gear allowed the engine to rev hard, and the target 170bhp was eventually achieved at 7,000rpm. This gave the new engine a very different character from its P6 parent, which achieved its peak power at 5,000rpm or 5,500rpm, according to tune.

P10 was intended to have a 16-valve derivative of the Rover 2000's 4-cylinder engine. This was prototype no. 3, which survived with large intake trumpets. These would not have been fitted in production as they negated the saving in height achieved by canting the block over to one side.

The slant-4 engine under renovation in the British Motor Industry Heritage Trust (BMIHT) workshops during 1980. The engine is lying on its left side.

The cylinder head of the slant-4 engine clearly shows the sixteen valve ports and eight exhaust ports.

Wall and his team spent several months on the design of the P10 engine before the prototypes were commissioned and bench-testing began. By then, it had been agreed that there would be a twin-carburettor version for the mid-range car, and a single-carburettor version for the entry-level model. Prototype work started with the more powerful variant because this would be subjected to greater stresses, and it soon became clear that the SU carburettors traditionally favoured by Rover were not up to the task. Some consideration was given to using Webers, but the final choice fell on a pair of twin-choke Dellortos, largely because the supplier could offer the necessary technical back-up immediately.

On the bench, top-end power turned out to be poor while bottom-end torque was much better than expected. This imbalance was traced to overlong inlet tracts resulting from a miscalculation in the design of the water-heated manifold. Rather than hold things up while the manifold was redesigned and remanufactured, Wall's team decided to try the engine out with fuel injection, which looked like a particularly good idea because it would also save the under-bonnet space otherwise taken up by the manifold. It was with a Bosch L-Jetronic system that the engine achieved its design target of 170bhp. Note, by way of comparison, that the 3.5-litre V8 would have just 155bhp in carburettor form for the first production SD1 models.

However, decisions made outside the engine development section now affected the outcome. Before the 16-valve engine had clocked up 200 hours on the test bed, British Leyland management had decided that the two lower-level engines in the new Rover would be developments of the existing Triumph 6-cylinder type. So the new Rover engine – by this stage described in some documents as the RT1 engine – was axed in May 1971 before it had ever run in a car.

Dave Wall believed that five or six prototype engines had been built. At least seven cylinder heads were cast, in line with Rover's usual policy of making about 25 per cent spares, and all of these had the twin-carburettor manifold; the single-carburettor version never progressed beyond the drawing board. Only one engine ever ran on a test bed and that, still with its fuel injection system, now belongs to the museum collection at the Heritage Motor Centre in Gaydon after being restored in 1980. The other engines went to Dr Weaving at Jaguar in connection with his work on exhaust emissions control; cylinder head no. 5 still existed in 1987 when it was owned by Land Rover; and Wall himself bought no. 7 as a memento.

Changes within the structure of British Leyland and its constituent companies in the early 1970s meant that the dohc slant-4 engine commissioned for the P10 became the last engine ever to be designed by the old Rover Company.

The Triumph Dimension

While Rover were forging ahead with their P10 design and its new slant-4 engine, Triumph were also working on a new saloon design. The Rover 2000 and Triumph 2000 had been introduced at the same time in 1963 and had always been rivals in the executive-car market sector. The Rover had a staid but efficient 4-cylinder engine; the Triumph had a 6-cylinder engine and a rather more sporting demeanour. It was no surprise at all that Triumph should be thinking of replacing their saloon at about the same time as Rover.

At this stage, British Leyland had not fully got to grips with the variety of marques now under their control, and in most cases the formerly independent companies continued to behave as if they were still independent. So it was some time before top management dealt with the ridiculous situation of having two of its brands designing new cars to be launched at the same time in the same sector of the market. Whether each company knew of the other's plans is a moot point, but if they had it is highly unlikely that they would have done anything to resolve the situation; the old rivalries died hard.

Triumph's new executive saloon was code-named Puma, and some of its engineering was to be shared with other planned new Triumph models. However, by all accounts its design was running behind that of the Rover. The full story is unclear, but it looks as if Triumph had drawn up their own design, apparently with the aid of freelance designer William Towns, who had once worked at Rover. From some time in 1970, Triumph had also started work on a new 6-cylinder engine that was intended to power this car and others; the top model of the Puma range would meanwhile have a version of the Triumph V8, which would first be seen later that year in the Triumph Stag grand tourer.

This was the Triumph Puma proposal that lost out to David Bache's P10 themes at the design contest held in February 1971. The large glass area was striking, but the rear treatment looks a little odd in this picture.

RT1 – the Compromise Solution

By late 1970, top management had realized what was happening. Triumph were told that Rover would have priority in the executive-saloon class and that they could not continue with the Puma project. This may not have been too upsetting to Triumph's chief engineer, Spen King, who was fundamentally a Rover man and had been transferred to the rival marque in 1968, when BLMC made its first attempts to reorganize the multiple companies now under its control. The message probably got through to Rover fairly quickly, too, because Rover's technical director Peter Wilks was actually Spen King's cousin and the two had worked closely together on many Rover projects, including the P6 saloon.

Nevertheless, Triumph were not completely shut out of the new project. An internal design competition between the two divisions was arranged culminating in a presentation in February 1971 at which chairman Sir Donald Stokes and finance director John Barber made their choice between the styling models for the Rover P10 and the Triumph Puma. Triumph's proposal was the rather elegant but somewhat conventional three-box saloon design drawn up by William Towns; David Bache at Rover prepared at least six scale models, five of them hatchbacks and one a three-box saloon. There seems to have been no major disagreement between Barber and Stokes, who decided that Leyland's new executive car should be based on Bache's more advanced-looking hatchback designs.

More changes followed swiftly. The British Leyland board decided on a classic compromise for the powertrains of the two cars, which would see the top model powered by Rover's V8 and the mid-range and entry-level cars powered by the new Triumph 6-cylinder engine. Triumph were also working on a new five-speed gearbox and would be allowed to continue with that, not least because it could have future applications in cars throughout the British Leyland organization. From this point on, the new executive-car project was renamed RT1 to reflect the co-operation between the two divisions.

Further down the line, Rover and Triumph would be subsumed into a single business unit, the Specialist Division, while Austin and Morris would form the Volume Cars Division. Although this reorganization would not take place until early 1972, from April 1971 – in anticipation of the merger – the new executive-car project was renamed SD1.

In practice, there was considerable bitterness about the British Leyland changes on both the Rover and Triumph sides of the house. Although the engineers of the Specialist Division were theoretically united under a single banner, the reality was that they were very far from united. The old rivalries between the two marques would cause tensions and problems throughout the design phase of SD1.

It is interesting that the Rover V8 engine was only mildly revised for the new car. In its post-1973 production form, it developed 143bhp, which was increased to 155bhp for the SD1. (Note that earlier output figures quoted in Rover literature were to SAE standards rather than the stricter DIN figures used from 1973 and cannot be used for comparison.) The main changes were to the inlet valves and ports, and to the hydraulic tappets, which allowed the engine to rev higher than before. A Lucas Opus electronic ignition system, representing the latest technology, gave more reliable firing than older contact-breaker systems and demanded less maintenance.

As for the gearbox, this was an all-new design that was intended to be produced with both four and five speeds. The basic unit was a four-speed type, with the fifth or overdrive top gear being located in a bolt-on rear housing. The design would become known in both four-speed and five-speed forms as the 77mm type, 77mm being the distance between the axes of the mainshaft and the layshaft. Some years later it would take on the name LT77, the LT standing for Leyland Transmissions.

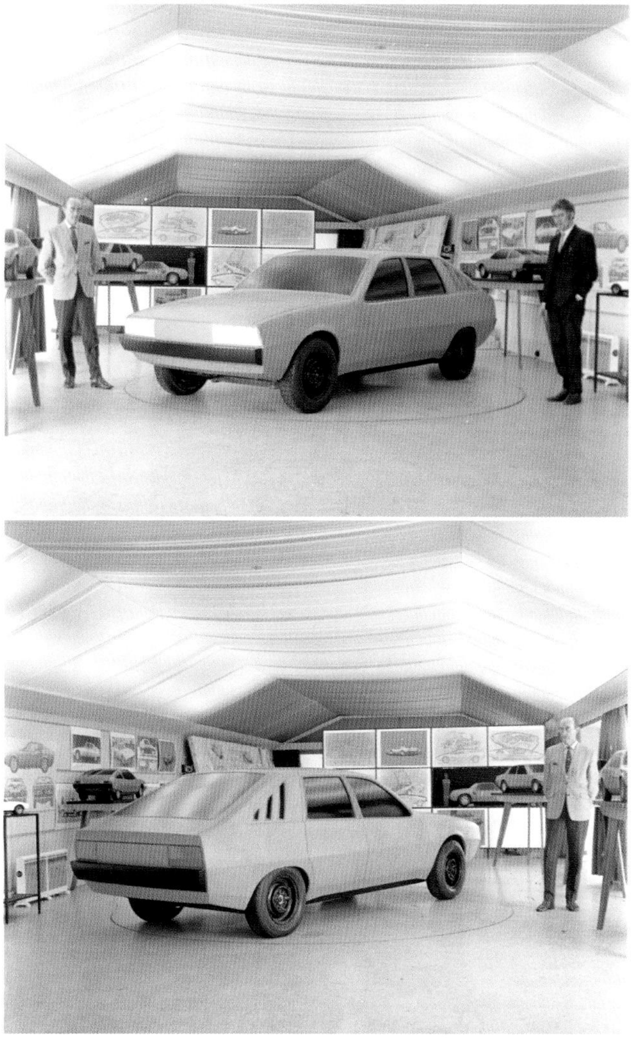

This full-size clay buck was prepared at the start of the SD1 period and shows the way the design was going by May 1971, when Lord Stokes reviewed progress. The styling studio staff were positioned to help give an impression of relative size.

SD1 Takes Shape

The SD1 project now went forward with Spen King, as technical director of Rover Triumph, in charge. (Rover's Peter Wilks had chosen to take early retirement from the top engineering position there during 1971. This was not as a result of the Rover Triumph reorganization; he was indeed ill, with a heart problem, and died a year later.) The rest of the team now gathered. David Bache was still in charge of styling, and Gordon Bashford remained responsible for the engineering package. British Leyland now saw the SD1 project as extremely important and were prepared to commit extensive resources to it. The job of chief programme engineer was entrusted to Mike Lewis, a Rover man. He had far greater responsibilities and a far larger team than had been the norm under Rover, when new cars were developed to production readiness by a project engineer, an assistant project engineer and one or two technical assistants, who were typically young engineers fresh from an apprenticeship. The development testing was done by teams of drivers working for Rex Marvin.

Further refined by July 1971, the initial SD1 design was not really progressing well (for further details, see Chapter 2). The design somehow lacked presence, but would nevertheless be used for the A-body prototype cars.

After more detail work, this was the September 1971 scale model for the car that had become the SD1 in April that year. It reflected Bache's overall outline and incorporated a hatchback.

There was strict control of costs from the very beginning, which – as Gordon Bashford recalled – encouraged the team to abandon any thoughts of independent rear suspension and to go for a cheaper 'live' rear axle. This would be manufactured by Triumph, who would also use it later in their TR7 sports car. The initial trials of the beam axle concept were done on a 'mule' prototype (known as a P7F), a Rover P6B prototype registered JXC 820D that had been fitted with the rear axle of a Vauxhall Ventora. Most of its trim was removed to simulate the target weight of the SD1, and the car was nicknamed the 'Lightweight Bomber' by the test engineers. It was tested both in the UK and on the Stelvio Pass in Italy.

Spen King wanted to separate the links counteracting axle wind-up from those providing longitudinal location, and so Gordon Bashford drew up a design that combined a torque tube (to resist wind-up) with radius rods and a Watt's linkage. King was also a believer in ride-levelling systems, having used one successfully on the Range Rover a few years earlier, and to maintain ride height and handling in an SD1 with a fully laden boot he specified twin Boge Nivomat self-levellers on the rear axle.

Rigid cost-control procedures were new to British Leyland. They had been brought in by the large numbers of former Ford people who had been headhunted to help make the organization lean and efficient. An August 1972 document from the Rover Triumph Vehicle Cost Control Department shows their effect. It analyses the projected manufacturing costs of the SD1 in minute detail, comparing them with those for the Rover P6 and Triumph 6-cylinder saloons that the new car was destined to replace. This comment, from a comparison of the new rear suspension with that of the Rover 2000TC, is typical:

> *SD1 uses more expensive springs £(0.20) and dampers £(0.29) but saves £15.67 on the De-Dion tube and all the associated links. A further saving of £0.14 is made on spring insulation.*

Further evidence of cost control was clear in the decision to fit drum brakes at the rear, even though the Rover P6 that the car would replace had featured disc brakes all round. There would of course be discs at the front; no credible new high-performance car could do without them in the mid-1970s. As for David Bache's gull-wing doors, they were always going to be expensive and complicated to manufacture and disappeared from the specification.

Quite a lot of the SD1 design was influenced by Triumph practice, too. There was now no question of base-unit construction, and the new car was to have a monocoque bodyshell with a subframe at the front, much like the existing Triumph 6-cylinder saloons. The front suspension followed Triumph practice in using space-efficient MacPherson struts, not least because neither the complex design for the Rover P8 nor that for the P6 – dictated by optimistic plans for a derivative with a gas turbine engine – was suitable for SD1. New for SD1, though, was that the rack-and-pinion steering gear would be mounted rigidly to the subframe, ahead of the transverse arms, one advantage of this arrangement being that any lateral deflection of the bushes would give safe understeer. To keep cost and weight to the minimum, the anti-roll bar was made an integral part of the transverse link. For safety, the steering was designed to incorporate a collapsible column.

Most of the basic engineering design for the SD1 was in place by mid-1972, and much of it was tested on some 'slave' prototypes based on other cars. The plan was to progress to two prototype stages, which were to be called the A-batch and B-batch cars. The A-batch cars were assembled in late 1972 at Solihull, and the very first one was slammed into a concrete block at the Motor Industry Research Association (MIRA) during 1972 to test the crashworthiness of the structure; the box overleaf gives details of the others and their uses.

SD1 PROTOTYPES – SDS AND A-BATCH

There were three groups of SD1 prototypes. These were the SDS (S for 'Slave') prototypes, the A-batch cars and the B-batch cars. The first two groups had varying degrees of resemblance to the eventual production models; details of the B-batch cars, which closely resembled the production types, are given in the next chapter.

SDS cars

The SDS prototypes were 'mules', built during 1972 and created by building elements of the proposed SD1 into existing cars. The known details are as follows:

SDS1 Triumph 2000 automatic registered RDU 479H. Fitted with SD1 front and rear suspensions, probably in early 1972. The car was used to test 6-cylinder engine mountings and the proposed fuel tank. In September 1972 the Stress Office and the Vehicle Safety Section ran a joint test using SDS1 for low-speed impact tests with sprung bumper mountings; photographs from these tests suggest that the bodyshell had been heavily modified both front and rear.

SDS2 Used for prototype rear-axle tests.

SDS4 Rover 3.5-litre (P5B) with SD1-type rear suspension and weight reduction to simulate SD1.

SDS5 Rover P8 with 3.5-litre V8 engine, registered BXC 760K. First registered on 7 June 1972; went to Boge at Eitdorf, West Germany, for work with the Nivomat ride-levelling system.

SDS6 Rover P8 with 3.5-litre V8 engine, registered HXC 800H on 10 October 1972. Use not known.

SDS7 Rover P8 with V8 engine, registered OXC 811E on 1 February 1972. Used for barrier crash test on 19 April 1973.

A-batch cars

The A-batch cars were first-stage prototypes and were built in late 1972. They had the original body design. Engineering documents reveal the following:

SD1-A1 Used for barrier crash test at MIRA (no. L69), for side intrusion tests and for roof intrusion tests.

SD1-A2/B In July 1973 this car was put through a 1,000-mile pavé durability test. The designation suggests it may have incorporated certain elements of the B-batch cars by that stage.

SD1-A3 This was the first fully running prototype and was described as having a '2.5-litre' Triumph 6-cylinder engine. It was used for interior noise tests (the Jaguar XJ6 was used as the benchmark), for engine shake tests and for road noise tests.

SD1-A4 Probably a V8-engined car, as it was compared with a Rover P6B V8 in cooling tests during November 1972.

Company registration records reveal details of two A-batch cars, one of which may be the car identified as SD1-A2/B above. Both were recorded as 'Cilroen' types (the spelling is correct; no doubt Rover planned to take advantage of the outline similarity between the new Rover and the Citroën CX saloon under development at the same time).

SD1-A-002 Registered on 1 November 1972 as MLY 375L. This was a blue V8-engined car with engine number 218227, which may be a mis-recording of '215/227'; the V8 engine was often identified as the '215' type (i.e. 215cu in, in its original Buick form), and 227 would be the engineering serial number. The car was tested on the roads using a canvas 'van' back to disguise the hatchback shape. However, later in life it was somewhat crudely converted to a three-box shape. It is likely that this was the car that survived into the 1980s as part of the Rover historic vehicle collection. Sadly, it was not retained when that collection was passed to BMIHT.

SD1-A-005 Registered on 16 November 1972 as MMV 110L. The engine number was 3.5 P8/7, which indicates a 3.5-litre V8; the 'P8/7' suggests this was a spare engine from the cancelled P8 programme.

An A-batch mock-up built by the research department was used in May 1972 for ventilation and heater defrost tests.

One of the A-body prototypes was slammed into a concrete block at MIRA to test the crashworthiness of the design. Test cars of all makes were given identifying numbers in the same sequence, and the initial letter corresponded to the registration letter then in force. The L-prefix therefore identifies this test as taking place between mid-1972 and mid-1973.

This is one of the A-body test prototypes, photographed in 1973. That canvas tilt concealed the most commercially sensitive part of the design, which was the fastback. The rear bumper appears to be the front bumper of a Range Rover!

CHAPTER TWO

FINAL DEVELOPMENT

Styling Issues

David Bache's design for a five-door hatchback had run into problems. By mid-1971, the styling team had made a full-size mock-up of the favoured design, but it had not scaled up well from the model that had gained the approval of Stokes and Barber in February. It was too angular, with an undistinguished nose design, and it looked quite dowdy next to the images of inspirational designs – Citroëns and the Alfa Romeo Montreal among them – that Bache had asked to be mounted on the wall of the styling studio.

Although this design was used to create the first SD1 prototypes, the A-batch cars, David Bache knew that his design was not maturing as it should. He seems to have been made painfully aware of this by lukewarm reactions from British Leyland management at their regular progress review sessions. To add insult to injury, top management called for an alternative proposal to be submitted from outside the company. This was and remains quite common practice in the automotive industry, the idea being to challenge existing thinking with a completely fresh look at the design.

At some point in the first half of 1971, the Michelotti studios in Turin – who had enjoyed a close relationship with Triumph during the 1960s – were given the package dimensions of the car and were asked to produce a design. Michelotti was well known for rapid turnaround times, and it seems likely that the call had gone out following a styling presentation to Stokes on 20 May.

The Michelotti proposal could hardly have been more different from David Bache's SD1 design. For a start, it was conceived as a more conventional three-box saloon. It was perhaps not one of Michelotti's more inspired designs, but it seems to have put the cat among the pigeons. In 1:3 model form, and wearing the Leyland badge on its grille, it was put forward for the next top management viewing of progress on SD1 styling, which took place on 8 July 1971.

No record has been found so far of that viewing's results, but later events strongly suggest that it was instrumental in provoking David Bache to take a fresh look at the SD1 design. Over that summer, he must have realized that minor alterations would not bring about the distinctive shape that he knew he could deliver and that the British Leyland top management wanted. The only answer was going to be a radical rethink. Tony Poole, who was then in charge of Land Rover styling under Bache and was only involved with SD1 styling as an in-house critic, remembered what happened:

> *[Bache] borrowed this Maserati [Indy] from his friend, who was the Bristol Motors chief. We were all asked to come in one weekend and do a crash job. We'd only got the car for the weekend.*
>
> *We took sections, like cardboard sections, and then walloped clay onto the SD1 clay model. We only had to add a couple of inches here, some more down there, and so on.*
>
> *Where we had to go into the clay, the original clay model, we did. Where we had to build out, we did. All my job was, was to cut cardboard templates and fasten them together on the Maserati. It was a rush job and it was Bache's idea and, by God, what we had there on Friday was nothing like what we'd got there on Monday.*
>
> *That was photographed in the clay without any ornamentation, and then from that photograph Kevin Spindler did a tracing and an illustration.*

As transferred to the SD1 clay, the curves borrowed from the Maserati worked very well. Bache also borrowed some design cues from another favourite design of his, the Ferrari Daytona, which inspired the wrap-around front sidelights and the scallop in the body side. The blending of these

ABOVE AND BELOW: Provocation? The Michelotti design called for by British Leyland top management in the early summer of 1971 certainly produced a reaction in the Rover styling studio. This scale model, with its prominent Leyland badges, has sometimes been misidentified as the Triumph Puma. The white model in the background is of the Rover P8, which was still 'live' at the time.

David Bache drew inspiration from two Italian supercars when he was improving the slightly dowdy A-body design. One was the 1972 Maserati Indy, with its body designed by Vignale, the other was the 1968 Ferrari 365 GTB4 Daytona, designed by Pininfarina.

This was how the SD1 full-size clay looked after its weekend of redesign inspired by Italian supercars. The improvement was simply enormous, even though no real work had been done on front and rear details when these photographs were taken on 25 November 1971.

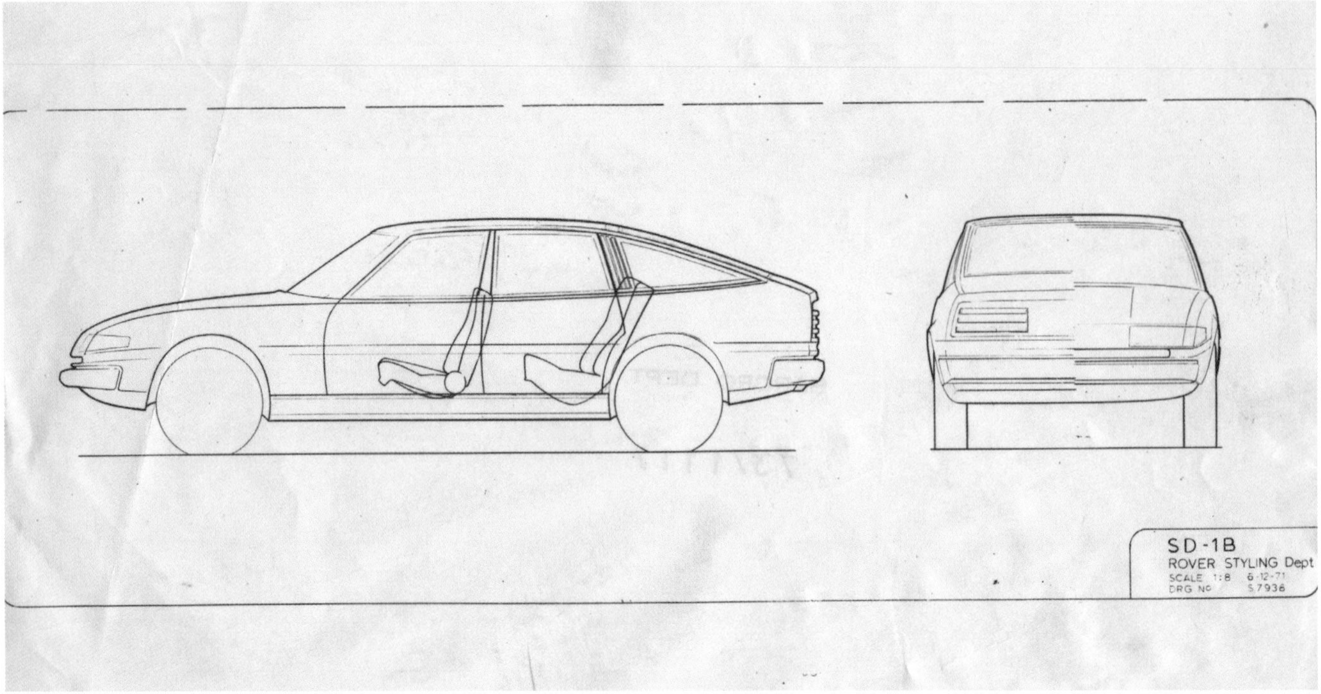

Progress with the new design was rapid: front and rear details were in place by the time of this styling department drawing dated 8 December 1971.

supercar elements with the basic SD1 body produced a stunning design, and the earliest photographs of the clay model (dated 25 November 1971 and still lacking any front and rear details) show just how good the overall shape looked.

Curvaceous, beautifully proportioned, and to this day utterly distinctive, the new design was turned into a more refined full-size clay during December. In February 1972, it won over the British Leyland management, and as a result all the B-batch cars would be built with the new body design. From that point on, everyone involved with the project realized that they had a winner on their hands.

The details of the design matured during 1972, and it was probably towards the end of that year that moulds were taken from the styling clay and two full-size 'see-through' fibreglass models were made. One was finished to represent the 'High-Line', or top models, of the new Rover, and was painted metallic gold; it had styled alloy wheels and was badged as a '3500A' ('A' for 'Automatic'). The other was finished to represent the 'Low-Line' models. This was finished in a darker, solid colour, and wore '2300M' badges ('M' for 'Manual'). Its wheels represented steel disc types, and had a rather attractive clover-leaf design of trim that was not carried through to production. (The production design would be settled over the summer of 1974.)

Bache wanted to make doubly sure that his new design – by this stage of course approved for production by the British Leyland board – really was as good as it needed to be. So one Saturday morning in May 1973, when few Rover employees would be around, he arranged a very special outdoor viewing session. He took the two fibreglass models and borrowed a large group of contemporary cars, lining them all up on the car park in front of Rover's main office block. The comparison exercise was shielded from unauthorized observers by a number of lorries parked behind the cars to act as a screen. The cars were of all shapes and sizes, from a Renault 5 to a pair of Maseratis, a Jensen Interceptor and a Mercedes SLC coupé. Bache came away from the viewing satisfied that his new design worked as it should. As he put it in a 1977 publicity brochure entitled *The Car of the Year, Today*:

> *Early clay styling mock-ups were put alongside cars like Maseratis and Ferraris. Despite the fact that it is a fully practical saloon car and not a cramped grand tourer, it looked perfectly in keeping.*

Two full-size clays had been developed in time for the next management viewing in February 1972. This was the 'Low-Line' model, with a rather attractive wheel design that did not make it through to production.

First thoughts on the 'High-Line' model featured alloy wheels and a streamlined exterior mirror design.

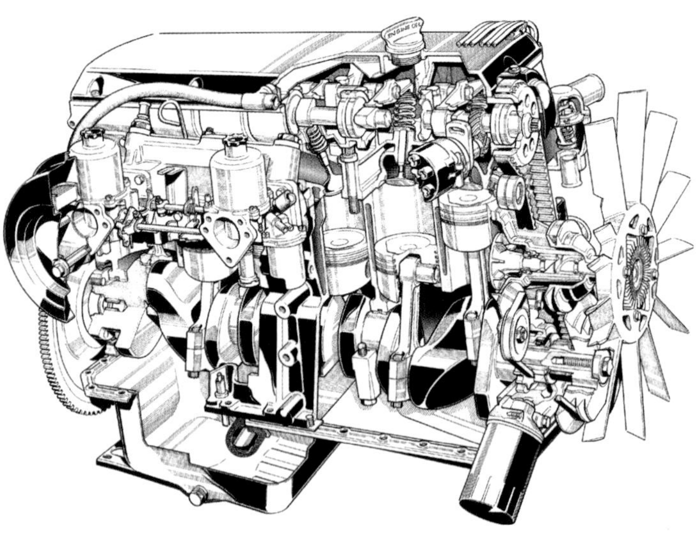

The six-cylinder engines were drawn up by the former Triumph design staff. This cutaway drawing shows the layout of the 2600 which, like the 2300, had a belt-driven single overhead camshaft.

Photographed in November 1974, the full-size '3500A' GRP styling model on the right is seen here alongside the model for the smaller SD2, planned as a replacement for the Triumph Dolomite saloons and designed with deliberate visual similarities to the new Rover.

With the shape settled, the practical features of the SD1's body could be developed. There were two particularly interesting features. To reduce sill corrosion, which was a big problem in many older monocoque designs, the sills were ventilated. Air was ducted from the main plenum of the heater-ventilator unit to flow down through the door hinge pillars and into the hollow sills, from where it escaped through a slot just forward of the rear wheel arch. However, bizarrely, the heater unit (which was shared with the Triumph TR7) was designed without a ram-air setting so that its fan had to be running all the time.

The second interesting feature was that the big windscreen was made of Triplex Ten-Twenty safety glass, a special type originally designed for aircraft cockpits and resistant to shattering. This windscreen was not rubber-glazed to the car but was bonded to the bodyshell, so adding to the torsional rigidity of the complete structure. The bonding process used was called Solbit, and during assembly a ribbon of sealing rubber was placed around the windscreen frame before the windscreen was fitted. A permanent bond was achieved by heating the rubber electrically by means of a wire running through it.

The 6-Cylinder Engines

As explained in Chapter 1, Rover's plan for P10 had incorporated an extensively re-engineered version of their 4-cylinder engine, but when the Rover P10 and Triumph Puma projects were effectively merged in 1972, Triumph were given the job of designing a pair of 6-cylinder engines and the Rover engine was cancelled.

In fact, Triumph had been working on a new 6-cylinder design since 1970, several months before the new Rover became a joint Rover Triumph project. They needed a new 6-cylinder engine for their planned Puma saloon and the smaller Bobcat intended to replace the Dolomite range, and the plan was to introduce it as an upgrade for the last few years of Innsbruck (Triumph 2000 and 2500) production as well.

Spen King, Triumph's chief engineer, influenced the design to a considerable extent. King was a minimalist engineer, who hated unnecessary complication, and when leading the design team on the 4-valve engine for the Triumph Dolomite Sprint, he had suggested an ingenious valve-gear design. Instead of using separate inlet and exhaust camshafts, the Sprint engine had a single overhead camshaft that acted directly on the inlet valves through bucket tappets, while operating the corresponding exhaust valve through a rocker arm. For the new 6-cylinder engine, King therefore proposed adapting this design for a two-valve layout and using it to convert the existing 6-cylinder Triumph engine to an ohc layout.

The job of drawing up this conversion of the older engine was given to Mike Loasby, who had joined Triumph from Alvis and would later have a distinguished career with Aston Martin. However, the plan seems not to have gone beyond the design stage before Triumph increased the budget for the new engine in early 1972. By this stage, Puma and Bobcat had been cancelled, but the engine was still expected to appear in the final models of the Innsbruck saloons. It was also going to be the principal power unit for the SD1.

The additional budget allowed a redesign of the cylinder block around repositioned bores, which could now be enlarged from the 74.7mm of the existing engine to 81mm. At this stage, the engine was being developed with a 76mm stroke to give a 2.3-litre swept volume. It had most likely already been given its internal type code of PE146, standing for Petrol Engine, 140cu in (roughly 2.3 litres), 6 cylinders. Again, King influenced the design by asking for the crankshaft to run in four main bearings instead of the seven that were the norm in 6-cylinder engines. This had the benefit of reducing internal friction as well as cost and complication. King also asked for the bottom end to be made very strong, to guarantee durability.

A second, larger-capacity version of the engine was created in late 1972. Its type code was PE166, indicating a swept volume of approximately 160cu in (2.6 litres). Still in keeping with King's vision of simplicity, the engine was to differ from the 2.3-litre type only in its crankshaft and pistons. Both sizes were to use the conrods from the Dolomite Sprint engine, and the decision to do that led to a reduction in the height of the cylinder block.

Just like the Sprint engine, the new 6-cylinder was designed with a pent-roof combustion chamber formed partly in the head and partly in the piston crown. However, it also incorporated new features. A die-cast aluminium alloy camshaft carrier above the cylinder head simplified the design by removing the need for separate bearings, and instead of a roller chain to drive the camshaft, the PE146 and PE166 engines were designed with a toothed rubber belt drive – the first time this had ever been used in an engine from the Leyland group.

In 1973, the plan to re-engine the Innsbruck models was dropped. Space under the Innsbruck bonnet had restricted the overall length of the new 6-cylinder engine, but there was more room in the SD1 engine bay and so the block could be lengthened. An extra 20mm enabled the designers to incorporate water passages between all the cylinders and an enlarged 86mm bore now became feasible, using the siamese bores of the original design. This would have given a 2928cc swept volume, but in the event was never used.

When the design was presented to Beans Industries at Tipton in Staffordshire, who had been doing Triumph's heavy castings since the mid-1950s, a further redesign became necessary. Beans asked to reduce the height of the water jacket to enable them to cast the block satisfactorily. So, to avoid the high piston temperatures that they feared would result, the Triumph designers ran an oilway through the conrods to spray cooling oil on the underside of each piston. The redesigned conrods replaced those shared with the Dolomite Sprint engine, although their major dimensions were unchanged.

There were inevitably delays in the programme, and the Rover and Triumph people of course blamed each other. Relations between the two sides were certainly difficult, and Rover's Gerry Boucher was seconded to Triumph to help out on engines because, as he remembered it, the Triumph people would not do as they were told! Stories abounded: *Cars & Car Conversions* magazine for June 1978 had heard that 'the principal delay on the launch had something to do with the fact that these sixes proved reluctant to better the V8's remarkable economy'. A more balanced explanation reached Karen Pender later on: she was told that the company contracted to machine the prototype cylinder blocks

> *went bust in the middle of the job. There was also a problem with the introduction of the early production machinery while development was sorted out. Parts were delayed, and the timing of the whole project was thrown off course.*

Some sources claim that one version of the 6-cylinder engine gave a very encouraging 150bhp on test. For production, some detuning was done (to 123bhp for the 2.3-litre and 136bhp for the 2.6-litre), partly to improve durability and partly to give appropriate differentiation between models in the SD1 range. Ian Elliott, product and technical PR manager for Leyland Cars at the time, confirms that:

There was a bit of concern when the first performance figures for the 2600 were issued by engineering before the launch – they seemed rather too close to the 3500 for comfort! Nothing was ever officially admitted, but I suspect that production 2600s were slightly de-tuned.

B-Batch Prototype Testing

The first B-batch prototypes were built towards the end of 1973 and in early 1974, somewhat later than planned because, in circumstances typical of the era, their completion was delayed by a dispute in the drawing office at Pressed Steel Fisher in Castle Bromwich, who were to build the bodies.

There was only so much testing that could be done behind the walls of the MIRA proving ground at Nuneaton. The SD1 had to be tested in real-world conditions on the European continent. So several of these B-batch prototypes went out on the road, looking as inconspicuous as possible – which was not easy for a large car that had such an unusual shape.

The test cars were finished in matt black, were given dummy front ends to disguise their sloping noses and carried a canvas 'tilt' to cover the whole rear body behind the B-pillars. From a distance, they looked like pick-up trucks. From close to, it was obvious that they were disguised prototypes, but any onlookers would have needed to get very close indeed to the cars to discover that the 'tilt' concealed the sloping tail of a hatchback design.

One of the prototypes, TLB 258M, was taken to the Stelvio Pass in northern Italy for some brake testing, and with it went Jim Shaw, who was Rover's brake specialist. Shaw remembered that the Rover was hit by a car coming the other way during one of the test runs, and although the damage was only slight, the test crew decided to take action. Reasoning that the black camouflage made the car less visible, they stuck some bright yellow tape to the front to form a simulated radiator grille. The finishing touch was a name badge, made with a logo cut from a magazine. There is a photograph of one of the Stelvio tests on the website set up by Jim Shaw's son James, at http://www.jshawmsc.f2s.com/rover.htm.

Another car – or possibly even the same one – was occasionally used by development chief Rex Marvin for commuting to and from work. Fellow engineer Geof Miller, who worked on the Land Rover side of the business, remembers

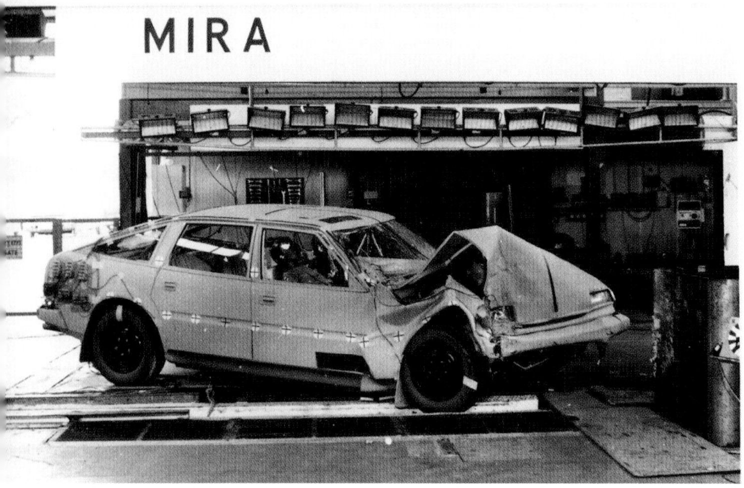

Crash-testing was of course an important element in the development process, and the actual tests were carried out at MIRA. This picture shows an SD1 after a 30mph one-third overlap impact test against a rigid barrier. The front end has absorbed all the impact, leaving the passenger cell intact. Interestingly, this early car has the sunroof that would not become available in production until 1978.

This is a late prototype on cold-weather test in Ontario, Canada. The photograph was taken by Geof Miller, the engineer who had led Range Rover development. The cold-weather test had to be overseen by an engineer of the appropriate grade. Although Geof was a Land Rover engineer, he got the job.

SD1 PROTOTYPES – B-BATCH

The B-batch prototypes were always intended as the final SD1 engineering prototypes and incorporated the improved components identified as a result of testing the SDS and A-batch cars. They also had the revised production body style and were probably all built by Pressed Steel Fisher in late 1973 and early 1974. The next stage in the build process was the pilot-build cars.

Engineering documents reveal that there were at least twelve B-batch cars, and provide the following information about them.

SD1-B1 Built as a V8 automatic. Initially (October 1973) used for 500-mile pavé durability test, which was suspended after 163 miles because of structural failures. Barrier-tested at MIRA (test number M88). Used for side intrusion tests to meet US regulations (FMVSS 214 standards).

SD1-B2 Manual gearbox with Triumph PE166 engine. Used for steering 'niggle' tests and for road noise work.

SD1-B3 To Levajok in northern Norway for cold climate testing, and in connection with front suspension strut tower design problems.

SD1-B4 Used for door intrusion tests to FMVSS 214, then by research department to devise a standard test for suspension strut tower testing. Also probably used to devise improvements to D-post design to improve roof crush resistance.

SD1-B5 Prototype head restraints were tested on this car.

SD1-B6 Used for rear axle compliance and vibration tests, and for road noise tests. Improved D-post design to improve roof crush resistance.

SD1-B10 Used for road noise tests.

SD1-B11 Used in 1975 for pavé test and to test body structure vibration.

SD1-B12 V8 automatic with sunroof. Used in simulated road noise tests during April 1975.

Seven of the B-batch cars were registered with TLB-M numbers, and their details survive in company vehicle records. Unfortunately, it is not possible at present to tie these numbers to individual prototypes with any confidence. It is likely, for example, that the car identified as SD1-002R is the same as SD1-B2 because its engine number X1323E is for a Triumph experimental engine and SD1-B2 is known to have had a Triumph engine.

In company regitstration records, the TLB-registered cars are all described as 'SD1 (Allied)', which is presumably a reference to the alliance between Rover and Triumph. The entry under 'Identity' is in effect the car's VIN – although prototypes had special identity numbers allocated by the engineering department. Note the variety of different number types recorded.

TLB 253M and TLB 254M were Triumph TR7 prototypes.

Registration	Identity	Date registered	Engine no	Fate
TLB 251M	SD1-0032	24 September 1973	SD1-B3	Scrapped, 13 June 1977
TLB 252M	SD1-002R	2 October 1973	X1323E	Scrapped, 28 May 1976
TLB 255M	SD1-005L	7 March 1974	SD1-B5	Barrier crash, 21 February 1977
TLB 256M	SD1-006L	18 December 1973	SD1-B6	Scrapped, 28 June 1976
TLB 257M	SD1-010Z	12 February 1974	SD1-B10G	Barrier crash, 11 April 1978
TLB 258M	SD1- no.8	1 March 1974	SD1-B8G	Scrapped, 20 June 1977
TLB 259M	SD1-014L	17 July 1974	SD1-17	Scrapped, 4 August 1977

sharing the car with him when they travelled in together. He also remembers that the car (or one of them, at least) had a cylinder shut-off system that enabled it to run on just four of its eight cylinders when cruising. Eric Branson, who was then working for Rex Marvin, remembers working on this system, which was intended to save fuel but was not taken through to production. Engines man Gerry Boucher believes that fears about damage to the 'dry' cylinders put paid to the idea.

Journalist Doug Nye recounted one story he had heard about the development testing in *Road & Track* for August 1976:

> *During development one car was dispatched on a Continental journey, disguised with Lancia plates. When it returned to Dover a hefty docker was impressed. 'Goor, that's nice, what is it then?' he asked. Leyland's slightly embarrassed engineer explained the badges were on the back. The docker looked, then rushed up and grabbed him by the lapels. Nose-to-nose he grated, 'It's blokes like you who're wrecking this country's economy!'*

One interesting observation comes out of this period. It must have been obvious early on that the SD1's sleek fastback shape would give a good aerodynamic performance, which in turn would reduce fuel consumption at high speed. However, there seems not to have been a deliberately scientific approach to this. Bache's SD1 shape was not tested in the wind tunnel at MIRA until early 1976, when a scale model gave a drag coefficient of 0.395, which was good for the time but surprisingly poor by later standards. Other cars on the market were already as good if not better in this respect, among them the Citroën CX, which had been introduced in 1975 – and it may have been the arrival of this car, whose very name is derived from the French equivalent (Cx) of the English abbreviation (Cd) for drag coefficient, that prompted the MIRA tests.

Interior Design

Rover traditionalists found the interior design of the SD1 its most disappointing feature when the car went on sale. The Rover name was associated with wood and leather and, although the P6 had used fake wood veneer and had normally come with fabric seat trim in recent years, leather had always been available. The SD1 was drawn up with neither wood nor leather in its specification. Instead, it had acres of plastic trim and velour upholstery. At a pre-launch 'customer clinic', where potential customers were invited to assess the new car against its obvious rivals, Rover had advance warning that all might not be well. Some invitees said that its interior was insufficiently conservative for their tastes.

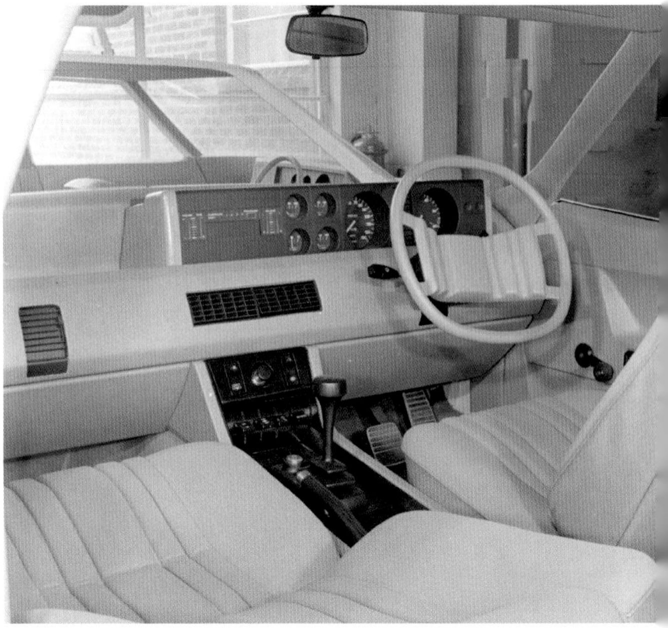

Bache's team had their interior proposals in place by February 1972.

The design was deliberately simple and minimalist, and the concept came from David Bache. It fitted into the overall ethos of simple design that Spen King had established for the SD1, and it was certainly ultra-modern in concept. Bache's team drew up a wide, sculpted facia that could be used for both left-hand-drive and right-hand-drive cars: the aperture for the steering column became a passenger's side air vent when the steering switched sides, while the instrument 'box' could be placed on either side to suit, leaving a wide parcel shelf ahead of the passenger.

That instrument box was drawn up as a modular unit, with major dials, subsidiary dials, warning lights and switches all in separate sections. The idea seems to have been that these sections could easily change places or be replaced with updated versions – and in practice the instrument panel of the 2.3-litre models was created by omitting the rev counter section of the 2.6-litre and 3.5-litre cars. However, the fully modular design tended to creak in use, and so some compromises were made for production. As it transpired, poor build quality completely subverted what was otherwise an advanced and viable concept.

The design of the steering wheel required an unconventional solution. The SD1's low roofline had its impact on the driving position and on the design of the seats, and it became clear that a steering wheel of the appropriate size would leave insufficient space for the driver's legs. So Bache's team designed a wheel with a flattened bottom section to provide the missing thigh room, and careful design of the central crash pad and spokes meant that the unusual shape of the rim was not immediately apparent.

Nevertheless, British Leyland were acutely aware of the public furore caused by the infamous 'quartic' steering wheel of the 1973 Austin Allegro. A few months before the SD1 was introduced in 1976, top management in British Leyland were sent a defensive briefing sheet with the following instruction:

> Do not mention *the steering wheel* at all *unless the subject is broached to you. If questioned simply state that steering wheel/steering ratio are perfectly matched.*

That quartic wheel, incidentally, may have appeared first on the Allegro, but its origins were in the Rover design studio. The story goes that Austin Morris chief George Turnbull had seen an early sketch in David Bache's studio and had asked for the design to be used on the Allegro; in fact, photographs prove that the quartic wheel was originally designed for the aborted P8 saloon. Ironically, the Allegro had reverted to a conventional round wheel in 1975, before the SD1 was launched, but it was too late to make any changes for the Rover.

Geoff Purkiss worked on aspects of the interior under David Bache, and he told Karen Pender (*Rover SD1: The Complete Story*) that the main influence on elements such the seat shapes, door panels and armrests was the Ferrari Berlinetta Boxer. The sculpted shapes of the Ferrari's door panels certainly could have inspired the hollowed-out shapes of the SD1's door trims. Purkiss also recalled that the sloping roof line caused some compromises for the rear seat passengers, which eventually robbed them of some legroom. He also noted that Bache had spent a lot of time getting the three-way range of adjustment right for the driver's seat; this was originally intended to have a pressed steel frame, but after July 1973 it was switched to a tubular type when costs began to go over-budget.

Purkiss attributed some of the interior design's failings to a shortage of skilled interior-trim designers, which led to the programme running late. As a result, some detail development may have been omitted or rushed. However, it was the trim materials that compromised the interior most. There was nothing inherently wrong with the choice of a velour nylon fabric for the upholstery (except, perhaps, that it was not leather), and this was developed specially for the car. However, despite sculpted panels on the seat cushions, it did tend to look rather plain. Another problem was the choice of headlining material. This was a nylon fabric glued to a moulded foam base, made for ease of assembly. Unfortunately, as was already becoming apparent from Range Rovers, which used a similar headlining, the glue tended to fail and allow the fabric to come away from its backing. The moulded door trims, too, felt flimsy even though their design was undoubtedly modernistic.

Nevertheless, the folding rear seat vindicated David Bache's hatchback concept by extending the carrying space available in the rear of an SD1 to something approaching that of an estate car. Detail design saw the spare wheel concealed in a well under the boot floor, which also provided some additional stowage space, and there was a hinged parcel shelf that concealed the load area but lifted with the tailgate to give excellent access.

The SD1 Assembly Hall and Paint Shop

Rover and Triumph looked at their existing assembly facilities early in the SD1 project to decide where to build the new car, but there was no space at either Rover's Solihull factory or Triumph's Canley plant. One problem was that both the Rover P6 and the Triumph 2000/2500 cars were expected to remain in production for a while after the SD1 was introduced, which meant that neither of those assembly halls could be used.

It rapidly became clear that a new assembly hall would be needed. A potential site was located within the Solihull factory, although it would mean cutting through the existing test track where new Rovers and Land Rovers were given their first shakedown runs. British Leyland saw in the new Solihull assembly hall the chance to build a vast complex

The new assembly plant and paint shop for SD1 was the largest of its type then built in Europe. In this aerial photograph, it dwarfs the other buildings on the Solihull factory site. Note the new-car test track running around the perimeter.

that might be used for other models later, and decided to back the scheme wholeheartedly. In the end, it cost them £31 million and became the largest investment yet made by the new company and the biggest single new development by any British car manufacturer for forty years – facts which rather give the lie to the widely held view that all of British Leyland's cash was being pumped into its Austin Morris division at this stage.

Rover Triumph produced their own estimates of the SD1's sales potential as part of the planning process for the new assembly hall. Those figures have not been discovered, but they were probably in the region of 70,000 to 75,000 cars a year, a figure that would have represented the average annual sales of Rover P6 and Triumph Innsbruck saloons combined, plus a percentage of anticipated improvement. However, many of the BL central staff were former Austin Morris men, and that company's policy had always been to set high production targets. Where the policy of the old Rover Company had been to put quality before quantity, Austin Morris people put quantity first. Encouraged by British Leyland's finance director, John Barber, who had been recruited from volume-focused Ford, they set figures of 3,000 cars a week (over 150,000 a year) for the new model, and the new factory was planned with three assembly lines to achieve build quantities of that order. It never did, and never came remotely near doing so.

At this stage, the British government was still encouraging manufacturers of all kinds to build new factories in depressed areas of the country. Rover had encountered that policy ten years earlier when they had been obliged to build a new gearbox plant in Pengam, South Wales, in return for agreement to build the new P6 assembly building at Solihull. Now British Leyland were refused an industrial development certificate for the size of assembly plant they wanted to create at Solihull.

They decided to outsource assembly of the SD1 bodyshells to Pressed Steel Fisher at Castle Bromwich, the old Fisher & Ludlow plant formerly owned by BMC. This reduced the size of the new building required at Solihull to a level acceptable to the government, and an industrial development certificate was granted in 1972; town planning consent followed in February 1973. However, it also introduced unwelcome complications in the production process. The bodies-in-white (unpainted bodyshells) had to be delivered by road from Castle Bromwich to Solihull, thus adding cost and time into the overall manufacturing process and also – fatally – exposing those unpainted bodyshells to the British weather for long periods of time.

The first plans for the new assembly hall envisaged a two-storey building with the paint shop upstairs, but these caused local alarm when they were made public. Solihull residents were concerned that they would be an eyesore, and even nearby Elmdon airport worried that they might present a hazard for incoming aircraft. After Rover Triumph chairman A. B. Smith had chaired a public consultation in Solihull, a compromise was agreed. Rover would reduce the height of the buildings, and would use spoil to construct man-made hills that would help to screen the site.

The new assembly hall was duly built within the Solihull factory grounds; the assembly hall covered 23 acres (9.3ha) and the three-storey paint plant a further 12 acres (4.86ha).

The assembly hall itself was 1,900ft (580m) long and 500ft (152m) wide. The whole complex was simply vast, and its size not only gave the production planners plenty of scope for an efficient layout but also enabled them to arrange for the car to be built using the latest techniques. It was planned that SD1 assembly would use a number of robots, which were then quite new in the industry – and were to some extent mistrusted by the labour unions as a threat to employment.

Early days in the new paint shop at Solihull, as SD1 shells progress down the line. The third shell from the camera is actually a Rover P6: the final examples of the SD1's predecessor were also painted in the new paint shop from approximately spring 1976.

ABOVE AND BELOW: **Bodyshells shipped in from Castle Bromwich were chemically cleaned and prepared for painting.**

Even though this was a modern paint plant, the SD1 bodies were still sprayed by hand.

Freshly painted bodies await their turn on the assembly lines.

The new assembly hall would not be entirely responsible for SD1 manufacture, however: far from it. It was intended only to handle final assembly of the cars, including painting. Elements of the SD1 would reach Solihull from a variety of suppliers. Bodyshells, for example, would come from Pressed Steel Fisher in Castle Bromwich, itself receiving pressings and sub-assemblies from Pressed Steel at Swindon. Gearboxes would be manufactured at the Rover transmissions plant in Pengam, South Wales, which ten years earlier had satisfied the government's need to create new jobs in deprived areas.

Early cars pictured on the assembly line at Solihull. Assembly was still labour-intensive as this was before the widespread use of robots.

Some of the first SD1s reach the final stages of the assembly line.

A car to be proud of: this metallic silver (Platinum) car is probably one of the pre-production models built in 1975.

ONE THAT GOT AWAY

A series of sketches prepared by David Bache in March and April 1975 show an interesting variation on the SD1 theme – a three-box saloon rather than a hatchback. Only the side profile is shown. There is no indication why these sketches were prepared, but they may well have fed into a scale model of a three-box SD1 that was made in the styling studio in June 1976, about a fortnight before the SD1 was released to the public. The sketches show a six-light design; the model is a four-light.

Particularly interesting is that this scale model is not only a three-box variation of the SD1 but also carries a Daimler grille and other identification. At this stage, Daimler (and its parent company Jaguar) were part of the Large Cars Division of Leyland Cars, as was Rover Triumph. Presumably, the scale model and the design work that preceded it were part of a plan to use the SD1 as the basis of a new model for Daimler; this would be quite logical in the context of the time, when British Leyland was trying to merge its formerly separate large car marques into a homogenous whole.

Exactly what the Daimler and Jaguar people thought of this proposal is not clear, and no reference to it has yet been found within the records of those marques, but it is highly unlikely that they were enthusiastic about it. In practice, the proposal seems to have gone no further.

Possibly connected with this exercise was a series of sketches that David Bache produced some time around March 1976, which supposedly showed alternative body styles for SD1. The freewheeling ideas showed a four-door saloon, a two-door fastback coupé and a four-door fastback saloon. None seem to have progressed beyond the original sketches.

This sketch, possibly by Charles Coldham in David Bache's styling studio, was dated 27 March 1975. It shows a three-box adaptation of the SD1 shape that seems to work rather well.

Recorded in the Rover photographic archive as a 'Daimler SD1', this three-box SD1 derivative must have shocked the people at Jaguar's Daimler subsidiary – if they ever got to see it.

CHAPTER THREE

THE FIRST CARS, 1976–1979

Rover had been hoping to release the SD1 in October 1975, which would have been just a year after the intended launch of its P10 predecessor. Mike Lewis's engineering team handed the car over to the production engineers in autumn 1974, by which time work had already started on manufacture of the body tooling. The first off-tools bodyshells were completed in April 1975, and pre-production cars swiftly followed.

However, that planned launch date proved to be excessively optimistic. There was a major delay in the 6-cylinder engine programme, and it must have been during 1975 that a decision was made to launch the car in 3500 form first with the V8 engine and to introduce the two 6-cylinder models later. Further delays meant that even the V8 models would not be ready in time for an October 1975 introduction. The whole programme slipped. In the end, SD1 was launched, in 3500 form only, at the end of June 1976.

This delay caused no special difficulties. If all had gone according to plan, production of V8-engined Rover P6B saloons would probably have ended over the summer of 1975, leaving the 4-cylinder models in production for a while. Over at Triumph, a similar plan to overlap the run-out of the less expensive Innsbruck saloons with the start of SD1 sales was probably in place. So all that happened was that both Rover and Triumph carried on building their existing models longer than they might otherwise have done.

In the meantime, the new paint shop that had been built as part of the SD1 plant on Rover's Solihull factory site was commissioned. The largest and most technically advanced ever to have been built in the UK, it was also designed to use a new thermoplastic paint process, in which the paint flowed and smoothed itself in order to reduce the need for cutting back and polishing later. The plant was bedded-in

LOE 103P was one of the launch cars, photographed here on a hill within the factory grounds, overlooking the new SD1 assembly plant. It is wearing the optional alloy wheels.

over the summer of 1975, although at this stage it was used for only a handful of pre-production SD1 bodies and Rover gained experience of the new processes by putting the 1976-model P6 and P6B bodies through the new plant. These cars were made available with the new paint colours that were intended for the first production SD1s. Unfortunately, the new paint process had teething troubles that had not been solved by the time SD1 production began in earnest. As a result, both the P6s and SD1s for the 1976 and 1977 model years suffered from paint problems.

Pre-Production Cars

The first off-tools bodies for SD1 became available in April 1975. During June 1975 the first five of these went through the new paint shop and were assembled into complete cars. These were not yet full production models, but they made their contribution to testing the production processes for the new Rover. Those first five pre-production SD1s were followed by a trickle of others as the plant worked up to full production of 1976-model P6 and P6B saloons. There were three more in July, four in August, seven in September and three in October.

Rover needed to build examples of as many different types as possible, and some of these pre-production cars had right-hand drive and some had left-hand drive; some had manual gearboxes and some had automatics. The majority had V8 engines, but build records show that six of the first twenty-one cars had been planned as 6-cylinder models. Five were to have had the 2.6-litre engine and one was to have been a 2.3-litre model, but there were no engines available and so the cars were completed without them. There appear still to have been no 6-cylinder engines by early December 1975.

Most of these early cars were allocated to engineering development work, a couple went to the quality control department, and there was one for the 'methods build' team, whose job was to make sure that the car would be built in the most efficient and practical way. There was then a pause in November, when no SD1s were built, and December saw volumes increase as the big pre-production batch began to appear. These were cars for the service training, technical publications and marketing departments, and several of them also became the first cars for the Rover press fleet.

During this period, minor elements of the specification were still changing. The early plan was to have a neat twin coachline that followed the main contours of the body at waist height. Several of the pre-production cars had this, and Rover's photographer Alan Luckett went to the Netherlands and to Switzerland to photograph and film them, probably in early spring 1976. Those photographs were intended to become the launch photographs, but none of

This photograph of an early pre-production car was taken in Holland, against an appropriate background. The car was wearing side decals, which were dropped from the production specification, so all the launch photographs had to be reshot.

them were issued because the coachlines were dropped from the specification and the launch photography had to be redone. Whether the coachlines were dropped in order to trim assembly costs, or because there were problems in adding them, is still unclear today. However, the coachlines were not lost altogether: they reappeared on the 1980 V8-S and the more expensive 1981-model SD1s.

There was another last-minute alteration, probably to save costs: the low-coolant warning system was dropped, although the warning light remained (unconnected) on the instrument pack. As a result, the first sales brochures (publication no. 3207) had to be withdrawn and replaced with an amended version (no. 3207/A). A further cost-saving change was made in March-April 1977 after production had been running for some time, when the original four interior colours were trimmed to just three. Amontillado disappeared from the options list; perhaps this orange-brown colour had been an unpopular choice.

Although overseas branches of Leyland Cars would eventually have their own press demonstrator cars, these were drawn from supplies of production models. The worldwide press launch was to be held in the UK, and it was therefore the responsibility of the UK press office to provide the cars for journalists to sample at the event. There were probably around twenty of these, and the majority were registered in the sequence LOE 93P to LOE 109P. All were 3500 models, most of them with automatic gearboxes but some with the five-speed manual type, and some had alloy wheels while others had the standard steel type. These were the cars that would be photographed for the press pack issued to the media, and it was these cars that would figure in the first published driving impressions and road tests of the SD1. They had to be as near flawless as possible, and no doubt were very carefully prepared for their job of presenting the new Rover to the world.

One of the launch cars, LOE 93P, featured in a series of press photos. It is wearing the standard steel wheels with their painted 'clover-leaf' stainless-steel trims.

LOE 93P shows the clean lines that made the SD1 design such a success. Four mudflaps were standard wear from the beginning.

The big hatchback was a novel and stylish feature. The boot floor has been removed in this picture, showing the spare wheel stowage below. All early cars, like this one, had a single supporting strap for the parcel shelf. Those are air extractor vents in the underside of the tailgate.

SD1 and the Press

Keen to launch the SD1 against a favourable background, Leyland Cars chose to base the worldwide press launch at Chateau Impney near Droitwich, an impressive-looking Grade II listed hotel built during the nineteenth century in the style of an elaborate French chateau. Members of the design team were on hand to talk about the new car, and journalists typically spent a day there, trying out one car in the afternoon of their arrival and a second one in the morning before they left, and covering around 200 miles (320km) on the road in the Midlands and Wales. All reports were embargoed until 30 June 1976.

Veteran *Motor Sport* journalist Bill Boddy shared a car with Alan Henry of *Motoring News* and was deeply impressed from the start of his drive. Just a couple of hundred yards after setting out, he reported (in the July 1976 issue of *Motor Sport*):

> *I had an instant conclusion: 'This, Alan, is a* proper *motor car. I want one!'*

Boddy was also favoured with a few days' loan of an early pre-production car (RRWVF7AA-000003, LOK 700P, a Midas Gold five-speed car originally allocated to the engineering department), and he drove this for a further 1,200 miles (1,900km). He liked the car very much:

> *I have been able to confirm both my own ecstatically enthusiastic reaction to my 200-mile Press launch drive and Leyland's own Press release superlatives.*

Doug Nye reported on the launch for the US magazine *Road & Track*. He was also favourably impressed, although he found the automatic model less than memorable:

> *I tried the manual, and it all came to life!... Now I could position the big car for the turns, squat it low under power and drive it like a sports car.... At 3,000rpm in 5th the 3500 snored along at 85mph, and though Leyland claims 24–25mpg, the press trial cars were returning 26–28mpg in many cases, and a pair of Dutchmen managed 31.*

Autocar delivered a full road test of an automatic model in its issue dated 31 July 1976 (the day of the car's official availability through UK showrooms). They concluded that 'the new 3500 is superb and deserving of the highest praise'. It had significant advantages over all the obvious competitors – Opel Commodore, Peugeot 604, Renault 30, Toyota Crown, Volvo 264 and Reliant Scimitar – and was 'the "best buy" in its class'. They added that 'the Rover has its flaws – but we believe that these can and should be easily rectifiable as running changes'. Sadly, as explained below, this initial impression soon turned sour.

Early Production

During the first half of 1976, production volumes gradually increased and by the time of the car's announcement at the end of June 2,946 cars had been built to provide dealers with a launch stock. Launch-stock cars continued to come from the lines over the summer, and records suggest that the first car actually ordered by a dealer – as distinct from those allocated automatically – had no. 3517. This was a Pendelican (white) 3500 with Coriander interior, and was passed from production to sales on 23 August.

The first car with electric windows (prototypes apart) seems to have been built in October 1976, just in time for the Earls Court Motor Show that month, where the cars would be seen in public for the first time. A total of six cars were designated as Motor Show exhibits, and records show these as no. 4810 (in Pendelican) and nos. 4898–4902 (of which the last two were both in Caribbean).

The first two Methods Build 6-cylinder cars had meanwhile been assembled in July 1976, car no. 3411 becoming the 2300 and no. 3412 becoming the 2600; both were painted in Pendelican. Assembly for sales began slowly in August 1976, the first cars apparently being no. 3993 (a 2600) and no. 4029 (a 2300), and a slow trickle of 2600s left the assembly lines that autumn.

With volume production of the 3500 models solidly established and running on two separate assembly tracks at Solihull, Leyland Cars was now able to begin looking at special derivatives. Among these were a number of black cars for the Government Car Service, the first of which were built in August 1976. So it was that, towards the end of the year, SD1s began to be seen as the transport of Prime Minister Jim Callaghan and of some of his senior colleagues. December also brought assembly of the first export models, including left-hand-drive cars, for the roll-out of the SD1 in continental Europe at the start of 1977 (see Chapter 8).

The SD1 was launched with just one engine option at first – the 3.5-litre V8. Here it is under the bonnet of an early car, which for some reason has lost the wire mesh panels that normally cover the air intakes in the scuttle.

Although the V8 engine was familiar from earlier Rovers, it had been re-worked for its new application. Rover hammered the fact home with this ingenious 'exploded view' model.

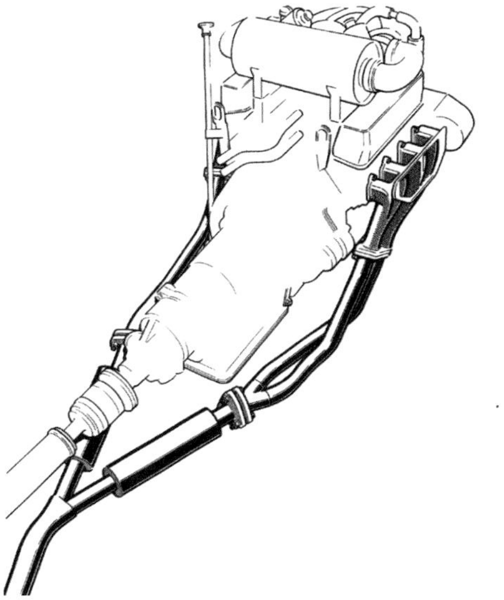

A free-flow exhaust system allowed the V8 to breathe more freely than in any previous Rover installation.

Triumph engineers had been responsible for the new '77mm' five-speed gearbox, seen here as a demonstration cutaway. The gear lever was mounted remotely, as the picture makes clear.

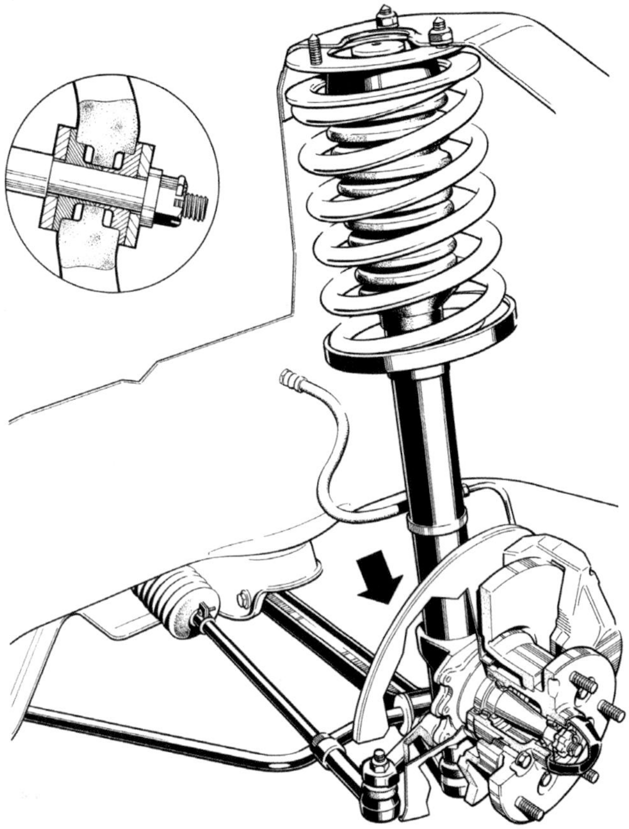

Strut suspension was new on a Rover, but it had been seen on the big Triumphs that the SD1 replaced.

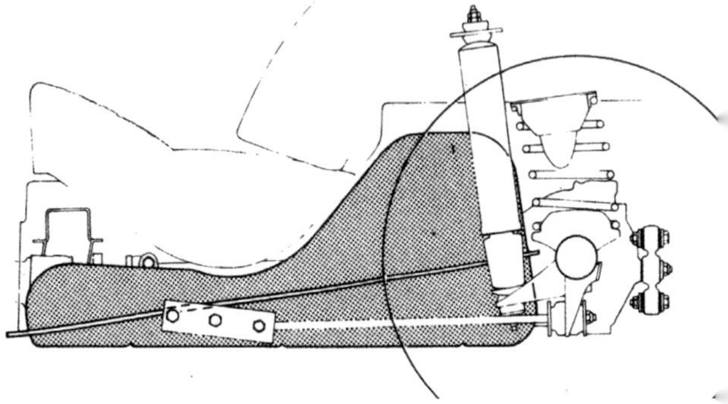

The fuel tank was mounted ahead of the rear axle, where it was safe from damage in a rear-end shunt. The fuel pump was inside the tank and shut off automatically in the case of engine stoppage, to reduce the risk of fire in a collision.

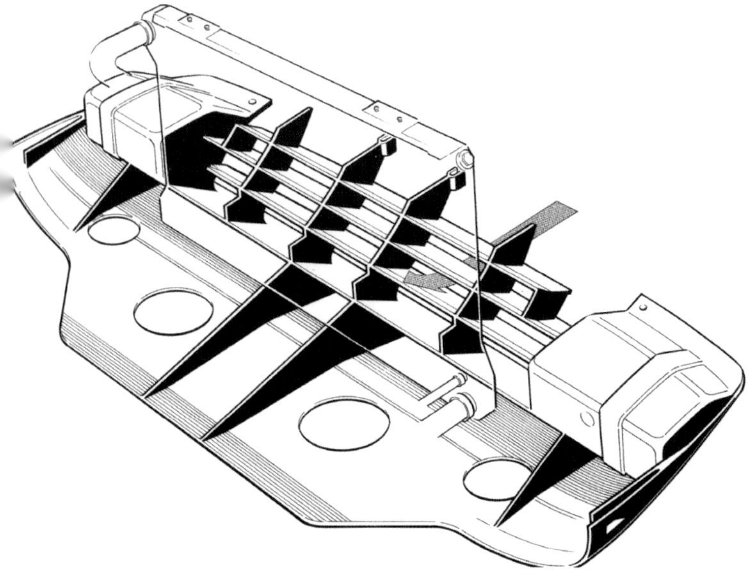

Well aware of the risk of underbody corrosion, Rover designed a plastic undertray for the nose of the SD1.

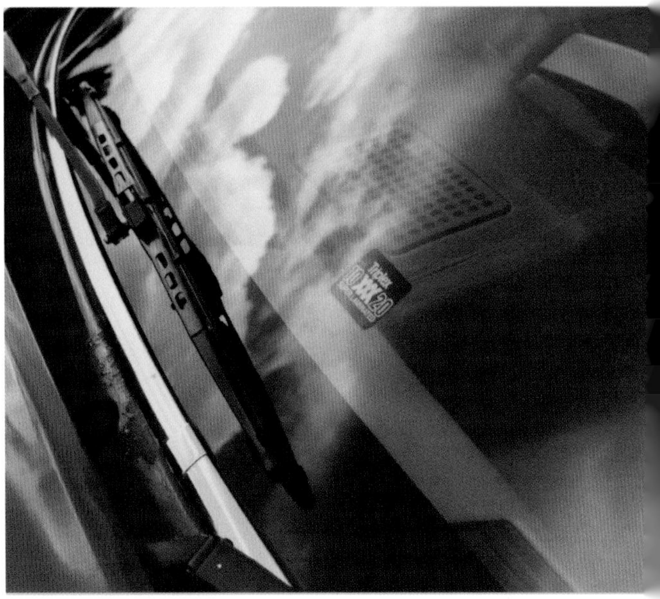

Even the windscreen brought new technology, in the shape of Triplex Ten-Twenty safety glass.

The Denovo Option

From the start of the 1974 model year in autumn 1973, the Rover P6B models became the first production cars in the world to be available with Dunlop's new Denovo run-flat tyres. These were an extra-cost option, which must have limited their popularity from the start. However, Rover were wedded to the safety benefits of the run-flat tyre, and it was probably at about this time that they decided to make Denovos an option on the SD1 which was then under development. So Denovo wheels and tyres were available from the very start of SD1 sales in 1976. Surviving records suggest that the first car to have them fitted had serial no. 4743 and was passed to sales in August 1976.

The Denovo was a low-profile tyre that could sustain a complete loss of air pressure at high speed with almost no effect on the stability of the car. Its secret was a special lubricant, carried in canisters attached to the wheel rim inside the tyres, that was released automatically when the tyre deflated. The lubricant reduced friction, kept the tyre temperature down, sealed any small punctures and partially reinflated the tyre, all in the space of a few seconds. The tyre was then capable of travelling limited distances at speeds up to 50mph (80km/h) in deflated condition and, after repair at an appointed service centre, would be fully operational again.

The Denovo wheels were as special as the tyres, and were made in two parts that were bolted together. At this stage, only steel wheels were available, and these were identified as special by a red band around the rim. They came with moulded plastic trims that had a modified version of the standard SD1 clover-leaf design. The trims unfortunately had a rather cheapening effect on the car, which probably did not encourage many customers to take up the Denovo option. At the start of the 1980 model year, alloy Denovo wheels became available, with a design similar to but subtly different from the standard SD1 type.

The Denovo alloy wheel was also similar to the standard type, but subtly different.

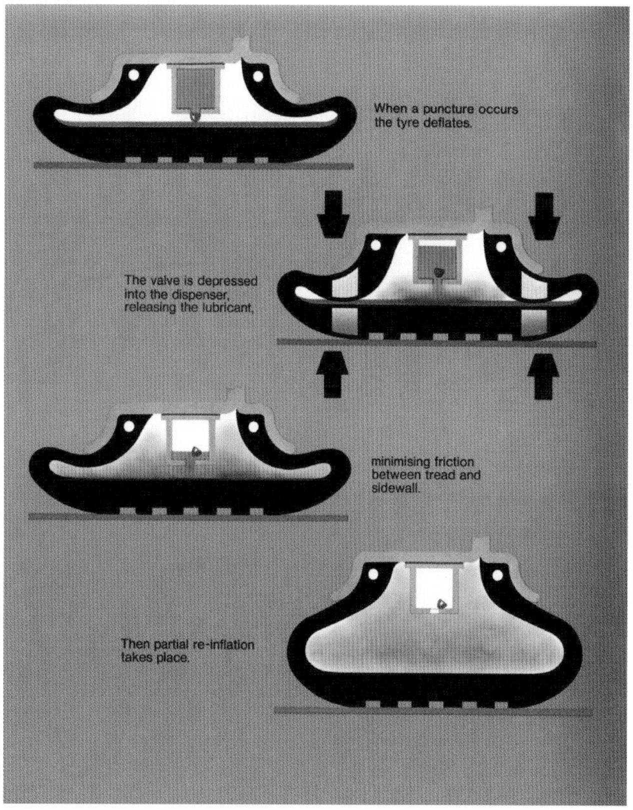

This was the principle of the Denovo tyre's operation. The special rims had several canisters containing the special fluid that sealed and then reinflated the tyre.

The Denovo steel wheels had a special and distinctive trim, which echoed the style of the standard trims.

A MILITARY SD1

Early on, the Ministry of Defence took an interest in the SD1. Car OHP 186P (RRWVF7AA-000218) was sent to the Fighting Vehicles Research and Development Establishment at Chertsey for evaluation. It was probably examined mainly to see if it would be suitable as VIP transport. The SD1 never did find widespread acceptance with the British military, one reason perhaps being a lack of headroom for tall passengers sitting in the back seat.

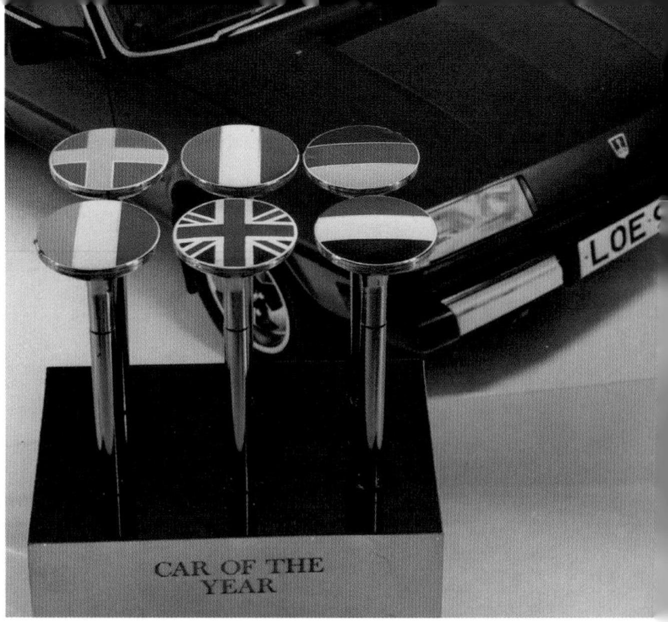

SD1 got off to a flying start by winning the 1977 Car of the Year award. However, the photographic department were clearly caught on the hop when asked to prepare this press release picture: the award has been grafted onto a photograph of launch car LOE 93P, suitably airbrushed to reflect the R-suffix registrations current at the start of 1977.

In theory, there was no need for a spare wheel, so SD1s with the Denovo option were supplied without one. All the Denovo-equipped cars also came with a temporary repair kit for small punctures. However, there was too much distrust of a car with no spare wheel for the Denovos to become a popular choice. The tyres themselves also gained a reputation for wearing quickly in service.

Awards

The SD1 was born into an era when the motor industry was increasingly gaining media attention through a series of awards – for the most part handed out by the media themselves and primarily intended as another means of gaining favourable publicity. Various high-profile figures from the motoring media and motoring industry were drafted in to act as judges, and the results gained the winning cars more column inches in the press.

It was the job of the public relations team at Rover to prepare the formal submissions for these awards, and the job of putting the SD1 forward for three of them fell to Ian Elliott, who had become the new product and technical PR manager for Leyland Cars on its formation in late 1975. One submission, for the Design Award, was unsuccessful, and Elliott puts this down to 'politics' with two of the judges. The other two, however, were successful. The major coup was winning the Car of the Year trophy in early 1977, an award given to the European car judged to be the best one released in the previous twelve months. The judges, comprising forty-nine motoring journalists working for magazines in fifteen European countries, gave the Rover 157 points to put it well ahead of the runner-up, the Audi 100 (138 points).

Leyland Cars made much of that award, as this later show stand, complete with cutaway demonstration SD1, makes clear. The event appears to be in Ireland as the name of Belfast dealer Charles Hurst is just visible on one of the stands.

The SD1 design team won the Midlander of the Year Award. Here they are, from left to right: Mike Lewis (chief development engineer), David Bache (styling), Spen King (technical director) and Gordon Bashford (chief design engineer).

The award was presented on 25 January 1977 to British Leyland's chief executive, Alex Park, at a ceremony held in Rome. Journalist Paul Frère, president of the award's organizing committee, said that:

> *The Rover 3500 is the first British car for years with a worldwide appeal. It is lavishly equipped, very economical for its size and performance (which is excellent) and offers a good blend of handling and comfort.*

The next award that fell to the SD1 was the Don Safety Trophy, and again Ian Elliott prepared the submission for this, which was presented in May 1977. This time, the judges argued that the car was a leader in both primary and secondary safety, and their unanimous verdict was that 'no other car producer for the first time in 1976 appears to have so many safety measures clearly incorporated at the design stage'.

Next came an AA Gold Medal (for 'a major contribution to the safety, comfort, economy, enjoyment and advancement of motoring'); the Style Auto award (given by a panel of leading European car designers); and then in April 1979 the 3500 became *What Car* magazine's choice as the best model in the director's car class. Small wonder, then, that publicity for the 1980 model year took to describing the 3500 as 'the outstanding British car that has won more awards than any other'.

Inklings of Reality

However, was the SD1 really as good as all these professional assessors of cars believed? The answer is only partially a Yes. The SD1 certainly did behave very well on the road, and as a piece of engineering and design it was unquestionably a triumphant success. The problem was that the workforce at Solihull seemed unable to build it to the necessary high standard.

The author vividly remembers a visit to the dentist in early autumn 1976, and discovering with some excitement that a brand-new Pendelican (white) SD1 was sitting in the drive outside the house. 'Yes, of course, look all you like,' said the dentist in reply to an enquiry. 'It's not locked.' It then rapidly became clear that one reason for the car not being locked was that the dentist hoped somebody might steal it. He was deeply unimpressed with his new acquisition.

Not long after that, a next-door neighbour bought a new SD1 to replace his 1968 Rover 3.5-litre coupé. It lasted about a week before he took it back to the dealership and demanded his money back. He bought an Audi instead. Something was clearly wrong with these early SD1s, and before long reports began coming in from all kinds of people that the build quality was atrocious.

None of that stopped waiting lists from building up, compounded by the Solihull factory's inability to build enough cars to meet a huge demand. The motoring press carried advertisements for delivery-mileage cars that were being sold at a premium over the list price, as some owners cashed in on public fascination with the new Rover. Somehow, the idea of the car – and, no doubt, those enthusiastic early press reports – had given a momentum to SD1 sales that would take some time to subside. In the meantime, a lot of customers were bitterly disappointed with what they had bought.

A prime example was George Fowkes, managing director of the company that owned *Autocar*. As reported in the magazine's 20 August 1977 issue, his ownership got off to a very bad start, and after only 750 miles he gave one of the journalists who had recommended the car an earful of his findings:

> *The finish of the car on delivery was poor by any standards but by those of a near-£5000 motor car, it was downright disgusting.... significant disappointments included out of balance wheels, ill-fitting items of trim, numerous creaks and rattles, clonks from suspension, steering and transmission, a misaligned selector gate [...], a sticky throttle linkage, jerky electric window action and very poor cold starting accompanied by serious loss of power during the first mile or so of running after a cold start.*

Bill Boddy at *Motor Sport* also managed to get an SD1 as a company car, and reported on its first 10,000 miles in the magazine's March 1978 issue. He was less than impressed when it arrived to discover that it had manual windows and no sunroof, not to mention an automatic gearbox rather than the manual he had requested and cloth upholstery rather than leather. Boddy was no fan of the instrument assembly's design, but that was a question of taste. More serious was that it revealed a problem that would become characteristic of the early SD1:

> *It is a clever idea to accommodate the electrical fuses at the left-side end of it, or would be if the lid wasn't secured by a single, small plastic catch, so that it frequently falls off. [He was] disappointed to find a big piece of trim hanging from the off-side wall, inside the boot, and to hear a tinkle from inside the off-side driver's door. The former has never been rectified at subsequent services and the latter is still faintly evident.*

This kind of poor service from a dealer was by no means confined to those who specialized in Rovers at the time, but it did hint at another problem. And that problem was highlighted further when the Rover's fuel pump failed after just 5,739 miles (9,236km). Whether the failure was uncharacteristic is neither here nor there, but the local dealer's inability to locate and fit a new pump before a week had passed was quite typical of the problems that early SD1 owners faced.

There is no one simple explanation for these problems. The poor build quality was probably caused by at least two factors. One was that Rover had recruited heavily to find staff for the new assembly plant at Solihull, and that the car was therefore being built by a largely inexperienced workforce. Another was that the SD1 was being built very strictly to a price, which had led to cost-cutting in some areas of the production design. That fuse cover on the end of the instrument assembly could have been made to stay in place by redesigning its fixings, but Leyland probably discouraged this on cost grounds.

A third factor also entered the equation, although it did not become apparent until the cars had been on sale for a year or so. Rover had chosen a new process for paint primer application, one that was believed at the time to be the best available in the industry and far better than the earlier 'dip' methods. This involved passing an electrical charge (typically 200–400V) through the body and a charge of the opposite polarity through the paint. The theory was that this would lead to improved paint adhesion, but it did not. It tended to generate gassing at the interface between steel and primer, which weakened the adhesion of the paint film to the metal. As paint adhesion is only ever as good as that of the first coat, it was not long before many bodies began to suffer from flaking paint and subsequent rusting. The situation was not helped by Rover's use of an acrylic top coat, which gave a very glossy but rather brittle finish.

Other car makers had similar problems with this new technology, and the paint makers eventually came up with

BUILD ISSUES – A PERSONAL EXPERIENCE

My first SD1 was a 1978 3500 with manual gearbox, SBK 240S, finished in Platinum. I bought it as a three-year-old car from a used-car dealer in London after looking at several other examples. Some of those were already showing problems; one in particular had had a lower-half respray, probably to cover the rust that had broken out in door bottoms and wheel arches.

The car was basically sound, although build quality problems were immediately obvious. The most glaring fault was an incorrectly fitted instrument pod, with a large gap between pod and outboard end panel, and a fuse-box cover at the other end which would not stay in place. (Blu-Tack eventually provided a reasonably long-lasting fix.) The boot leaked, too.

After a while, it became clear that even the tried-and-tested V8 engine was not giving its best. I remember being unable to keep up with a 1.6i Escort that was being driven with some enthusiasm on the M4 motorway. Perhaps the wrong spark plugs had been fitted (they had a different reach from those on earlier V8 engines); I never did find out.

About two years into ownership, rust became a real problem around the wheel arches. I also wanted to replace the standard telescopic radio aerial with an electrically operated aftermarket one, and was appalled to discover that the front wing had to come off first and was welded in place. The wing never did come off, of course; I hacked a hole in the side of the passenger's footwell and did the job that way.

After about three years, I had had enough. SD1s of that age were almost unsaleable, and I eventually put mine through the local auctions. I walked away with £650 for a car that had cost £2,750 three years earlier.

RIGHT: Note the massive gap between end panel and the main instrument panel. The fact that a car could be released with a build fault as glaring as this one (which was never corrected by a dealer, either) was a clear indication that something was badly wrong with the quality-control system at the SD1 plant. The additional circular warning light at the bottom of the instrument panel was a tell-tale for trailer lights.

AN UPHILL STRUGGLE

The Rover SD1 was both developed and launched in a period of dramatic change for its manufacturer, British Leyland. It was also a period in which the British Leyland name became a byword for strike action, and in many ways it was a miracle that the car ever entered production at all. Its early years were blighted by multiple strikes, with the effect that there were never enough cars to satisfy customer demand. BL's desperate need to build the car down to a price in order to make it competitive also led to cost-cutting in materials, equipment and, ultimately, in further development when the money nearly ran out altogether at the end of the 1970s.

A look at the problems that affected SD1 production in the first nine months of 1977 – the car's first full year on sale – makes the difficulties abundantly clear. In early 1977, the Castle Bromwich body plant went on strike, crippling production and undermining the launch of the SD1 in continental Europe when Rover had no cars to supply to their dealers. When normal working returned to the body plant, the British Leyland toolmakers walked out, bringing almost the whole of Leyland Cars to a standstill. Then, as the company began to recover from the effects of this, production was again hit by a ten-week strike in late summer by the toolmakers at Lucas Industries, who supplied vital components for the cars. All this had its own effect on the launch of the 2300 and 2600 models that was scheduled for October that year, and there were no 2300 models available in the showrooms until well into 1978.

CORPORATE REORGANIZATION (AGAIN)

When the SD1 was launched in mid-1976, Rover was one of the many marques under the common management of Leyland Cars, which had been established in 1975 as one of four operating divisions within a drastically restructured British Leyland after British Leyland had secured government support to prevent its insolvency. The managing director of British Leyland was now Alex Park, while the managing director of Leyland Cars was Derek Whittaker.

In 1977, the government brought in Michael Edwardes to run British Leyland. The hard-hitting South African took up office as chief executive on 1 November and almost immediately renamed the company BL Ltd. Park and Whittaker resigned, while Sir Donald Stokes retired and was elevated to the peerage as Lord Stokes. Ray Horrocks became managing director of British Leyland.

Edwardes reorganized Leyland Cars during 1978, hiving off Land Rover as a stand-alone business unit and dividing the rest of the organization into two semi-autonomous business units – Austin Morris and Jaguar Rover Triumph. They more or less (but not quite) corresponded to the earlier Volume Cars and Specialist Cars divisions, the key differences being that Land Rover was now separate and that MG now belonged to what was usually known as JRT.

JRT had its own management under chairman William Pratt Thompson, an American, and managing director Jeff Herbert. Jaguar was a very reluctant member of this division and always did its best to remain aloof from the Rover Triumph and MG side.

a modified system that reversed the polarity and made the car body the cathode instead of the anode as in the original process. The gassing problem disappeared. However, a lot of SD1s would be built before the revised paint process was introduced on the 1981-season cars; Rover had been unlucky to be commissioning its new paint plant just before a significantly improved technology became available.

Another important point is that morale was low within Leyland Cars generally by the mid-1970s. British Leyland, of which Leyland Cars was a component part, had been publicly and ingloriously bailed out by the government at the end of 1974 when it had run into a financial crisis. Leyland Cars itself had emerged from a restructuring of the various constituent companies, and one result was that the old workforce loyalties had been broken down. Rover, for example, no longer existed as a company, and those who worked at Solihull had seen so many organizational changes and changes in management since the start of the 1970s that they barely knew who they worked for any more. An inevitable result was that many of them no longer took, or had never developed, a pride in the cars they were assembling.

Press and public ridicule of British Leyland's failings cannot have helped, and it was already clear that British cars generally were falling further and further behind those built in Europe because complacency had led to a lack of investment in new products. In such circumstances, it must have been hard to feel involved with the assembly of the SD1; working on the production lines would have been nothing more than a job – and inevitably, there were those in the trades unions who wanted to exploit this disaffection for their own ends. Even Rover became used to stoppages and strikes, which were one reason why SD1 production took so long to reach acceptable volumes. By October 1977, when the 3500 had been on sale for more than a year, Roy Harry was able to write in the motoring section of the *Guardian* newspaper that the waiting list for the car still stood at about eight months.

The SD1 Estate – A Missed Opportunity?

Once the SD1 had successfully entered production, the next step was to see how the model range could be developed further. Responsibility for suggestions lay with the product planning department, which was then run by Alan Edis, and among the suggestions taken forward was one for an estate derivative of the SD1. It made a lot of sense: there had been an estate car derivative of the Triumph 2000/2500 range that the SD1 was replacing, and big estate cars from Ford (the Granada) and Volvo (the 244 and 264 models) were proving to be strong sellers.

The key period for the estate design was 1976 and 1977. The earliest serious work seems to have been done in May 1976, just before the SD1 saloon was announced, and photographs suggest that an estate rear end made from clay was added to the 'Low-Line' GRP model. A finished clay was ready by July, and then a GRP model was taken from this. Painted in Midas metallic gold, the model was ready in October, and it incorporated a raised roof at the rear and a wrap-over or 'clamshell' style of tailgate. The rear number plate was set into the tailgate panel.

An engineering prototype followed, and this was made from an early pre-production car that had been registered as LOE 99P on 17 February 1976. This, too, was finished in Midas, and it seems to have been turned into an estate at Rover soon after the GRP model was completed. The car had standard steel wheels and the stepped roof of the model remained, but there was a simplified tailgate that was inset from the sides of the body. The rear number plate was also relocated below the bumper, and a lifting handle for the tailgate was added, carrying rather small 'Rover 3500' identification. The interior was also properly developed, with a rearward-facing bench seat that folded into the floor of the load bay.

A second engineering prototype was built slightly later. The base model was again a 3500, this time registered SHP 549R on 20 January 1977. Bill Munro discovered, when writ-

RIGHT AND OVERLEAF, TOP LEFT: This appears to be the full-size GRP model of the estate car, dating from October 1977. Here it is on the viewing turntable in the styling studios. The blackout applied to the windows disguised the fact that the mock-up had no interior.

ABOVE RIGHT AND BELOW: The rear end was redesigned for the first running prototype: note that the number plate is now below the bumper rather than in the tailgate. The interior has now been reworked and includes a useful rearward-facing occasional seat that would have made the car a seven-seater and an ideal upmarket family holdall.

SD1 ESTATE PROTOTYPES

Michael Edwardes, who was appointed as British Leyland's chairman in late 1977, clearly thought highly of the SD1 estate project. He took SHP 549R for his personal transport and was often seen and photographed using it. By this time it had lost its alloy wheels and was wearing steel wheels, the dull trims visible in supposedly 'scoop' photographs published in the press suggesting the use of 2600-pattern plastic wheel trims.

Edwardes (by this time Sir Michael) left BL in September 1982, but before then SHP 549R had been given a major makeover to bring it into line with the 1981-season specification. This appears to have been done in late 1981 or early 1982, and the car took on Pharaoh Gold paint, bright metal mirror bodies, the latest bonnet badge and an interior with Vanden Plas-specification leather upholstery. The leather trim was extended to cover the rearward-facing third seat as well, and the car was put back on alloy wheels – this time Denovo alloys. Displaying a '3500E' designation above its rear number plate, it was then photographed at Windsor in February 1982.

One theory is that the car was updated so that management could take a second look at the SD1 estate project, but this is not very likely: it would surely have been updated with the planned 1982 specification if this were the case. Another possibility is that Michael Edwardes was still using the car and that he wanted it updated so that it looked more like the latest production SD1 models. However, the likelihood is once again that it would have been updated to 1982 specification if the BL chairman had wanted it to be more representative of the company's latest products.

One way or another, by the mid-1980s SHP 549R seems to have been in private hands. It was photographed in London, wearing steel wheels with 2000-style plastic trims, and looking more than a little down at heel. It was later acquired by the Haynes Motor Museum and is still on display there.

As for LOE 99P, taxation records show that it was not taxed after its initial twelve-month licence disc expired in February 1977. There is a story that it was used for a time by HRH Prince Charles, but the expiry of its tax disc in early 1977 means that his period of use must have been quite brief. It is possible that the story of SHP 549R being photographed at Windsor may somehow have been transformed into this suggestion that the Prince used one of the cars. LOE 99P was definitely at Solihull in July 1981, when the author photographed it on the Rover factory site (in the days when cameras were not forbidden). It has subsequently become part of the Heritage Motor Museum collection. The Museum believes that this car, not SHP 549R, was the one used by Michael Edwardes, but the photographs of the Edwardes car in London clearly show SHP 549R.

There was yet another rear-end redesign for the second prototype, which is seen here at Windsor in February 1982 after its 1981 update. This was the car used by BL chairman Michael Edwardes.

Another attractive estate car was created by an enthusiast in the UK, who grafted Volvo estate elements onto a red 1982 3500 saloon registered as TMK 428Y. This car was not part of the Rover project to create an estate version of the SD1.

ing his book *Carbodies, the Complete Story*, that the Coventry firm had some involvement with the SD1 estate project, and the photograph he found suggests that Carbodies built this second estate. Carbodies' involvement was logical, as they had been converting Triumph 2000/2500 saloon bodyshells to produce the estate versions which would go out of production in 1977. This second car followed more closely the lines of the original full-size mock-up, with a wrap-over tailgate that incorporated an inset number plate. It was again a metallic gold car, but this time seems to have worn alloy wheels from the start.

Enthusiasm for the SD1 estate was running high at Solihull in 1978–79, and product planning documents from about this time suggest that Rover were thinking of introducing it in autumn 1981, when the SD1 range would receive a midlife facelift. There are also photographs from March 1979 showing a wood and clay full-size model that is described as 'estate final'. However, this was a period when British Leyland were rapidly running out of money once again, and a number of promising new products had to be cancelled because there simply was no money to build them. The SD1 estate was one of the casualties; later product planning documents suggest that it had disappeared from the product plan before the end of 1979. The last trace of the project so far discovered was in 1980, when Carbodies were asked to provide costings for building the car – perhaps as a last-ditch attempt to revive what was clearly such a promising idea.

1978 Season Upgrades

The SD1 followed the plan laid out for it under Leyland Cars. The 6-cylinder models would join the range in October 1977, and at the same time some changes were made to the existing 3500 model. On the 1977 models, a passenger's door mirror had been an extra-cost option, but it was now made standard on 3500 and 2600 variants. The optional electric windows were now made standard, too, along with a four-speaker radio cassette system. All these were probably responses to customer feedback, and the truth was that charging extra for such items on a car of the SD1's pretensions had been an unforgivable example of cost-paring by accountants somewhere within British Leyland. Another example of cost-paring had been rectified out of necessity: the first cars had a single supporting strap for the rear parcel shelf, which allowed the shelf to wobble when the tailgate was open. The new models had two supporting straps – a far more satisfactory solution.

There were colour changes for the 1978 season, too. Caribbean (a dark metallic blue) was withdrawn and two new metallic colours were introduced. These were Persian Aqua, a strikingly effective light blue metallic, and Poseidon, a dark green metallic, which did not prove very popular in the UK but would remain available until summer 1980. Meanwhile, Rover was already planning to introduce the leather that so many customers had already requested. That would become available at extra cost in April 1978, although only in Nutmeg, a rather sombre dark brown.

The leather interior had been advertised in SD1 sales brochures from the start of the 1978 season. Those same sales brochures also advertised a second desirable extra-cost option, a sliding steel sunroof. Like the leather, however, this did not actually become available until April 1978, even though build records show that small numbers of cars with sunroofs had been built as early as mid-September 1976. Perhaps early ones had given trouble. It was becoming clear that the Solihull factory was not only having problems with getting the cars built, but also with getting changes implemented on production.

The 6-cylinder Cars

By the summer of 1977, volume production of the Triumph 6-cylinder engines had been established, and in mid-October Leyland Cars was able to announce the two companion models for the 3500 version of the SD1 as the Rover 2300 and 2600. Or, at least, that was how it appeared. In practice, although the 2300 was announced at the same time as the 2600, none reached the showrooms until May 1978. This left Leyland Cars with a yawning gap in their model range for well over six months, because the last of the Rover 2200 cars had been built in the early summer of 1977.

Nevertheless, both cars were introduced to the UK press at an event based at the Gosforth Park Hotel in Newcastle. 'It was well placed for a super route into the Cheviot Hills up to Jedburgh and beyond,' remembers Ian Elliott. ' I can't be categoric about the number of 2300 cars we had, but we *did* major on the 2600.'

The 2600 was really the replacement for the 2.5-litre Triumph saloons, and in Britain it slotted neatly into that sector of the market. With 136bhp at 5,000rpm and 152lb ft of torque at 3,750rpm, it offered plenty of performance and did not lag too far behind the 3500. To keep its price down, it lacked several elements of the 3500's standard equipment, but overall it was a well-rounded package with good customer appeal.

The 2300, on the other hand, may have replaced the Rover 2200 in the showrooms but was in fact aimed squarely at fleet buyers and was intended to compete head-on with Ford's strong-selling 2.3-litre Granada. To that end, it was very much a stripped-out 'fleet special', and unfortunately the early cars came across exactly like that. With just 123bhp at 5,000rpm and 134lb ft of torque at 4,000rpm, it sounded promising on paper but in practice lacked low-down torque. Its non-availability until summer 1978 simply allowed Ford to get an even stronger grip on the fleet market; Leyland promoted their Princess 2200 in the 2.3-litre bracket, but without much success because the car was already controversial on account of both its looks and its poor build quality.

Both cars came with the same 3.45:1 final drive gearing, lower than in the 3500 in order to compensate for their lower-powered engines. Although the 2600 came with the same five-speed gearbox as the 3500, the 2300 had a four-speed variant of the same design as standard, the five-speed box being an extra-cost option. Both could be had with the Borg Warner 65 three-speed automatic at extra cost, and both could be had with power-assisted steering, again at extra cost. The 2600 shared the 3500's self-levelling rear suspension, but the 2300 had ordinary telescopic rear dampers with variable-rate coil springs.

The simple way of recognizing the two cars was of course by their tail badges, which read either '2300' or '2600'. There were other superficial differences from the 3500. Neither car had fog lamps or tinted glass, although both could be so equipped at extra cost. The 2600 had rather dull grey plastic wheel trims with the clover-leaf design seen on the 3500, but the 2300 simply had very dreary looking plain grey plastic trims, with black instead of chromed wheel nuts. There were no mudflaps, unless the customer paid extra for them, and both cars had narrower, 175 HR 14 tyres than the 3500 – steel-braced on the 2600 but textile-braced on the 2300.

Neither 2600 nor 2300 came with central locking. Metallic paint, rear seat belts, and an upgraded radio cassette player with four speakers were also extra-cost options. The 2300 normally had tungsten headlamps unless ordered with

The 6-cylinder models followed the V8 into production during 1977. This was the 2600, the 2600, normally distinguished externally from the 3500 by the absence of foglamps (although this car has them), by painted plastic wheel trims, and by the absence of mudflaps. Note the absence of a passenger's side mirror, too.

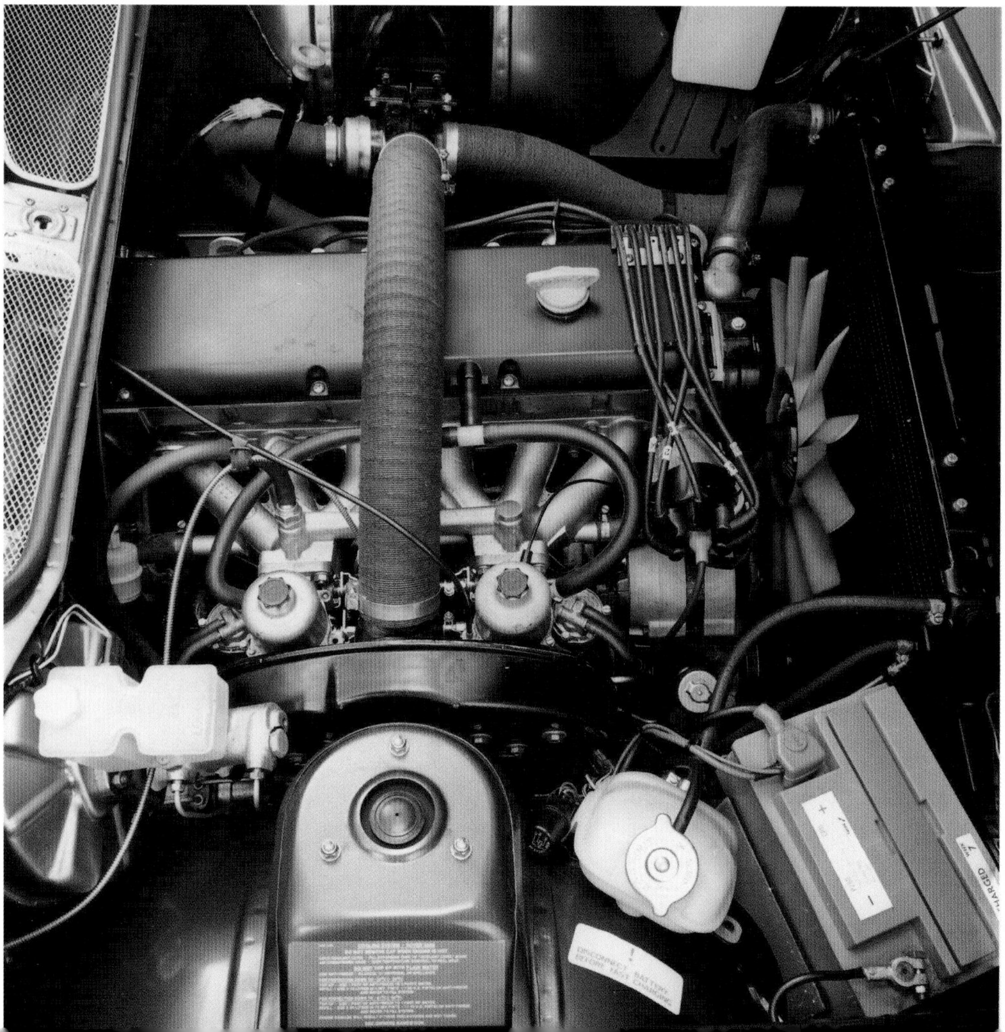

This was the 2300 entry-level model. Unpainted plastic wheel trims were the most obvious visual difference from the 2600.

The underbonnet view was exactly the same on both 2300 and 2600 models. The 6-cylinder engines were canted slightly backwards.

The interior layout of the 2600 models, seen here on the right, was essentially the same as on the V8s. However, the 2300 models (on the left) had a smaller instrument pod without a rev counter, and they had unique pleating on the seats. A close look shows that this 2300 had the optional five-speed gearbox; a four-speed was standard.

the quartz-halogen type fitted to the 2600 and 3500 – in which case there was again a cost penalty. It could not be had even optionally with the electric window lifts available on the 2600 and by now standard on the 3500. Only a driver's door mirror was standard, and there were other cheapening features on these early 2300s: no glovebox lamps, passenger's map-reading lamp or door-open lamps; different seat pleating and armrest coverings; a smaller instrument panel with no rev counter and fewer warning lights; rubber instead of carpet in the boot; and so on.

The 2300, 2600 and the Press

In many ways, it was a shame that the 3500 had been launched before the other two cars. It tended to overshadow them, and their later arrival inevitably made commentators focus on what had been dropped from the 3500 specification. If all three models had been launched together, there can be little doubt that public perceptions would have been very different.

Practical Motorist reported on a 2600 in its February 1978 issue. POK 25R was one of the Rover press fleet cars, with an automatic transmission. The magazine really liked the car, describing it as 'one of the sweetest cars we've driven' even though it had some imperfections.

> *It's quiet, comfortable, quite quick, and handles impeccably. At £5,800 it isn't exactly a gift, but if we had that sort of money, we wouldn't buy anything else.*

A fault with the brake warning lamp led the testers to disconnect it, and they 'were not impressed with the gear selector gate which was imprecise'. Performance was good, though, with 0–60mph in 12.9sec and a maximum on the banked track at MIRA of just under 110mph (177km/h). Fuel consumption worked out at 22.7mpg (12.5ltr/100km) overall.

> *The 2600 feels a little sluggish at first [and] a lighter throttle would make the Rover much less wearing around town. [However,] if you give the accelerator*

> *full boot, the 2600 accelerates like a Jumbo Jet on take-off – slowly at first, but gathering speed remarkably quickly as the revs rise . . . upward gearchanges are smooth and quick with more than 80mph available in second gear if you allow the transmission to make up its own mind, over 90mph if you hold second gear manually and let the revs rise to the red line at 6,000rpm.*

Handling was 'first class':

> *Even the slightly artificial feel of the power steering doesn't spoil the sense of security when you corner the car fast. The wide steel-braced radial tyres mean that it needs to be cornered very hard before breakaway is reached, and when this happens, it's a safe understeer that is corrected by lifting off the throttle.*

Cars & Car Conversions borrowed POK 19R, with five-speed gearbox, and reported on it in their June 1978 issue:

> *Driving behind a good 6-cylinder engine is a real pleasure, and that bestowed on the Rover is really good. . . . The torque band is very wide and low speed flexibility . . . is outstanding. . . . Revved hard, the unit responds eagerly, accompanied by a stimulating, though well controlled, growl which produces deceptively fast sprints.*

They recorded 0–60mph in under 11sec and a maximum speed of just under 120mph (193km/h). 'The 2600 is as refined as the V8, perhaps even more so. As a high speed cruiser it has much to offer, and passenger comfort is most impressive.'

Autocar tested a 2300 in its issue of 3 June 1978. Its overall praise of the SD1 design was unstinted, and good points were that the 2300 offered 'exceptionally quiet cruising, and the expected excellent SD1 steering, handling and ride qualities'. On the debit side, 'the 2300 has nothing remarkable in the way of mid-range performance (prospective towing owners please note)'. The model was also very close in price to the 2600 and offered a lot less.

> *Disregarding the less important options fitted to our test car but including power steering and five-speed transmission, its price is still over £6,000 and within £200 of a similarly equipped 2600, which has much better instrumentation and self-levelling suspension. Bearing this in mind, and the lack of any practical economy gains from the smaller engine, the 2600 would seem a far better buy.*

Worth adding here is a personal reminiscence of the 2600 from Ian Elliott, Leyland Cars' product and technical PR manager when the cars were new.

> *At the time that I had my first pre-launch drive of a 2600, I was using a Triumph 2500. The contrast was very marked – the old Triumph engine was smoother and quieter than the 2600 (mainly because it was necessary to use fairly hard engine mounts on the 2600 – the big ram pipes on the intake manifold meant that engine rock had to be constrained) but the Innsbruck was a really soggy pudding to drive after the nimble SD1.*

On the differences between the two 6-cylinder Rovers, he adds:

> *The short stroke 2300 version was significantly smoother than the 2600, I thought, and although relatively slow, it just beat the main competitor, the Granada 2.3.*

The 1979 Models

Not many changes were made to the SD1 range for the 1979 season. Like the 3500, the 2300 and 2600 could have leather upholstery at extra cost from April 1978, although very few actually did so. Power steering became standard on the 2600 in October 1978 for the 1979 season, and on the 3500 inertia-reel rear seat belts moved from the options list to the standard specification, while metallic paint became a no-cost option.

Dealers were advised in August 1978 that Black (gloss black) paint was being made available for a trial period, and by October 1978 the paint shop at Solihull had a production target of thirty black cars a week, although the new paint was not made public until February 1979, when it was touted as a 'special option'. In fact, a number of black cars had already been supplied in the third quarter of 1976 to special order for Prime Minister Jim Callaghan and for official use by the Government Car Service.

PAINT AND TRIM OPTIONS – 1976–1979

June 1976 to September 1977

There were initially nine paint colours, of which three were metallics. These were accompanied by four upholstery and interior colours. Amontillado was discontinued in March-April 1977, leaving just three interior options.

Colour name	Description	Interior options
Atlantis	Dark blue	Caviar or Coriander
Avocado	Bright green	Coriander or Nutmeg
Brazilia	Dark brown	Amontillado or Coriander
Caribbean	Dark blue metallic	Amontillado, Caviar or Coriander
Midas	Light gold metallic	Caviar or Nutmeg
Pendelican	White	Amontillado, Caviar or Nutmeg
Platinum	Silver metallic	Caviar or Nutmeg
Richelieu	Rich red	Caviar or Coriander
Turmeric	Yellow	Caviar or Coriander

October 1977 to September 1978

From October 1977, when the 2300 and 2600 were announced, the paint options were changed. Caribbean was withdrawn and two new metallic colours (Persian Aqua and Poseidon) were introduced. These ten exterior colours were accompanied by the same three interior colours.

Colour name	Description	Interior options
Atlantis	Dark blue	Caviar or Coriander
Avocado	Bright green	Coriander or Nutmeg
Brazilia	Dark brown	Coriander
Midas	Light gold metallic	Caviar or Nutmeg
Pendelican	White	Caviar or Nutmeg
Persian Aqua	Light blue metallic	Caviar or Coriander
Platinum	Silver metallic	Caviar or Nutmeg
Poseidon	Dark green metallic	Coriander or Nutmeg
Richelieu	Rich red	Caviar or Coriander
Turmeric	Yellow	Caviar or Coriander

October 1978 to June 1979

From October 1978, there were eleven paint options. Black was initially added to the list for a trial period and then became available as a 'special option' from February 1979. There were again three interior colours, although some cars from late 1978 were trimmed in Amontillado, possibly as a way of using up remaining stocks of this interior trim. Leather upholstery now became optional; it was always in Nutmeg.

Colour name	Description	Interior options
Atlantis	Dark blue	Caviar or Coriander
Avocado	Bright green	Coriander or Nutmeg
Black	Gloss black	Caviar, Coriander or Nutmeg
Brazilia	Dark brown	Coriander
Midas	Light gold metallic	Caviar or Nutmeg
Pendelican	White	Caviar or Nutmeg
Persian Aqua	Light blue metallic	Caviar or Coriander
Platinum	Silver metallic	Caviar or Nutmeg
Poseidon	Dark green metallic	Coriander or Nutmeg
Richelieu	Rich red	Caviar or Coriander
Turmeric	Yellow	Caviar or Coriander

TECHNICAL SPECIFICATIONS
ROVER SDI, 1976–1979

Engines

2300
Type PE 146 6-cylinder petrol
2350cc (81 x 76mm)
Single overhead camshaft
Four-bearing crankshaft
Compression ratio 9.25:1
Two SU HS6 carburettors
123bhp at 5,000rpm
134lb ft at 4,000rpm

2600
Type PE 166 6-cylinder petrol
2597cc (81 x 84mm)
Single overhead camshaft
Four-bearing crankshaft
Compression ratio 9.25:1
Two SU HS6 carburettors
136bhp at 5,000rpm
152lb ft at 3,750rpm

3500
V8-cylinder petrol
3528cc (88.9 x 71.1mm)
Single overhead camshaft
Five-bearing crankshaft
Compression ratio 9.35:1
Two SU HIF6 carburettors
155bhp at 5,250rpm
198lb ft at 2,500rpm

(Some export V8 engines had an 8.13:1 compression ratio with two Zenith-Stromberg 175CD carburettors and 133bhp. For further details, see Chapter 8.)

Transmission
Five-speed manual gearbox standard on 2600 and 3500
Ratios 3.32:1, 2.08:1, 1.39:1, 1.00:1, 0.83:1; reverse 3.43:1
Four-speed manual gearbox standard on 2300
Ratios 3.32:1, 2.08:1, 1.39:1, 1.00:1; reverse 3.43:1
Three-speed Borg Warner type 65 automatic gearbox optional
Ratios 2.39:1, 1.45:1, 1.00:1; reverse 1.92:1

Axle ratio

3500	3.08:1
2300	3.45:1
2600	3.45:1

Suspension, steering and brakes
Front suspension with MacPherson struts, lower links and anti-roll bar
Rear axle with torque tube, trailing arms, Watt's linkage and coil springs
Rack-and-pinion steering; power assistance standard on 3500 and optional on 2300 and 2600
Disc brakes at front with 258mm (10.13in) diameter; drum brakes at rear with 229mm (9in) diameter; vacuum servo assistance standard

Dimensions

Overall length	185in (4,699mm)
Overall width	70in (1,778mm)
Overall height	55in (1,397mm)
Wheelbase	110.8in (2,814mm)
Front track	59in (1,499mm)
Rear track	59in (1,499mm)

Wheels and tyres
14in five-bolt steel wheels with 5.5in rims (2300 and 2600); 14in five-bolt steel wheels with 6in rims (3500); 14in five-bolt alloy wheels with 6in rims optional on 2600 and 3500
Steel wheels with 175 HR 14 tyres (2300 and 2600) or 185 HR 14 tyres (3500)
Alloy wheels with 195/70 HR 14 tyres

Kerb weights
(depending on options fitted)

2300	2,787–2,912lb (1,264–1,321kg)
2600	2,866–2,972lb (1,300–1,348kg)
3500	2,877–2,989lb (1,305–1,356kg)

The styling department continued to work on possible improvements to keep the car fresh. This dates from around 1978 and adds a contrasting body side indentation, bright wheel-arch highlights, and a twin-panel glass sunroof. None of these proposals entered production.

Rover Triumph ran a competition through the employees' magazine, *Specialist Car*, to name the black paint, and this was won by Anne Sharp, a production and material control trainee then working at BL Cars' Coventry office. She won a bottle of Champagne for her suggestion of Maraschino, although that name was not used in sales material until July 1979 and the start of the 1980 season. Strangely, when Black first became available, it was priced at £88.55 on the 2300 and 2600 models but only £33.87 on a 3500 – a very effective deterrent to would-be owners of black cars who had set their sights on a 6-cylinder Rover.

CHAPTER FOUR

THE 1980 AND 1981 MODELS

Ever since the SD1 had been launched, there had been an undercurrent of criticism that it was insufficiently 'Rover', and did not embody many of the characteristics that the buying public expected of a car with that badge. They did not want a homogenized Leyland product; they wanted a Rover to look and feel like a Rover, even if it did have an ultra-modern shape.

Leyland Cars had to respond to criticisms like these, because there was an unquantifiable risk that they were working against sales. The public had not taken kindly to David Bache's 'skeletal' Rover badge, so that would have to go. They wanted a more upmarket interior with leather seat facings – and those had arrived as an option in April 1978. Then the Black paint option made available from autumn 1978 had added sobriety to the Rover's modern looks.

The mounting pressure to give the car a more traditional Rover feel with a higher level of equipment and luxury coincided with Leyland's programme to sell the car in the USA. US customers were going to want such improvements, and the two sets of requirements were wrapped up together as the Rover designers worked on higher specification levels for SD1 in the later 1970s.

Air Conditioning

By this time, a satisfactory air-conditioning system had become essential for any car with luxury pretensions in many markets around the world. Leyland therefore had to wait until such a system was available before announcing the SD1 in overseas markets such as the USA and the Middle East. Meanwhile, the Rover engineers worked with the SU-Butec division of Pressed Steel Fisher to develop a system that could be built into the SD1 on the assembly lines rather than added as an aftermarket accessory. That had been the only realistic solution for Australia (see Chapter 8), where the importers had settled for an add-on system from Alpinair to meet demand until Solihull could come up with the real thing.

The SU-Butec system was developed to be as similar as possible to the US-made automotive air-conditioning systems on which expectations were based in most world markets. Even its controls copied the style and layout of American systems, so that buyers of an SD1 with air conditioning would have no difficulty in adapting to that element of the car. In practice, many of the system's components were directly sourced from General Motors in the USA, the compressor, for example, being a GM Harrison item and the VIR (Valve-In-Receiver) unit being extensively used in GM cars of the period.

The plan was to introduce the system to the UK first, partly in order to gain experience of it in service before it was released to overseas markets. In order to do that, Rover's product planners came up with the idea of a new top-of-the-range model that would have the new air-conditioning system as standard and would also have distinctive styling, trim and equipment features to set it apart from the rest of the range.

THE V8-S

Rover's new top-of-the-range model was introduced on 2 July 1979. A launch stock of 900 cars ensured that every Rover Triumph outlet in the UK would have at least one example to sell. Those first cars came with metallic paint in one of three colours (Midas, Persian Aqua or garish new Triton), but the plan was to make the V8-S available with the full range of SD1 colours after these had been sold.

Both manual and automatic models were made available, the latter of course costing extra. In Britain, the car certainly was expensive: the manual model cost £10,699.22 (£8,588 base price plus £715.67 Special Car Tax and £1,395.55 VAT), while the automatic cost £10,929.22 after tax.

This car, bearing a 1977–78 registration number, was used for styling development of the V8-S. The bright Triton green metallic paint and the black bumpers are already in place, and so is the extra air intake for the air-conditioning system, but the bonnet badge simply has a red background and the rear badging has not been settled.

The only visible change to the bodyshell was a small air intake slot in the front panel just below the bonnet, added so that cooling air could be forced through the condenser radiator for the SU-Butec system. All cars had the sliding manual sunroof as standard, too. The distinctive exterior features were all cosmetic, beginning with black bumpers, double coachlines on the flanks – in the form of adhesive tape rather than hand-painted – and a chrome-plated exhaust tailpipe.

This early V8-S (note the T-suffix registration, current during summer 1979) was photographed at the entrance to Eastnor Castle in Herefordshire, where Land Rover did (and still does) much of its off-road testing. The bright blue Persian Aqua paint was not unique to the V8-S, but the gold-painted alloy wheels were.

The Scandinavian-pattern wash-wipe system was standardized on the V8-S for some markets, including the Italian-specification car pictured here.

Clearly visible on this left-hand-drive V8-S (again, the Italian car) are the twin coachlines and the compressor for the new air-conditioning system. The V8-S came with gas struts to support the bonnet, instead of a metal prop.

Further distinction was added by gold-painted alloy wheels, which looked much better in practice than the description suggests. (If a car was ordered with Platinum silver paint, the wheels were finished in silver rather than gold.) Then there was a special version of the Triplex Ten-Twenty windscreen with a 4in band of graduated tint at the top. This was intended to reduce glare for the driver, and the V8-S was the first UK-built volume-production car to have such a feature.

There were special badges, too. All cars carried a bright metal V8 motif low down on each front wing, and the rear badges had black backgrounds with silver lettering in what Rover called 'stylized Euroscript'. The S of V8-S was highlighted in red. On the nose, the skeletal bonnet badge was replaced by a more traditional-looking Rover Viking ship emblem, and although it was not clear yet, this badge would become standard on the 1981 models in autumn 1980. Stylish though it may have been, David Bache's modern interpretation of the Viking ship emblem had not gone down well with Rover customers, many of whom were traditionalists at heart.

David Bache's team had seen the V8-S as an opportunity to try out a number of new ideas, and the interior was again distinctive. Against a background of Nutmeg carpets and plastic trim, the seats were upholstered in a new velvet material that came in either Beige or Bronze. The rear seats came with their own head restraints, and all four head restraints had press-studs to take detachable cushions. The carpets, though in a familiar colour, had a fashionably deep shagpile, and there were cloth facings on the door armrests.

Sadly, however, it was clear that Rover had built the V8-S down to a price. The bright trim that Bache had used to frame the centre console, the air vents, the facia and the interior door locks turned out to be chromed plastic – and that 'chrome' tended to wear off after a while. Similarly, although all four head restraints had fittings for cushions, only two cushions were included in the car's price. Those tape side-stripes were another example of cost-cutting. It is certainly arguable that the V8-S would have had a more pronounced feeling of quality about it if money had been spent on some of these areas rather than on replacing the standard mechanical bonnet prop with self-supporting gas struts.

At the launch of the V8-S, Rover claimed to be aiming for production of 140 cars a week, a figure that presumably included equivalent models for overseas markets. In practice, air-conditioned SD1s took some time to be rolled out in markets outside the UK. Switzerland began to take delivery of cars in February 1980, and here (as in West Germany) they were called 3500S models in some sales literature, although the V8-S badging was always the same as on home-market cars. Italy introduced the V8-S in March, and the US model SD1 arrived at the same time. However, the V8-S itself lasted only one year in production, the last examples being built over the summer of 1980. Figures from the archives at the Heritage Motor Centre in Gaydon suggest that no more than 1,040 examples were built, which makes the V8-S one of the rarest of all SD1 models.

A more traditional Rover badge was central to the 'Roverisation' that came with the V8-S in summer 1979.

Although the V8-S was a step in the right direction as far as equipment levels were concerned, it was not – yet – the 'conservative' Rover that many customers in Britain wanted to see. That would come later.

THE 1980 MODELS

3500, 2600, 2300

The mainstream models for the 1980 model year were altogether less adventurous than the V8-S, although they did incorporate some mechanical changes. Most important was that a Borg Warner type 66 automatic gearbox replaced the earlier type 65. This was essentially an updated version of the old gearbox, and came with the same internal ratios as before. The power-steering system now had a new integral pump and reservoir, and the air conditioning pioneered on the V8-S became optional at extra cost on other models. A headlamp wash-wipe system became optional, having originally been developed for Scandinavian countries where regulations required one. Revised settings for the self-levelling struts on cars that had them gave a softer ride than before. On the inside, there was now carpet material on the rear parcel shelf, intended to prevent items stowed there from sliding about as they had done on the earlier plastic surface.

The specification of the 3500 models was adjusted just after the start of the 1980 model year, when alloy wheels became part of the standard equipment. To match that, an alloy version of the Denovo wheel was also made available. This had a design very similar to that of the standard alloy wheel, but was very slightly different. Like the Denovo steel wheels, it also had a distinctive red band around the rim. However, the Denovo wheels never did become popular, and these alloy versions seem to have been particularly rare; probably rarest of all is the gold-finish Denovo alloy wheel that was made available for the V8-S from January 1980. January 1980 also saw a change in the specification of the optional leather interiors: originally available with leather only on the seat facings, they now became available with leather on the sides of the seats and on the head restraints as well.

Sales of the 1980 models were affected by the slump in sales of large cars that followed major fuel price increases in 1979. Stories were told of fields full of unsold cars, and many of the cars that had stood out in all weathers later became early victims of rust. Over the summer of 1980, dealer stocks were discounted heavily to help clear showrooms of the old models in time for the arrival of the upgraded 1981 models.

The general turn against large cars was also affecting prices of used SD1s. When *Autocar* ran a 'Buying Secondhand' guide for the SD1 range in its issue of 23 February 1980, it noted that there were plenty of used 3500s on the market at the time, partly because:

At the start of the 1980 model year, which introduced V-suffix registrations in the UK, the standard cars looked much the same as they always had. This is a 3500 with the optional alloy wheels.

The two 6-cylinder cars were also much as before for 1980. The press photos give the impression that not a lot of effort had gone into the choice of locations.

This was styling director David Bache's own SD1, which of course incorporated several ideas from the styling department. A front spoiler, two-tone paint and painted alloy wheels are matched by four head restraints with detachable cushions (as would later appear on the V8-S) and by the larger badge lettering that would arrive on 1980 models. Note the silver V8 lettering and associated hatching on the rear-quarter glass and the discreet rear spoiler.

many first owners have become worried by the way in which their secondhand values have continued to plummet in the last year or so; for that you can partly blame BL's own 'image' problem, although the fuel-thirsty image is difficult to live down as well.

The magazine also quoted examples:

Six-month-old V8-S models which cost £11,000 when new are now only worth about £6,500 as 'trade-ins', and you would be able to buy one in a showroom for not more than £7,500. Can you come to terms with a car which has depreciated £3,500 in six months? 1979 model 3500s, too, sell for at least £3,000 under list price, and you could certainly find 1976 3500s for a mere £3,200–£3,300.

The V8-S and the Press

The SD1 had been on sale for three years by the summer of 1979, and without major changes to its specification did not attract much attention from the motoring press. However, the V8-S model did merit a road test report in *Motor* dated 19 July 1980 – by which time it had been on sale for a year.

Another car from the press fleet, FRW 189T, received a brief but revealing write-up in *Thoroughbred & Classic Cars* magazine for February 1980.

When writer Brian Palmer turned the heater on, a stream of water emerged in the passenger's footwell. 'Whenever the fan was used this expensive douche would come into play – so we had to put up with steamed-up windows and cold/wet feet.' He took the car into the Rover dealership in Stirling, who 'proved thoroughly disinterested in the whole thing, eventually suggesting I could leave the car for an indefinite period until they might find time to look at it'.

Palmer did not leave the car with them, but pressed on to Oban, where a small local garage discovered that

rainwater was entering the air intake vents, passing where it shouldn't into the plenum chamber and then being drawn out by the fan. They could only offer a temporary remedy but this held up until the return journey.

Clearly, build quality was still not up to acceptable standards, though the car tested by *Motor*, FRW 192T, revealed no such problems:

If our test car was anything to go by, Rover have now achieved the standard of finish that the excellence

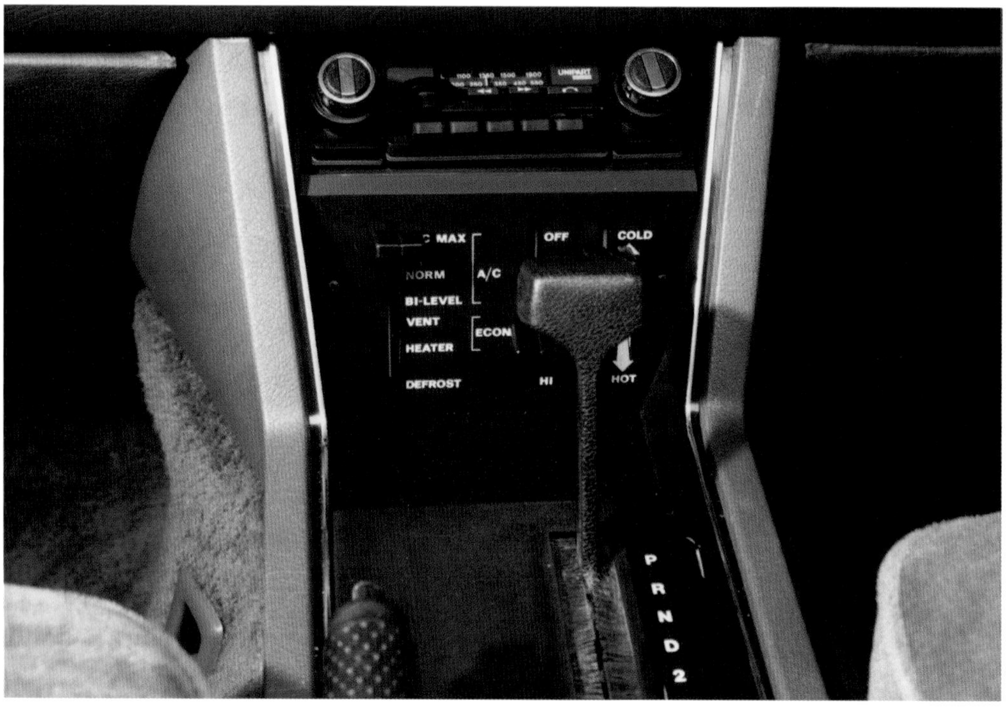

The controls for the new air-conditioning system were integrated within the existing heating and ventilation control panel. Note the bright highlights on the console that were characteristic of the V8-S.

The velour upholstery of the V8-S was very much of its time, but did offer at least the appearance of more luxury than the standard fabric. Four head restraints were standard, but it was typical of the cost-cutting atmosphere of the period that only two clip-on cushions were supplied.

of the basic design deserves. . . . Happily for BL the Rover as a basic design is still an impressive all-rounder. Refined, versatile and blessed with excellent road manners, it is virtually unrivalled as an economical long-distance express. It is also comfortable and lavishly equipped, although we have reservations about the 'S' package's value, given that air conditioning is so rarely needed in the British climate.

The Fuel-Injected V8

Critical to Leyland Cars' plans to introduce the SD1 in many markets around the world was the availability of an engine with exhaust-emissions control. Emissions-control equipment was notorious in this period for sapping engine power, so the only SD1 engine to which it could be satisfactorily applied was the most powerful one in the Rover stable, the 3.5-litre V8.

Product planning had originally hoped to launch the car in Canada first (where British cars tended to receive a warmer welcome) during autumn 1979 and then to follow up in the USA in spring 1980. However, the Canadian launch plan was abandoned and Rover decided to focus on a summer 1980 US launch.

One reason for this change of plan was that the development of the emissions-controlled engine had become entangled with plans to use it in the US-market Triumph TR8 sports car. The TR8 had been planned for a 1978 introduction, but had been delayed by strikes and had eventually reached the market as a 1980 model. There were unwelcome complications in its production: although most US states were content with an emissions-controlled carburettor engine (known as the 49-State type), stricter emissions regulations in California demanded finer control of fuelling. The only way this requirement could be met was by using fuel injection, and the Californian-specification engine was developed using a Bosch L-Jetronic injection system built under licence in the UK by Lucas, who called it an Airflow Meter System (it has also incorrectly been described as a Lucas L-type system). Bosch in fact supplied many of the parts, including the air flow meter, the injectors, the extra air valve and the coolant temperature

A COMPANION IN PRODUCTION

SD1 production never came near to filling the huge assembly hall that had been built for it, and British Leyland management decided to make use of some of the redundant space by moving Triumph TR7 production from the Triumph works at Canley into the Solihull works where the Rover was assembled. It made good sense: the SD1 and TR7 shared major components such as gearboxes and rear axles, and the TR7 was about to spawn a TR8 derivative that would share the Rover V8 engine in both carburettor (for Europe) and fuel-injection (for North America) forms.

So TR7 production was transferred to Solihull over the spring and summer of 1980. However, it was to be a short-lived experiment because production of the TR7 was halted in October 1981. The TR8 was to have come on-stream as a 1982 model, but only pre-production and press demonstrator cars had been built before production stopped.

sensor, although the electronic control unit (ECU) was made by Lucas and used custom-made integrated circuits supplied by Ferranti in the UK.

Having two different versions of the engine in production at the same time was a headache, so a plan was drawn up to do away with separate 49-State and Californian versions of the engine and to produce a single emissions-controlled V8 for the 1981 models that could be sold right across North America. This engine would obviously also suit the SD1 and its planned summer 1980 introduction to the USA – and all the more so because from summer 1980 TR8 (and TR7) production was to be transferred to the East Works at Solihull, where the two cars would be built alongside SD1s for all markets.

Pilot examples of the fuel-injected SD1 nevertheless existed long before the US launch date. Build records show that the first 'production' models were built in mid-July 1979, and that the first cars were destined for Canada – which was consistent with the original plan to launch the car in Canada first. Cars for the USA began to come off the lines in November 1979, although early examples were stored until shipments to the USA actually began in February 1980. The author saw a handful of early North American specification cars during an enthusiasts' club visit to the Solihull assembly lines on 15 September 1979 – when, sadly, the line was not operating because the plant was on a three-day working week. There was a particular irony about the occasion because the Solihull tour had been arranged as part of the celebrations surrounding seventy-five years of Rover car production.

THE NORTH AMERICAN SD1

Rover's track record in the USA was not a happy one. The company had struggled ever since the early 1950s to gain a foothold in this big market, but had come up against the problem of having too few dealers scattered across the country. Its Land Rovers had encountered the same problem, and although the company had made a determined effort in the 1960s to gain sales with Federalized versions of its P6 2000 and P6B 3500 saloons, it had achieved mediocre results. Faced with escalating development costs as US emissions and safety regulations tightened at the start of the 1970s, it had withdrawn its cars from the market in 1971. The Land Rover lingered three years longer, disappearing from North America in 1974.

As a result, the Rover name was not well known in North America by the time the SD1 began production, and where it was remembered, it was not always remembered very fondly. Nevertheless, Leyland Cars saw the latest Rover as an integral part of their North American product offensive for the early 1980s. A report in the June-July 1976 issue of *Automotive Engineer*, the magazine of the Institute of Mechanical Engineers, states that the car was designed so that it could be modified to meet US regulations, although it did not yet do so. What the report did not say was that David Bache's styling studio had been working on the necessary design modifications since the start of the year, and the earliest photographs of proposals so far found in fact date from February 1976. The earliest North American-specification car would be built in early 1977: described as 'NAS 33VM Methods Build', it had serial no. 9598.

The biggest challenge to the styling team was to integrate impact-absorbing bumpers into the design. It was a US requirement that none of the car's vital lights should be damaged in a low-speed impact, such as might occur when parking, and the easiest way of meeting this was by fitting bumpers mounted on hydraulic struts that absorbed the energy of the impact.

Several ideas were tried before the styling of the US-model SD1 was settled. This proposal used wire wheels, and that red stripe was matched by a similarly coloured interior.

US legislation gave the design engineers a hard time, and here it is in a pile on the bonnet of a 50,000-mile US-specification test car.

This proposal for the US car incorporated a small dummy grille as well as paired square headlamps. A special bonnet pressing would have been required.

By definition, such bumpers had to move inwards and towards the body of the car on impact, and that in turn meant they had to protrude quite a long way from it. Grafting such bumpers onto an existing design was bound to unbalance it – and on the SD1, it did. Fortunately, perhaps, Rover were not alone in facing this problem, and every European manufacturer trying to sell cars in the USA suffered in the same way. The results were frequently very far from pretty.

North American regulations also required that headlights should conform to one of a small number of standard designs, so that replacements could be bought at every car accessories store in the country and did not have to be ordered specially. After trying a design with four square headlamps, Bache's team settled on one with a pair of round lamps on each side of the car's nose. As these could not be covered by an additional glass lens, the lamps gave an odd, notched appearance to the front of the car, and of course the angular shape did further damage to the aerodynamics of the original design. Other North American lighting requirements led to all-amber wrap-around front turn-indicator lenses, which also contained side marker lights, and these were matched by red running lights let into the rear bumper wrap-arounds.

As the US design and the European V8-S high-specification car were being developed at more or less the same time, it was inevitable that there should be some cross-fertilization between them. In fact, the V8-S pioneered some features of the North American car, giving Rover some experience of these features in service before the SD1 was actually launched in the USA.

Key among those features were the SU-Butec air-conditioning system and cross-ribbed velvet upholstery from the V8-S. Also carried over from the V8-S were velour-trimmed door panels and bright highlights on the dash, console and air vents. However, the North American SD1 did not have rear head restraints, even as an option, and a sunroof was only available at extra cost. The alloy wheels were standard wear, but no Denovo option was offered. More regulations demanded side-impact beams in the doors, rear seat belts as standard and a chime to warn the driver if a seat was occupied but the relevant safety belt was not fastened.

Then there were some special features on the US car, notably a somewhat jingoistic Union flag emblem on each front wing and a twin coachline just above the swage line on the body sides, which continued around the rear of the car. Inside, there was a special three-spoke steering wheel, probably specified for fear that Americans would react adversely to the not-quite-round wheel of the standard cars. A cruise control was also standard and the speedometer was marked only to 85mph in accordance with contemporary US regulations.

Most of this extra equipment added weight, and the emissions-controlled engine with its twin catalytic converters lacked the power of the standard-issue SD1 V8. The actu-

The real thing, at last – this was one of the press release pictures for the SD1 in the USA. The huge bumpers did the appearance no favours. Just visible is the Union flag badge on the lower front wing – unique to these cars in the SD1 range.

A distinctive feature of the US-model SD1 was a round steering wheel – leather-rimmed, of course. The bright dashboard highlights were the same as those on the V8-S models for other markets.

As this brochure cover dated February 1980 shows, the new front end on the North American cars worked well enough – it was the side profile that did no favours to David Bache's sleek styling.

al figures, expressed in US-friendly SAE nett terms, were 133bhp at 5,000rpm with 165lb ft of torque at 3,250rpm, which immediately reveals how much power had been sacrificed to the cleaner exhaust. The North American 3500 was made available with the five-speed manual gearbox as standard, partly to give it a more sporty image, but with the three-speed automatic as an extra-cost option. In five-speed form, it took 10sec to reach 60mph from rest and could reach 116mph (187km/h). Though slow by comparison with the European model, it was quite respectable in comparison with other saloons available in North America at the time.

Despite high hopes in some quarters, the North American SD1 adventure failed dismally. By the time it was launched in summer 1980, British Leyland was running out of money again and did not put any real promotional effort behind the car. Quality control was no better on these cars than on their European equivalents, and US consumers expected more of a car that cost $15,900 when it was introduced; by way of comparison a 1981-model Cadillac Fleetwood Brougham sedan cost $15,564, while a 1981 Buick Century Limited (broadly the same size as an SD1) cost just $7,999.

The buyers stayed away. Figures currently available show that only 1,254 cars were sold before British Leyland decided to withdraw the SD1 from sale after a single year. More specifically, 480 cars were sold in the 1980 calendar year and 774 in the first half of 1981, by which time dealers were offering discounts as high as $2,000 just to get the cars out of their showrooms. It was an unqualified disaster.

PAINT AND TRIM OPTIONS NORTH AMERICAN SD1, 1980–1981

All paint colours were available with either Nutmeg/Bronze or Nutmeg/Beige interior trim.

There were ten paint options, as follows:

Atlantis Blue	Platinum Metallic
Brazilia Brown	Poseidon Green Metallic
Midas Gold Metallic	Richelieu Red
Pendelican White	Triton Green Metallic
Persian Aqua Metallic	Turmeric Yellow

Note that contemporary sales brochures consistently referred to 'Brazilia Brown Metallic'. The colour was in fact the standard 'solid' Brazilia Brown, with code BLVC 214.

SD1 and the North American Press

Even though the SD1 failed in North America, the motoring press had welcomed the car on its arrival in 1980. *Road & Track* magazine tested one for its April 1980 issue, concluding:

> *For the enthusiast driver whose needs dictate a 4-door family sedan, but whose heart is steeped in the joy of exciting performance and crisp handling, the Rover 3500 is like a dream come true.*

The magazine liked the car's shape, 'a pleasant overall design that succeeds from nearly all angles', although they felt that the special US headlamp installation did not look very good. The V8 engine was 'extremely smooth throughout the range', although the fuel pump was noisy at idle and the fan was noisy at all engine speeds. They concluded with a caveat:

> *It should do very well in the US, but, and it's a very big but, the car will stand or fall entirely on the standard of quality control at the factory and the standard of service and availability of parts at the dealerships.*

Sadly, that reservation was well founded.

Car and Driver tested the very same car (with licence plate DTM-68) for its May 1980 issue, achieving a better 0–60mph time of 9.8sec with a 117mph (188km/h) top speed. Used to German cars at the quality end of the market, the magazine was 'more than a little shocked to admit that the automotive surprise this spring comes from . . . England'.

> *The Rover 3500 has a warm, endearing, just slightly eccentric personality. It's a car one savors with the hope that there will always be an England.*

They thought the car was a 'unique and unprecedented blend', with looks that made it 'downright Italian the way it seduces you on first glance'. The interior was 'cavernous', although 'ergonomic perfection is lost on the instrument pod'. Overall, 'the most serious shortcoming you're likely to encounter in the Rover is its 15mpg fuel economy' (the US gallon is of course smaller than the Imperial gallon used in the UK, so this equates to about 18mpg).

TECHNICAL SPECIFICATIONS NORTH AMERICAN SD1, 1980–1981

Engine
V8-cylinder petrol
3528cc (88.9 x 71.1mm)
Single overhead camshaft
Five-bearing crankshaft
Compression ratio 8.13:1
Lucas fuel injection
133bhp (SAE nett) at 5,000rpm
165lb ft (SAE nett) at 3,250rpm

Transmission
Five-speed manual gearbox standard
Ratios 3.32:1, 2.08:1, 1.39:1, 1.00:1, 0.83:1; reverse 3.43:1
Three-speed Borg Warner type 66 automatic gearbox optional
Ratios 2.39:1, 1.45:1, 1.00:1; reverse 1.92:1

Axle ratio
3.08:1

Suspension, steering and brakes
Front suspension with MacPherson struts, lower links and anti-roll bar.
Rear axle with torque tube, trailing arms, Watt's linkage and coil springs.
Rack-and-pinion steering with standard power assistance.
Disc brakes at front with 258mm (10.13in) diameter; drum brakes at rear with 229mm (9in) diameter; vacuum servo assistance standard.

Dimensions

Overall length	185in (4,699mm)
Overall width	70in (1,778mm)
Overall height	55in (1,397mm)
Wheelbase	110.8in (2,814mm)
Front track	59in (1,499mm)
Rear track	59in (1,499mm)

Wheels and tyres
14in five-bolt alloy wheels
195/70 HR 14 tyres

Kerb weight
3,251lb (1,475kg) with manual gearbox
3,226lb (1,463kg) with automatic gearbox

THE 1981 MODELS

The 1980 calendar year was the worst ever for SD1 sales, with lower overall totals from the four models on sale (2300, 2600, 3500 and V8-S) than there had been in 1976 when there had been just a single model available. The worldwide reaction against large cars that followed the fuel price rises in 1979 was a major reason for this, but poor quality control was also a factor.

Three things were expected to improve SD1 sales for the 1981 season: a high-profile racing programme (*see* Chapter 9), the car's introduction to North America, and an improved model range. Although the US initiative was a failure, the other two did help to make a huge improvement in sales. From a miserable 25,619 cars in 1980, production rose in 1981 to 35,885 – a massive increase of over 40 per cent.

The 1981 models were introduced at the Motor Show in October 1980, and were immediately identifiable by the new pictorial Viking ship emblem on the nose, as pioneered on the V8-S. The range now consisted of five models instead of the previous four. As before, the entry-level model was the 2300, but above this was added a better-equipped version with the same engine and 2300S badges. The popular middle-range car now came with a higher specification than before and was called a 2600S, and the mainstream V8 model became a 3500SE while there was a new Rover Vanden Plas at the top of the range. This name had never previously been used on a Rover, but had become available to British Leyland through its acquisition of Austin, and of course had originally belonged to the high-quality coachbuilder that Austin had bought out in 1946.

New paint colours and bright housings for the door mirrors rejuvenated the exterior, and all models now had

For 1981, the new Vanden Plas model headed the Rover range, and always looked best in Bordeaux Red like this example. The rubber bump-strips in the side indentations and the dark finish for the alloy wheels were both unique Vanden Plas features. The ROV 1 registration number always belonged to Rover dealers Colliers of Birmingham, but was on permanent loan to the Rover Company and was generally applied to the car used by its managing director.

Leather finally returned to the standard Rover range for the Vanden Plas, which also had the bright dashboard highlights pioneered on the V8-S. This is the darker of the two leather options and, unusually, the car has a manual gearbox.

ABOVE AND BELOW: The twin coachlines on Vanden Plas and 3500SE models were very neat, even though they were only stuck on. They had been planned for the SD1 range from the start but, for cost-cutting reasons, were not used initially.

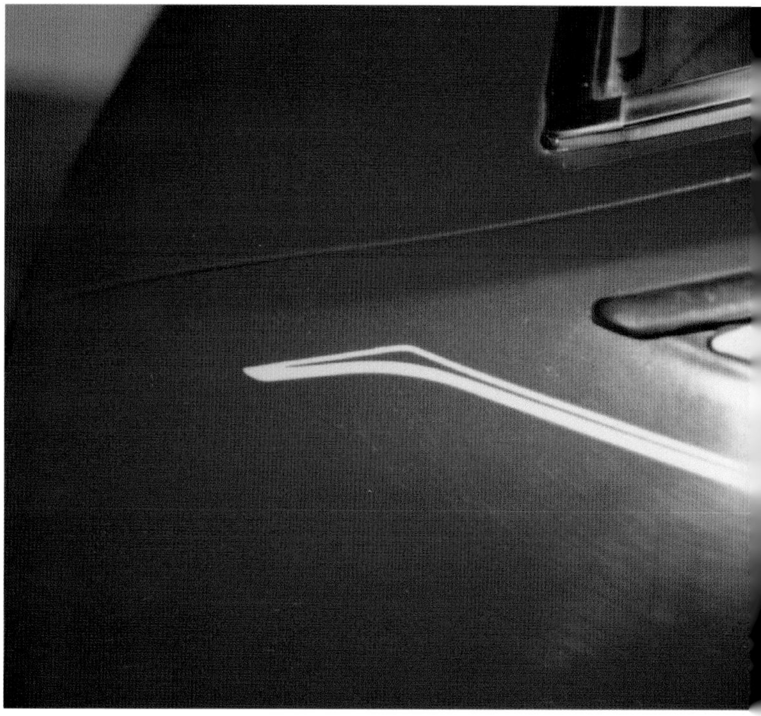

the extra frontal air intake introduced on the V8-S. Most important, however, was a major change in the paint process that guaranteed better paint adhesion than before and also improved the paint's resistance to stone chipping. The SD1 paint process had always depended on an electric charge being passed through the bodyshell and a similar charge (but with reversed polarity) being passed through the paint. The latest version of the process simply changed the body from the anode to the cathode, removing all the earlier problems at a stroke.

All wheel-cenre emblems now changed to a stylized outline of the traditional badge. The base-model 2300 gained a new style of silver plastic wheel trim with radial slots and a black centre. The two 'S' models, 2300S and 2600S, shared the stainless steel 'clover leaf' trim of the first 3500s, and the 3500SE came with alloys as standard. The Vanden Plas model also came with alloys as standard, but in this case the wheels were machined and their spokes were enamelled dark grey to achieve a striking contrast with the polished rims and centres. They gave the car a very distinguished appearance, which was exactly what was needed – for the

Vanden Plas was, at long last, the 'traditional' Rover that customers had been asking for since the SD1's launch in 1976. Denovo alloy wheels remained available for both V8 models (and were a no-cost option on the Vanden Plas), but seem to have been no more popular than before.

Other details changed on the 1981 models, too. There were additional identifying badges reading '2600' or 'V8' on the front wings of all models with those engines. All new cars had new rear badges with larger lettering, and the model-badge on the 3500 now described the car as a '3500 V8'. The Vanden Plas, meanwhile, had special black badges at the rear, together with a bright finish for its exhaust tail pipe. Like the 3500SE, it also had a rubber facing strip on both front and rear bumpers, and it was distinguished at the front by large overriders that contained washer jets for the headlamps. These were made available as an extra-cost option for the other models and replaced the earlier Scandinavian-pattern wash-wipe system, but were rarely ordered. The Vanden Plas also came with black rubber bump-strips in the body-side indentations, and it shared a V8-S-style twin coachline with the 3500SE. The two V8s had the sliding sunroof and tinted glass as standard, and these were both made available at extra cost on the other models. Sadly, the expensive Triplex Ten-Twenty windscreen slipped quietly from the specification, to be replaced on all models by a laminated one.

There were relatively few mechanical changes. The four-speed gearbox remained standard on both 2300 and 2300S models, and the entry-level 2300 came without the power steering that was standard on the 2300S. On the five-speed gearboxes, the ratio of the overdrive fifth gear was raised to give better fuel economy at cruising speeds, and a subsidiary result was that the V8 models with manual gearboxes became the highest-geared production cars in the world with an overall figure of 29.7mph (47.8km/h) per 1,000rpm. This made no difference to maximum speeds, although the Vanden Plas, which had put on a further 165lb (75kg) over the superseded V8-S, was now noticeably slower to accelerate than the 3500SE. Meanwhile, changes to the suspension of all models gave more compliance at the front to reduce harshness, while recalibrated rear self-levelling units with shorter coil springs gave a lower ride height and improved handling to the 2600S, 3500SE and Vanden Plas.

A great deal of effort had gone into improving the interior ambience of the 1981 models, and it is arguable that this was actually the biggest step forward on these cars. The old muddy browns all disappeared, and in their place came four new colours – blue, green, dark brown and light brown. The upholstery was now velvet, with pinstriped central and plain outer panels on all but the cheapest 2300 model and the most expensive Vanden Plas. The 2300 came with cropped velour upholstery in light or dark brown only, but the Vanden Plas staked its claim to being the 'traditional' Rover with leather upholstery in a choice of dark or light brown. Hairline woven velvet upholstery was also made a no-cost option for the top model.

This is a 1981-model 3500SE, showing its standard alloy wheels, twin coachlines and V8 front wing badge along with the new black-faced bumpers, bright mirror bodies and traditional Rover badge.

The new velour upholstery and front seat reclining adjusters made a huge improvement to the SD1. They are seen here in a 3500SE model.

PERSONAL EXPERIENCE: A 1981 VANDEN PLAS

When the opportunity arose to buy a 1981-model 3500 Vanden Plas automatic, I seized it with both hands. KOB 602W was in the ideal colour scheme of Bordeaux Red metallic with light Oatmeal leather, and its fit and finish were immeasurably improved as compared to the 1978 car I had owned earlier. In particular, the paint was excellent, and there were no signs of rust on the body. The car was around four years old.

The engine pulled strongly and provided all the performance I expected of a V8, and the three-speed automatic did everything it was supposed to do. There were failings, though. The cruise control never worked and the electric sunroof tended to jam, but I didn't feel it worth spending the money to fix either. In addition, the car had been fitted with the approved Unipart rear wash-wipe. I don't know if this had been installed by a dealer, but the installation was hardly professional, and the motor was partly held to the tailgate by brown parcel tape!

Of course, the car leaked. The boot was forever wet (I spent a whole weekend drying it out after buying the car) and the sunroof drain channels had become blocked. I found this out the hard way, when a sudden stop delivered a large quantity of cold rainwater into my lap. That was probably the final straw – although I did miss that car after I'd sold it.

Although Leyland Cars had bravely pretended that the sloping tail window remained clear in rain, it did not. This was the Unipart solution, although the parcel tape suggests that it had not been fitted very professionally.

The Unipart rear wash-wipe came with its own washer bottle. The dark stains on the carpets were caused by chronic water leaks into the boot.

This was the 1981-model 2300S, now with the stainless steel wheel trims from the earlier 3500 but still lacking mudflaps as standard. There was no model designation badge on the front wings of these cars.

Front seats had an adjustable lumbar pad – though, again, not on the 2300 – and their reshaped backrests gave more legroom for rear-seat passengers, who also benefited from recontoured seats to give them more headroom. Improved reclining mechanisms with a turnwheel control for the front seats also gave these a finer adjustment.

At the same time, the instrument pod casings were coloured to match the upholstery. The switchgear, although essentially similar to that on earlier SD1s, was now illuminated at night, and the low-coolant warning light (present but not connected after it was removed from the specification just before the 1976 launch) was now connected. At long last, the heating and ventilating system was given a ram-air setting, and there were improved carpets (although the 2300 still had rubber in the boot) plus a leather-bound steering wheel and a fully carpeted rear parcel shelf. New kick plates on the door sills advertised the Rover name, and there was extra sound-deadening material on the floor and under the bonnet. The automatic models gained a much-improved selector lever with a neat push-button release in place of the old T-handle, and the two V8s came with rear seat belts and a four-speaker radio cassette system as standard; both items could be had at extra cost on the other models. Electric window lifts were standard on the 2600S and above, but the base-model 2300 still made do without even central locking.

The Vanden Plas came with its own special luxury features. Its sunroof was electrically powered, and there was electric adjustment and heating for the door mirrors too. There were shagpile footwell over-mats, four head restraints (each with a detachable cushion), a cruise control (made by Dana and also available on the 3500SE) and the zone-tinted windscreen first seen on the V8-S. The V8-S style of bright trim on the facia was also carried over for the new top model.

THE SD1 AND ITS RIVALS

According to figures used in a presentation by Ray Horrocks, chairman of BL Cars, at the launch of the 1982-model SD1s, Rover's share of the executive-car market in Britain increased in this period. BL's own figures showed that it went up to 15.1 per cent in 1981 from 12.6 per cent the year before. At the same time, the share of its main rival, the Ford Granada, fell from 19.2 per cent to 14.2 per cent. At this stage, some 75 per cent of all SD1 sales in Britain were to companies rather than to private individuals.

This 1981-model 2600S shows the larger letters introduced for the rear badges a year earlier, and the discreet '2600' badge low down on the front wing.

The 1981 Models and the Press

Although the motoring press dutifully reported on the model changes, the real interest was in the Vanden Plas. 'Living up to the old traditions' was the subtitle that *Autocar* gave to its road test of one in the 26 March 1981 issue, perfectly capturing what Rover had tried to achieve with the car. Strangely, however, they did not follow this up with any comments linking the car's luxury levels to the Rovers of old.

The car they tested had the five-speed manual gearbox, but the extra weight seems to have counted because the overall fuel consumption was a rather poor 20.7mpg (13.7ltr/100 km). Maximum speed of 123mph (198km/h) was achieved in fourth gear, the best available in fifth being 118mph (190km/h) flat out, and the Vanden Plas needed 9.7sec to reach 60mph from rest. Autocar reported that:

> *The outstanding features are the relaxed cruising at speed, and the low noise level, but [the Rover] finds tough competition when such matters as ride comfort*

A MANUFACTURING CHANGE

Since 1979, British Leyland had been working on a major retrenchment programme right across the board in order to stem its losses. This programme was known as CORE (it stood for Coordination of Resources, and is explained in detail in Michael Edwardes' essential book, *Back from the Brink*) and its aim was to reduce expenditure in order to protect really vital projects such as the forthcoming Metro. One of the changes made under CORE was to SD1 manufacturing, when BL decided to mothball the still underutilized plant at Solihull and move assembly to Cowley. At the same time, body production would move from Castle Bromwich to a new plant within the Cowley works. Having body assembly on the same site as final build would make huge differences in transport costs, production time and manning costs, as well as boosting quality.

The first Cowley-built shells were made in June 1981, in preparation for the complete transfer of SD1 assembly to Cowley from Solihull and in anticipation of facelifted models being introduced for the 1982 model year. That 1982 model-year introduction was subsequently put back from autumn 1981 until January 1982, and so the 1981-model SD1s were built until the end of the 1981 calendar year.

For a time in the second half of 1981, bodyshells were being manufactured at both Castle Bromwich and Cowley. There were also some interesting anomalies in this period. Some very late 1981-model bodies were painted in the new colours planned for the 1982 season (these appear to have been sent for export, to territories where there would be a delay before the facelifted models became available). In addition, the first of the 1982 'facelift' cars were actually built at Solihull right at the end of 1981.

CLEARING THE SHOWROOMS

Around a fortnight before the announcement of the facelifted 1982 models, BL issued a revised SD1 price list in the UK, with a 4 per cent increase in prices of the old models. As *Autocar* of 23 January 1982 commented:

> *We noticed that while the list price – that is the price before Special Car Tax and VAT have been added – had been increased, the amount of Special Car Tax payable had not.*

The explanation was that BL had been trying to close the gap between the prices of the old models and those of the new, more expensive, facelifted cars. The Special Car Tax, a figure agreed with the relevant government authorities and based on a 'factory gate' price, did not change because that 'factory gate' price had not changed.

As *Autocar* commented, this left room for dealers to offer some very attractive discounts on the old models – and indeed they did. At two Wadham Stringer dealerships in Hampshire, a 1981-model Vanden Plas could be had for £11,265 instead of the normal on-the-road price of £14,665, while a five-speed 2300 carried a price tag of £6,629 instead of £8,133. Those prices were to last until stocks of the 1981 models were exhausted.

> *on a poor road and ultimate handling are considered. The undoubted limitations of a live rear axle then make themselves felt.*

Autocar felt that the five-speed gearbox was not the best match for the Vanden Plas' character:

> *Buyers would do best to choose the automatic transmission version unless they are the particularly keen sort of drivers who like the feel of a good gearbox, are happy to do a lot of gear-changing, and will appreciate the long-legged cruising ability of the car with this very high gearing.*

At the conclusion of the report, the magazine compared the Vanden Plas with similarly priced rivals – Audi 200 Turbo, BMW 732i, Mercedes-Benz 280E, Opel Senator and Volvo 264 GLE. Ride quality apart, the Rover

> *has redeeming features which make it a very strong competitor in the class, and has the distinction of being the best-equipped car of them all. Add to this, the fact that it has a much more useful potential for carrying awkward loads, and that it proved the most economical of the group, and one begins to see sound reasons for choosing the Rover Vanden Plas. It's not the best all-rounder, but it's the one that comes out on top when all aspects are weighed up.*

PAINT AND TRIM OPTIONS – 1980–1981 MODELS

July 1979 to September 1980

There were twelve paint colours for the 1980 season, Triton being a new colour announced with the V8-S in July 1979. Maraschino was the new name for Black, which had become available during the 1979 season. Metallic paint still cost extra on 2300 and 2600 models. There were three colours for the standard cross-ribbed velvet upholstery; the V8-S models came with cropped velour upholstery in either Beige or Bronze; and Nutmeg leather was an optional extra across the range.

Colour name	*Description*	*Interior options*
Atlantis	Dark blue	Caviar or Coriander
Avocado	Bright green	Coriander or Nutmeg
Brazilia	Dark brown	Coriander
Maraschino	Gloss black	Caviar, Coriander or Nutmeg
Midas	Light gold metallic	Caviar or Nutmeg
Pendelican	White	Caviar or Nutmeg
Persian Aqua	Light blue metallic	Caviar or Coriander
Platinum	Silver metallic	Caviar or Nutmeg
Poseidon	Dark green metallic	Coriander or Nutmeg
Richelieu	Rich red	Caviar or Coriander
Triton	Bright green metallic	Coriander or Nutmeg
Turmeric	Yellow	Caviar or Coriander

October 1980 to February 1982

There were eleven paint colours for the 1981 season, which was extended to the end of the 1981 calendar year. Eight of these were new. Note that there is also evidence of cars built late in 1981 having paint colours from the 1982 model year 'facelift' palette (see Chapter 6).

The 2300 models came with plain velour upholstery, which was available in Caviar or Oatmeal with all exterior colours. The 2300S, 2600S and 3500SE came with plain and pinstripe velvet upholstery (P&P) in a number of exterior/interior colour combinations, as shown in the table below. The Vanden Plas models came with leather upholstery as standard, which was available in Caviar or Oatmeal with all exterior colours. Optional for the Vanden Plas models was Hairline Velvet upholstery (HV), with availability as shown in the table below.

Of the interior colours, Bayleaf was green, Caviar was dark brown, Oatmeal was light brown and Prussian was blue.

Colour name	*Description*	*Interior options*
Aran Beige	Light beige	P&P: Bayleaf or Oatmeal HV: Caviar or Oatmeal
Argent Silver	Silver metallic	P&P: Bayleaf, Caviar or Prussian HV: Caviar, Prussian or Oatmeal
Barley Yellow	Bright yellow	P&P: Caviar or Oatmeal HV: Caviar or Oatmeal
Bordeaux Red	Dark red metallic	P&P: Caviar or Oatmeal HV: Caviar, Prussian or Oatmeal
Carnelian Red	Bright red	P&P: Oatmeal or Prussian HV: Caviar, Prussian or Oatmeal
Cavalry Blue	Dark blue	P&P: Oatmeal or Prussian HV: Caviar, Oatmeal or Prussian
Maraschino	Gloss black	P&P: Bayleaf, Caviar, Oatmeal or Prussian HV: Caviar, Prussian or Oatmeal
Pendelican	White	P&P: Bayleaf or Caviar HV: Caviar, Prussian or Oatmeal
Persian Aqua	Light blue metallic	P&P: Oatmeal or Prussian HV: Caviar, Oatmeal or Prussian
Pharoah Gold	Dark gold metallic	P&P: Caviar or Oatmeal HV: Caviar or Oatmeal
Sylvan Green	Light green metallic	P&P: Bayleaf or Caviar HV: Caviar or Oatmeal

TECHNICAL SPECIFICATIONS ROVER SD1, 1980–1981

Engines

2300
Type PE 146 6-cylinder petrol
2350cc (81 x 76mm)
Single overhead camshaft
Four-bearing crankshaft
Compression ratio 9.25:1
Two SU HS6 carburettors
123bhp at 5,000rpm
134lb ft at 4,000rpm

2600
Type PE 166 6-cylinder petrol
2597cc (81 x 84mm)
Single overhead camshaft
Four-bearing crankshaft
Compression ratio 9.25:1
Two SU HS6 carburettors
136bhp at 5,000rpm
152lb ft at 3,750rpm

3500
V8-cylinder petrol
3528cc (88.9 x 71.1mm)
Single overhead camshaft
Five-bearing crankshaft
Compression ratio 9.35:1
Two SU HIF6 carburettors
155bhp at 5,250rpm
198lb ft at 2,500rpm

Transmission
Five-speed manual gearbox standard on 2600 and 3500
Ratios 3.32:1, 2.08:1, 1.39:1, 1.00:1, 0.83:1; reverse 3.43:1
Fifth gear ratio changed to 0.79:1 for 1981 models.
Four-speed manual gearbox standard on 2300
Ratios 3.32:1, 2.08:1, 1.39:1, 1.00:1; reverse 3.43:1
Three-speed Borg Warner type 66 automatic gearbox optional
Ratios 2.39:1, 1.45:1, 1.00:1; reverse 1.92:1

Axle ratio

3500	3.08:1
2300	3.45:1
2600	3.45:1

Suspension, steering and brakes
Front suspension with MacPherson struts, lower links and anti-roll bar
Rear axle with torque tube, trailing arms, Watt's linkage and coil springs
Rack-and-pinion steering; power assistance optional
Disc brakes at front with 258mm (10.13in) diameter; drum brakes at rear with 229mm (9in) diameter; vacuum servo assistance standard

Dimensions

Overall length	185in (4,699mm)
Overall width	70in (1,778mm)
Overall height	55in (1,397mm)
Wheelbase	110.8in (2,814mm)
Front track	59in (1,499mm)
Rear track	59in (1,499mm)

Wheels and tyres
14in five-bolt steel wheels with 5.5in rims (2300 and 2600); 14in five-bolt steel wheels with 6in rims (3500); 14in five-bolt alloy wheels with 6in rims optional on 2600 and 3500
Steel wheels with 175 HR 14 tyres (2300 and 2600) or 185 HR 14 tyres (3500)
Alloy wheels with 195/70 HR 14 tyres

Kerb weight
Not quoted in Rover sales literature.

CHAPTER FIVE

THE FACELIFT MODELS, 1982–1986

When Michael Edwardes took over as chairman and chief executive of British Leyland in 1977, he asked his product planners to take a good hard look at what products the company needed and to draw up a coherent strategy. The existing plan to put SD1 into the North American market was part of that strategy, and a second element in it was a plan to improve sales in Europe. By the late 1970s, it was clear that success in the large-car market in most European countries (Germany was an exception at the time) would depend on the availability of a diesel engine, and so the plan for the SD1 range came to include a diesel derivative.

The second major factor that influenced the SD1 in the 1980s was that British Leyland top management finally lost patience with the Solihull assembly plant. It had been built to handle far higher volumes than SD1 ever achieved, or now seemed likely to achieve, and even bringing Triumph TR7 production into it during 1980 did not provide the whole answer. The problem was that British Leyland decided to withdraw from the traditional sports car market altogether, and Triumph production was then scheduled to end in mid-1981. So a plan was hatched to mothball the Solihull plant (it would eventually be reused by Land Rover, whose activities were expanding) and to move SD1 production to the old Morris works at Cowley.

A third element in the product plan saw the SD1 range being expanded downwards with the introduction of a model using the 2-litre Austin Morris O-series engine. There were clear reasons for this. The SD1 was expected to remain in production until at least mid-1984 so sales had to be maintained, at the very least, and ideally increased. Sales of the big-engined cars were slowing down as a result of the increases in the cost of fuel during 1979, so a logical way forward was to introduce a smaller-engined model to help maintain overall volumes. There had been a very noticeable switch to cars with engines of around 2 litres in the large executive-car market, from which the rival Ford Granada range was already benefiting. Rover also hoped that a cheaper SD1 would

Painted SD1 bodyshells awaiting entry to the assembly hall at Cowley in 1983. They are protected with clear plastic sheeting. Note also the Austin Ambassador shells in the compound.

This picture shows a stage in the design process for the facelifted cars. Elements of the final design are already in place.

This was another stage on the way to the facelift. The enlarged rear window is already in place. Note that the car is labelled 'SD1 1983'; in practice, the facelift was introduced midway through the 1982 season.

This was another 1983 proposal, with redesigned tail lights and tail panel.

The selected design, pictured in this case on the 3500 Vanden Plas model that was at the top of the facelifted range.

The new dashboard was a vast improvement over the original. The blue one belongs to a 2600S and the beige one to a 3500SE. The main difference is the addition of a trip computer control panel on the more expensive car, just visible below the heater controls on the centre console. The radio head units are also different.

have greater appeal to private buyers in Britain, where a majority of SD1s were being bought by companies.

All these elements came together at the same time as a major facelift planned for the 1982-model SD1s. Although originally intended for autumn 1981, the facelift was delayed – largely because of the move to Cowley – and the cars were actually introduced in January 1982. The 1981 models remained in production for most of the last quarter of 1981, although the first of the facelifted cars were actually built at the end of the year at Solihull, before the transfer of production was complete. The facelift was reported as having cost around £7 million, which was a relatively small investment by motor industry standards of the time.

In the meantime, further changes were taking place within the British Leyland organization. From 1978, Land Rover had been established as a standalone business unit, which took it out of the Jaguar Rover Triumph division where it had been sitting somewhat uncomfortably. Jaguar, meanwhile, did its best to remain aloof from its stablemates, and in 1984 would be sold off as an independent concern. That left Rover and Triumph, and from mid-1981 the Triumph marque ceased to exist. Rover was thus left on its own, and more or less naturally migrated towards the old volume cars group that incorporated Austin, MG and Morris. This group was renamed the Austin Rover Group (ARG) from mid-1982.

NEW MODELS

Diesel SD1

British Leyland did not have a diesel engine that was even remotely suitable for the job of powering the SD1, nor were there any under development. To design a new engine from scratch would be very expensive and would take longer than was ideal in terms of the corporate business plan. The product planners therefore recommended buying in a suitable engine as a short-term strategy, setting a target on-sale date for the diesel SD1 as summer 1981.

Two avenues of enquiry were pursued. One was with Peugeot-Citroën in France, who had a highly regarded 2.3-litre turbocharged diesel engine, and the other was with Stabilimenti Meccanici VM in Italy. VM had been pushing their range of modular diesel engines since the mid-1970s and probably initiated the contact with British Leyland. John Bilton was the powertrain strategy manager for Jaguar Rover Triumph at the time, and he remembered putting together a strategy that would have seen the 2.4-litre 4-cylinder VM engine in SD1, the 3-litre 5-cylinder in the Range Rover and the 3.6-litre 6-cylinder in the Jaguar XJ range. Circumstanc-

When the diesel model arrived, it took on the S specification. From this angle it was almost indistinguishable from the contemporary 2300S and 2600S models, although sharp eyes would spot the '2400' badges on the wings. By the time it was launched, fog lights had become part of the S specification.

The SD Turbo was more easily identified from the rear, where the plinth below the number-plate carried appropriate badges. Those are the standard S specification wheel trims.

The VM diesel engine was one of a modular family of indirect-injection diesels. A later version, with intercooler, would be used in the diesel Range Rover from 1986.

The diesel engine was installed with a very noticeable rearward slant. The separate cylinder heads are clear in this picture.

es worked against the latter two proposals, but the plan to use the VM engine in the SD1 did materialize as proposed.

As work progressed on the VM-engined SD1, British Leyland also began work on its own large-capacity car diesel engine, which was known as Iceberg. This was nothing more nor less than a diesel derivative of the 3.5-litre petrol V8, and for SD1 the product planners saw it as a possibility for autumn 1983 introduction. However, Iceberg (see box over the page) never did go into the SD1, and never did reach production either.

The diesel-engined SD1 was finally introduced in the second quarter of 1982, as a model in the facelifted range. It took the name of 2400SD Turbo, the numeral obviously corresponding to the engine's capacity, the S representing the S specification (as seen on 2300S and 2600S models), the D standing for Diesel and the Turbo making it sound both modern and a little exciting. In practice, sales in Britain would always be minimal, and only selected Rover dealers had staff trained to service the model, but the 2400SD

Even though the engine was supplied by VM, it carried Rover identification on the inlet manifold. This is a left-hand-drive car.

THE ICEBERG DIESEL V8

The possibility of making the SD1 available with a diesel version of the Rover V8 that was known as the Iceberg engine was under consideration from about 1980. Rover did not have any modern diesel engines of its own at the time, which was why the VM engine had to be bought in to create the 2400SD Turbo in 1982. Spen King suggested that a suitable engine might be created from the 3.5-litre V8 petrol engine, and a joint project to develop such an engine was established with Perkins, the leading British builder of diesel engines at the time. The project leader at Perkins was Alex Stephenson, who would later move to Land Rover to run engine development.

Iceberg was developed as a turbocharged 3.5-litre engine, with a target output of 125bhp. The top priority to receive it was the Range Rover, but the engine was expected to become available for British Leyland's large cars as well and Perkins used at least one SD1 for prototype testing. Development of the engine unfortunately proved much more complicated than originally anticipated. One problem was with developing a rotary fuel pump suitable for an 8-cylinder engine, and it proved necessary to redesign the cylinder block as well. All this introduced costly delays.

By mid-1982, there were those at Rover who were convinced that Iceberg would never enter production, but everyone was taken aback when Perkins announced its impending availability at the Paris Motor Show that autumn. In reality, the engine was far from ready for production, and Perkins were simply hoping to drum up some advance orders.

Product planners had earlier envisaged that the Iceberg V8 would have been available to create a new derivative of the SD1 from autumn 1983. However, by that time responsibility for all V8 engine manufacture had been given to Land Rover. As former product planner John Bilton recalled:

An early naturally aspirated prototype of the Iceberg diesel engine was tested in an SD1, which was registered SDU 279R. The radiator has been removed for clarity in this photograph.

As this exhibition engine shows, the turbochargers were eventually sited at the back, on top of the inlet manifold. This would have presented problems for the SD1 installation.

It was perfectly obvious that Land Rover's cash flow, their business position, was now almost dire....It was probably breaking even in '81, '82 but losing money in '83 and indeed again in '84 while things were sorted out. But at that point, there was obviously very, very severe pressure on the funding for V8 diesel.

Tony Gilroy was brought in as Land Rover's managing director during 1983, and his first priority was to make the company profitable again. One of his solutions was to close a number of the satellite factories that fed the Land Rover production lines and to relocate their work in the old SD1 assembly plant at Solihull that had been standing idle since early 1982. Among the plants he closed was that at Acocks Green, where V8 engines were assembled. The engine line was brought to Solihull and co-located with Land Rover 4-cylinder engine assembly in the existing engine plant in the North Block. As John Bilton remembers:

It only made sense to bring the V8 under the same roof. There was room for only one of the lines that we had and, quite simply, we weren't going to take the risk of not building the petrol! So the logic, then, of a windfall programme in the form of the V8 diesel built on existing plant and equipment . . . disappeared and we were just not able to justify it.

The result was that Tony Gilroy had the Iceberg engine cancelled during 1983 before it was ready for production.

A single prototype of the engine, in Range Rover tune, survives in the collection of the Heritage Motor Centre at Gaydon.

Turbo did help to give the Rover marque a stronger presence in France, Italy and, to a lesser extent, other continental European countries.

The VM diesel engine was known as the HR492HT type, and had oversquare cylinder dimensions with overhead valves and a chain-driven camshaft. A key characteristic, resulting from its modular design, was that each cylinder had a separate cylinder-head casting. The exhaust-driven turbocharger was made by KKK and had a maximum boost pressure of 10psi, which was controlled by a wastegate. Fuel was supplied by a Bosch mechanical system to pre-combustion chambers in the cylinder heads and, as installed in the Rover, the VM engine was canted slightly backwards and sat on hydraulic front mountings to damp out the characteristic vibration of a diesel engine. Maximum power was 90bhp at a low 4,000rpm, and the respectable torque figure of 142lb ft was developed at just 2,350rpm – lower down the rev range than any other SD1 engine – which helped to give the 2400SD Turbo a rather better performance than most people expected. An oil cooler, twin cooling fans and two heavy-duty 12V batteries were all included in the production specification.

The engine was some 160lb (73kg) heavier than the 2.6-litre 6-cylinder, and there was additional weight at the front from twin 12V batteries. As a result, the car had stiffer front springs. Overall, it was quite heavy, weighing some 330lb (150kg) more than a 2000, and so the 2000's low 3.9:1 axle ratio was employed to help acceleration figures. However, the diesel engine was red-lined at 4,500rpm, so in order to give a more acceptable top speed the fifth gear ratio was raised. The results were overall gearing of 23.9mph (38.5km/h) per 1,000rpm, good cruising fuel economy and a maximum speed of just over 100mph (161km/h).

2-litre SD1

Like the diesel model, the new 2-litre SD1 was originally planned for introduction in or around summer 1981; in practice, its launch was delayed until the whole facelifted range arrived in January 1982. Like the diesel model, it also featured a 4-cylinder engine, although this time fuelled by petrol and not turbocharged.

By comparison with the more expensive models, the 2000 appeared very plain; the 2300 was visually similar. Like all the facelifted cars, they had the larger rear window with standard wash-wipe.

The O-series 4-cylinder engine in the 2000 models had twin carburettors and put out 101bhp but looked rather lost within the SD1's engine bay.

DESCENDANTS OF THE O-SERIES ENGINE

During the 1980s, the O-series engine was further developed as the M-series (often called the M16) with a 4-valve cylinder head. The O-series was also developed into a diesel engine in collaboration with Perkins, and in this guise was known as the Perkins Prima engine. The M-series was then further developed as the T-series, and in this guise powered versions of the Rover 800 saloon; entry-level models of the Rover 800 were also briefly available with the O-series 2-valve version of the engine.

Austin Rover put a turbocharged version of the 2-litre O-series engine into the MG Montego Turbo in 1985, and that version of the engine delivered 150bhp. There were some thoughts of using a similar turbocharged engine in the Rover 2000, and a certain amount of development work was done for Austin Rover on such a car by Broadspeed.

The original idea for a turbocharged Rover 2000 came from Graham Atkin, a former Lotus man who had joined Austin Rover as chief engineer for engines. However, the idea was never taken forward to production, probably largely because the SD1 was nearing the end of its life and a 150bhp turbocharged 2000 would have created awkward overlaps with other models in the range; the 2300 had only 123bhp, the 2600 had 136bhp, and even the carburettor V8 had only 155bhp.

The choice of the Austin Morris O-series engine for this new entry-level SD1 showed that the product planners were earning their keep by doing some joined-up thinking about potential synergies among the multiple British Leyland marques. In earlier times, it would have been unthinkable to use an engine from the Austin Morris volume cars division to power an upmarket Rover. But times were changing, although it is doubtful whether traditional Rover owners ever accepted the new model as a proper Rover, whatever the badges said.

The O-series engine had been designed within the Austin Morris division as a successor to the old BMC B-series engine family. It was first produced in 1.7-litre size for the rear-wheel-drive Morris Marina Series 3 and the front-wheel-drive Austin Princess in 1978, and was thus available for both transverse and north-south installations. By 1980 it had been enlarged to 2 litres for the automatic-gearbox versions of the Morris Ital. All these engines had the same basic design, with an aluminium cylinder head and a belt-driven single overhead camshaft.

At about the same time as the plan to use this engine in the SD1 was formulated, the product planners were also suggesting that it should replace the 2-litre Triumph engine in the TR7 sports car and the B-series engine in the MGB. These ideas made perfect sense but came to nothing when British Leyland decided to end sports car manufacture in mid-1981. The SD1 plan, known to the product planners as Project RT 014, was the only element of this set of proposals to survive.

The most powerful version of this engine available before its introduction in the Rover was the 2-litre size used in the Morris Ital 2.0 HLS from autumn 1980. This had a single carburettor and put out 90bhp and 114lb ft of torque. However, a twin-carburettor version had been developed for eventual use in the MGB and TR7, and it was this that went into the SD1. With 101bhp and 120lb ft of torque, it was still very much less powerful than any other SD1 engine (the VM diesel excepted), but allied to a lower final drive it proved able to give the car quite respectable performance. Not surprisingly, the new 2-litre car was given the name of Rover 2000, echoing that of the original Rover P6 saloon that had been introduced in 1963.

Equally unsurprising was that some extensive sound-deadening was added to the model in an attempt to maintain the levels of refinement expected of a Rover. An electric cooling fan and remote air filter were other ways in which engine noise was reduced, while a larger-diameter propshaft was added to reduce driveline resonance. The Rover engineers specified softer front springs and dampers to suit the lighter engine, and the car was designed to have variable-rate rear springs like the 2300 models.

THE 1982 FACELIFT MODELS

The diesel model was held over when the facelifted SD1 models were introduced at the start of 1982. It was announced at the Turin Motor Show in April and was initially released in France and Italy, where preferential tax rates made the sale of diesel cars particularly strong. Andy Barr, ARG's managing director at the time, said that he anticipated incremental sales of around 2,000 cars as a result. In the UK, where diesel models still accounted for less than 1 per cent of passenger car sales, the 2400SD Turbo would not be released until the autumn – but BL's prediction was that UK sales of diesel cars would begin to rise in the second half of the 1980s and would hit 15 per cent by 1990.

So it was that by early spring 1982 the SD1 range embraced no fewer than five engine options. These went into models that were badged as 2000, 2300S, 2400SD Turbo, 2600S, 2600SE, 3500SE and 3500 Vanden Plas. The hope was that the revised range would maintain and possibly even improve SD1 sales towards the end of the car's life. At this stage, SD1 was to have just over four and a half years longer in production.

External Changes

Styling changes gave the 1982 models a fresher, more modern look. The headlamps were now flush with the bonnet panel, and a bright trim strip ran above them and along the lower edge of the bonnet. A black plastic radiator air-intake grille ran across the full width of the car to give the front end further definition. The sidelights were now incorporated in the headlamps (and the 2300 at last gained quartz lamps as standard), and the front turn-indicator lenses wrapped all the way round, like those introduced in 1980 for the North American SD1s.

Front and rear, the cars now had new wrap-around bumpers made of black polyurethane, and at the front all except the new 2000 and the 2300 had bright trim on the top surface of these bumpers. Similarly, 2300S and above had a deformable plastic apron spoiler at the front that was painted to match the body. This spoiler contained apertures for fog lamps, which were standard on the two V8 models.

All models had a new rear window, enlarged downwards to improve the view for reversing (which had always been a problem on the earlier cars) and equipped as standard with a wash-wipe system. There was also a new full-width badge plinth at the rear, with appropriate badge letters to distinguish one model from another. The Vanden Plas model had a

The entry-level specification of the 2000 and 2300 models is shown here on a 2000. There is no front spoiler and the bumper has no bright trim.

With the S specification of the 2300S and 2600S, a spoiler was added and the bumpers gained bright trim.

The SE specification was distinguished by front fog lights, although these were also available as an optional extra on the S models.

The Vanden Plas was the only model to come with headlamp washers as standard when the facelifted cars were first launched.

black side rubbing strip mounted below the body-side indentation, with a bright insert that continued the bumper line.

Wheels were mostly new, too. Although the 2000 took on the steel wheels with plastic trims of the old 2300, the three S-specification cars (2300S, 2400SD Turbo and 2600S) gained stainless-steel trims of a new design that featured oval blackout sections. Alloy wheels were standard on the two V8 models and an extra-cost option elsewhere, and they now came with a new style that was designed to be easier to clean than the earlier type. On the Vanden Plas, they once again had a machined and painted finish.

Both V8-engined models now had '3500' badges on the lower front wings (actually made of chromed plastic rather than metal), and twin coachlines. Both also came with bronze tinted glass instead of the green Sundym glass on earlier cars, and both came with mudflaps as standard, these features being available only at extra cost on other models. The Vanden Plas had headlamp washers mounted in its front overriders, and these too could be ordered at extra cost on the other facelifted cars. All models had a new windscreen-wash system with a vigorous fan-shaped spray, which was more effective at speed than the earlier type.

Interior Changes

Upholstery remained essentially the same as on the 1981 models, but 3500SE models now had as standard the hairline velvet trim that was optional on the Vanden Plas. All models now had safety belts colour-keyed to the interior. Rover publicity claimed that head and legroom in the front had been increased, but the extra few millimetres made no discernible difference. The 1982 door trims were better quality mouldings with a neater design than before, and on the 2300S models and above came with wood inserts – another traditional Rover feature that customers had repeatedly requested. On the three S models, these wood inserts had

Entry-level interior trim, on 2000 and 2300 models, was Plain Velvet.

The S-level trim was attractive Plain & Pinstripe Velvet.

The SE trim was Hairline Velvet.

The S-level trim was attractive Plain & Pinstripe Velvet.

a satin finish and on the two V8s they were of burr walnut; the Vanden Plas maintained its superiority with a burr walnut panel running across the facia.

Although the basic design of the facia shelf was unchanged, it now carried a completely redesigned instrument binnacle, wider and much neater than before. Among its revised instruments was now a digital clock with an elapsed-time function, supplemented on Vanden Plas models by a multi-function trip computer that could be ordered at extra cost on other models. Controls for clock and computer were sited on the revised console, which also had improved heater controls, a lidded trinket box (which was also ideal for storing cassettes in cars fitted with a radio cassette player) and a neater gear lever and gaiter for cars with the manual gearbox. A map-reading light in the dashboard was standard across the range, and the redesigned steering wheel now bore a bright nameplate. Column stalks had swapped sides to meet the latest ISO standards, and from 2300S upwards all models had central locking as standard and the luxury of a sunroof.

As before, some features were reserved for the Vanden Plas model. This came with electric sunroof operation, map pockets behind the front seats and a three-band radio cassette player. The 3500SE still had a two-band head unit, although with the four speakers and electric aerial also standard on the Vanden Plas. The 2600S and cheaper models came with only two speakers, but the additional pair could of course be fitted at extra cost. Both the V8s had a courtesy lamps delay, a second cigarette lighter in the rear and rear seat reading lamps.

Mechanical Changes

There had been mechanical changes, too. All manual gearboxes now had five speeds, and all the 6- and 8-cylinder engines had an automatic choke. The 2600S and both V8 models had recalibrated self-levelling struts to give a better controlled ride and tauter handling, and all models had a bigger brake servo for improved stopping and a new master cylinder for better pedal 'feel'. All models also now had pad-wear sensors on the front brakes. On those fitted with self-levelling rear suspension, the struts had been stiffened to a level more or less midway between the original 1977 specification and the softer settings introduced on 1980 models.

The 6-cylinder engines took on a remote air cleaner to cut down induction roar, while the V8s had stiffened cylinder blocks to reduce noise and Solex instead of SU carburettors;

REPLACING THE SD1: PROJECT BRAVO AND LM15

After 1979, the plan was to replace SD1 by a car called Project Bravo, but it appears that little progress was ever made on that even though some product planning documents optimistically expected it to be introduced as early as mid-1984. Project Bravo ground to a halt some time in 1980, apparently disappearing from the future product plan when JRT was dissolved.

Bravo was conceived at a time when British Leyland was short of cash again but needed multiple new products in order to remain competitive. Product planning documents show that it was to be smaller than SD1, with a 105in (2,667mm) wheelbase. The mid-section of the body was to be similar to SD1, while the front end and front suspension were to be derived from TR7/TR8 components and the rear end and axle were to combine elements of the SD1 and the Triumph Lynx (a stillborn 2 + 2 fixed-head coupé). The first release would be a four-door saloon, and a five-door hatchback would follow a year or so later.

Engines were envisaged as 2-litre O-series, the 2.6-litre 6-cylinder from the SD1 and a bought-in 4-cylinder turbocharged diesel. All would have the 77mm gearbox. The 3.5-litre V8 engine would not be in the initial release, but would appear in the five-door models, which would replace SD1 in North America. Other options were also under consideration.

After Project Bravo, when the Rover brand belonged to the new Light-Medium Cars division of British Leyland, a new future product plan was drawn up. This included a model known as LM15, which was intended as the new Rover and was an enlarged derivative of LM11, which would later become the Austin Montego. However, LM15 did not last long. Michael Edwardes had forged an alliance with Honda in 1979, and in late 1981 British Leyland and Honda signed an agreement to work together on the design of a new large car. This replaced LM15 in the product plan, was developed as Project XX, and reached showrooms as the Rover 800 in 1986.

The two 6-cylinder engines looked the same as before, and the same as each other. On the original photo, it is possible to read the car's VIN (top left on the scuttle), which shows that this is the engine bay of a 2300S model.

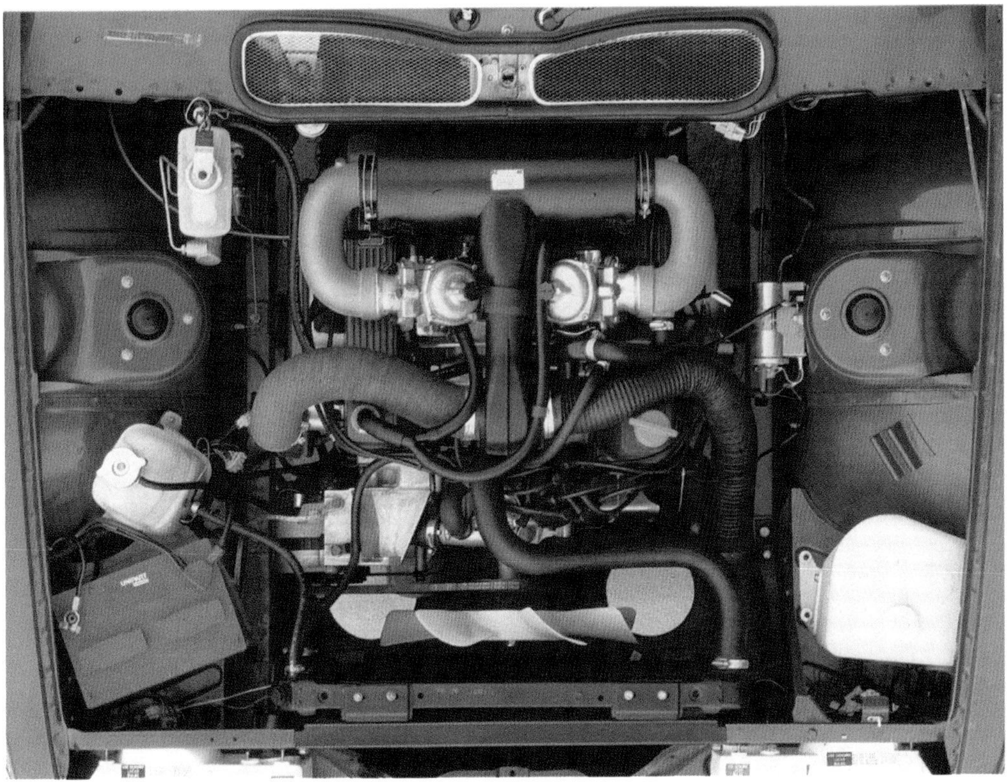

The 3.5-litre V8 engine now had Solex carburettors instead of the SUs on earlier cars.

these were said to improve fuel economy. Minor changes to the 6-cylinder engines also improved fuel economy, and the service intervals for all engines were now extended to 12,000 miles. A redesigned electrical system led to improved reliability and to more consistent operation of the central locking.

The 1982 Facelift Models and the Press

The facelifted SD1s were introduced to the world's press during January 1982 at a ride-and-drive event held in Biarritz, where many of the cars had left-hand drive despite their UK registrations. These were in the LOV ---X series, which was also used for other new BL models of the time, such as the Austin Ambassador.

There was a favourable flurry of comments about the revisions to the range, but the UK press generally avoided full road tests of the established 6-cylinder and V8 models, preferring to focus on the new 2000 model and, when it became available in April, the new 2400SD Turbo. Both of these represented extensions of the existing SD1 range into new territory and were therefore likely to attract more readers. *Motor* magazine, meanwhile, took a 3500SE on long-term test and would report on it later.

2000 and 2600 Models

The *Guardian* newspaper's correspondent managed to get BL Cars chairman Ray Horrocks to admit that he had had some misgivings about the new 4-cylinder model in the beginning: 'I thought it would be a dog.... But it wasn't, by any means,' he was reported to have said. In the newspaper's issue of 20 January 1982, the verdict was that

> *the performance of the new 2000 model was surprisingly good.... The 4-cylinder engine has a different, harder note compared with the big sixes, but it pulls quite well. Even in the high fifth gear. It did not feel strained cruising at an indicated 100mph.*

Of the new range, the *Guardian* saw the mid-range 2600S variant as the most attractive purchase.

Autocar briefly reported on its initial drive in its issue dated 23 January 1982, noting that the car had a very different character from the 6-cylinder and V8 models. The engine emitted 'a deep 'thrumb' when called upon to work hard', and the car was overgeared in fifth, 'which requires a down-change to maintain speed on a motorway incline'. Nevertheless, 'for Rover comfort and style at a lower price, the 2000 achieves its object'. Overall, the 2600S once again came out as the best model to buy.

Autocar gave the 2000 model a thorough road test for its issue dated 20 March 1982. The car was a white one, registered LOV 729X, and had the optional power-assisted steering which, said the magazine, was 'an essential option for those who have experienced the 4.5 turns from lock to lock of manually steered cars'. Build quality generally was of a high order:

> *Paintwork and panel work on the test car were excellent. Much better trim fits were apparent and those people previously rather put off by the 'clang' that used to accompany door closure will notice the more solid-sounding door shut.*

It was sometimes necessary to work engine and gearbox hard to get the desired acceleration, but

> *once the driver re-tunes to a more leisurely rate of acceleration, he finds the car gets along very nicely, easily matching most of the 2-litre 'executive class' opposition on both straight line acceleration and mid-range performance.*

PERSONAL EXPERIENCE: A 1982 2600S

I bought my 1982 2600S as a three-year-old car from a specialist aftermarket SD1 dealer. DYB 634X was a manual-gearbox car in Cashmere Gold and had earlier been owned by a company. The car was completely standard except for the addition of side bump-strips, which were a practical addition that also improved the appearance.

This was everything a good SD1 should be. It was well built, comfortable, rapid and reliable, and was a superb long-distance cruiser. A small leak into the boot developed but was quickly rectified by resealing one of the light units.

The car survived an excursion into a ditch on a wet country lane, and was only sold on after being rammed from behind by an inattentive driver in a Japanese pick-up. I sold it to a fellow motoring journalist and the car promptly blotted its copybook when its engine succumbed to top-end oil starvation.

In addition:

> *Bar a suggestion of fluffiness when asking the engine to pull away from very low rpm, the engine is flexible and untemperamental. Power delivery is smooth . . . the main discouragement to hard use being the increasingly thrashy sound emanating from under the bonnet once revving above 4,500rpm.*

On the downside, overall fuel economy on test of 22.8mpg (12.4ltr/100km) meant that economy was no better than that of the 6-cylinder cars.

The magazine found the 2000's brakes very good indeed, and with good resistance to fade. The testers did note that the absence of a front spoiler made this version of the revised SD1 range just as susceptible to crosswinds as the earlier models had been.

Motor also tested a 2000, this time LOC 726X, finished in red and also featuring power-assisted steering: clearly the press office knew that unassisted steering was not going to be a selling point. The magazine had somewhat mixed views about the car:

> *We find the 2000 a difficult car to come to terms with. Undoubtedly an attractive alternative to the 4-cylinder Ford Granada and, indeed, a likeable car in its own right, the crudeness of the engine seems at odds with standards of refinement and luxury attained by the rest of its design. With neither performance nor economy to commend it, we can think of no good reason for not spending another £500 for the 6-cylinder 2300.*

Diesel 2400SD Turbo

In the UK, *Motor* was the first to test the new diesel model, in its issue dated 30 October. The magazine did not dispute Austin Rover's claim that the 2400SD Turbo was the fastest production diesel car then available on the UK market. Overall, they felt that the car

> *retains all the better attributes of the capable Rover range and while the driver is unlikely to forget he is sitting behind a diesel engine he can take comfort from the car's parsimonious thirst for fuel and the plushness of his surroundings. The diesel Rover will undoubtedly appeal to fleet operators looking for more economical cars for their executives; and the private owner who wants an economy luxury car, and isn't too bothered about performance, should also find the Rover a very attractive proposition.*

As for the diesel engine, it was

> *disappointingly lacking in response below about 2,000rpm (it feels particularly sluggish when pulling away from rest) but once the turbocharger starts working effectively, the engine revs eagerly through the gears – albeit with a noticeable diesel clatter – to its 4,500rpm red line.*

High-speed cruising showed the car at its best, but the well-chosen gear ratios meant that it was not difficult to keep the engine on boost to give respectable acceleration. Overall fuel consumption on test was 29.6mpg (9.6ltr/100km), which was quite exceptional for an SD1 of any kind, and *Motor* thought that 'most owners should find 35mpg within their grasp'. Diesel clatter apart, refinement was good, although there was 'a noticeable whistle from the turbocharger as the engine comes on boost at 2,000rpm'.

Autocar also tested the diesel Rover, in its issue of 6 November. Overall, the magazine could 'think of no significant drawback to running an SD Turbo as long as people are not put off by the slightly rougher than average tickover, and having to give the car an oil change at the suggested 3,000 mile intervals'.

Engine noise was actually 'a bit less than expected', and 'above 1,500rpm the engine smooths out noticeably', although it 'does sound rather busy if revved hard, and there is a perceptible exhaust resonance at around 3,500-4,000rpm which more often than not corresponds to one's chosen cruising speed'. The testers were surprised at the car's performance, which comfortably exceeded 100mph (160km/h) on the banked circuit at MIRA, and commented on the car's 'most un-diesel-like mid-range go'.

'On the road,' they said, 'one soon gets used to the fairly narrow power band and low revving nature of the engine.' The car was 'at its best on the open road where the minimum of gear changing and nippy overtaking is required to make decent progress'. *Autocar* achieved exactly the same 29.6mpg overall test figure as had *Motor*.

The 3500SE came with alloy wheels as standard but, initially at least, without headlamp washers.

The grey enamelled alloy wheels of the Vanden Plas are clear in this photograph, which also shows the special tail badge. Despite the UK registration, this is a left-hand-drive car, seen here in Biarritz in January 1982.

3500SE

For most potential buyers of a facelifted SD1, however, it was the comments made by *Motor* in the running report on its long-term 3500SE that were of the greatest value. The magazine was unimpressed to find the wrong driver's handbook had been provided, and that even when the right one turned up it did not contain helpful running-in instructions. Nevertheless, the car was 'substantially free of faults and blemishes' except for 'a loose surround to the locking knob on the driver's door'.

'I particularly liked the smoothness and excellent low-speed pull of the splendid V8 engine,' wrote editor Anthony Curtis, although he also noted that the automatic choke often caused the engine to falter immediately after a cold start. He commented on excessive wind noise at speed and on a whine from second and third gears, and that the dampers made the car 'feel vague, lurchy and untidy'.

In the first 5,000 miles (8,000km) of use, more problems showed up. The wind noise got worse, the tailgate developed a leak, the rear suspension knocked on left-hand bends, the brake-pad-wear warning light flickered and the temperature-gauge light developed a fault. The ignition key could not be relied upon to turn the starter first time. Headlamp adjustment seemed to be wrong – and was later traced to the car being fitted with a left-hand-drive headlamp on the driver's side. 'All these problems,' summarized Curtis, 'make me believe that my car, while perhaps sound in essentials, is below average in its quality.' Nonetheless, the car remained on the fleet and there were more reports.

A SAD END

After the old Light-Medium Cars division had transformed into Austin Rover during 1982, Harold Musgrove became the company chairman. Musgrove was notoriously forthright and did not take kindly to those who challenged him.

David Bache, by this time head of all styling for Austin Rover, was also very strong-willed. The two men clashed at a styling review for the forthcoming Austin Maestro in late 1982 and Musgrove sacked Bache on the spot. So the SD1, quite possibly Bache's masterpiece, lived through its final years in production without oversight from the man who had been responsible for its looks. The new head of Austin Rover styling was Roy Axe, who had been in charge of styling for Chrysler Europe until 1977 and had then taken over as head of styling for Chrysler in the USA.

THE 1983–1986 MODELS

1983 Models

The 1982 facelift was followed quite swiftly by a series of further changes, which delivered the 1983 models in October 1982. At this point, a new high-performance derivative called the Vitesse joined the range, and this is dealt with

The arrival of the 2600SE as a 1983 model reflected customer preference for high specification levels.

separately in Chapter 6. October also brought the first 2400SD Turbo models for the UK market. Meanwhile, the mainstream range was also swelled by an additional model. This was the 2600SE which, engine aside, had a specification almost identical to that of the 3500SE. Differences were the absence of a courtesy lamp delay, rear cigarette lighter, electric aerial and underbonnet lamps.

October 1982 also saw bronze-tinted glass standardized across the range, and carpeted lower door kick panels with plastic speaker covers on SE models and above. The 2000 gained central locking as standard. There were then two more changes during the 1983 model year. One was that motorized central locking replaced the solenoid type. The other, introduced at about the same time, was that the Borg Warner automatic gearboxes gave way to a new three-speed type built by General Motors in Strasbourg and known as the GM 180. Gear ratios were slightly different, but made no discernible difference in driving.

The 2.6-litre cars continued their upward rise in 1984 with the introduction of a 2600 Vanden Plas. This is a left-hand-drive car.

The leather and burr walnut of the Vanden Plas specification were unchanged for the 2.6-litre cars.

1984 Models

The changes for the 1984 model year were announced in July 1983. The major novelty was new interior trim. Colours and fabrics were now standardized as far as possible across the Austin Rover range. The 2000 and 2300 both took on Shetland Tweed upholstery, and the Vanden Plas option of Hairline Velvet gave way to Raschelle knitted fabric. Door trims on all models now incorporated a contrasting colour as well as the main interior hue. New air-conditioning and cruise-control systems were introduced for those cars so equipped. On the outside, the 1984-model SD1s were recognizable by black plastic surrounds on the door handles, which replaced the bright metal type used on earlier cars.

There was then a further realignment of the SD1 range in May 1984. Austin Rover simply called it an 'improved 1984 specification', but the changes were actually quite far-reaching and amounted to a range-wide improvement in specification levels. These improvements were clearly thought to be necessary to maintain sales of the SD1 in the face of increasingly strong competition from new rivals in its market sector. They also helped to focus public attention on the Rover name, which from June 1984 was to be used on the new 200 series, a much smaller car based on the latest Honda Ballade and destined to replace the Triumph Acclaim, which would be the last model to wear Triumph badges.

Most significant was that the 2600SE and 3500SE models were discontinued, while a new 2600 Vanden Plas model was introduced with an equipment specification corresponding to that of the existing 3500 Vanden Plas. There was a new top-of-the-range model as well, which combined the fuel-injected engine from the Vitesse with the Vanden Plas equipment specification and was called the Vanden Plas EFi (see Chapter 6).

The other models were generally given higher levels of equipment. The 2000 gained the same stainless-steel wheel trims as the S models, together with bright trim around its

A DIESEL RECORD-BREAKER

On 5 and 6 December 1983, a standard 2400SD Turbo was used to set new 24-hour distance records for diesel cars, held at that stage by a Ford Granada, which had set them in 1978. The record attempt was organized by the Williams Grand Prix team (of which BL was a sponsor), with sponsorship from a number of companies, including TAG (Techniques d'Avant Garde), another sponsor of the Williams team, Austin Rover, Goodyear and Mobil.

The car used was a standard production example, without even a rollover cage or racing seat belts. However, it was fitted with 175 SR 14 Goodyear Grand Prix S tyres and was decked out with sponsors' logos.

The event was held at the Snetterton race track and was observed by RAC timekeepers. Black ice delayed the start on the first day, but the car later comfortably took fourteen records, its only problem being a broken throttle cable that had to be changed.

ABOVE RIGHT: A subtle change on the 1985 models was to introduce black plastic air grilles in place of the earlier wire-mesh type. They are seen here on a diesel model.

From May 1984, a black badge plinth replaced the bright type on all models. Here it is on a diesel.

An even more subtle change made in May 1984 was to the shape of the door mirror bases. The earlier type is seen here above, with the more curved type below.

bumpers. Its interior went back to plain velvet upholstery, and gained adjustable lumbar support for its front seats, plus walnut veneer on the doors, passenger grab handles, electric windows and a four-speaker MW/LW stereo radio cassette system.

From May 1984, all the SD1 models also took on black badge plinths at the rear, as pioneered on the Vitesse in 1982. The shape of the door mirror bases was changed to reduce wind noise, and black plastic grilles replaced the wire-mesh type below the windscreen.

1985 Models

As described in the box on page 102, Austin Rover had hoped to introduce the Project Bravo car as a replacement for the SD1 over the summer of 1984, but the switch to Project XX and a joint design with Honda had changed the timing on that. By the summer of 1984, the SD1 had been on the market for eight years, and Austin Rover management judged that frequent 'product actions' – changes and improvements – were necessary to maintain sales of what was now an elderly design until its replacement was ready in 1986. In fact, the SD1 still looked fresh, thanks to David Bache's superbly executed original design. However, sales were now past their peak, and during the 1984 calendar year they began to slide.

All this helps to explain why there were additional changes in October 1984 for the 1985 models. The 2000 was further upgraded with power-assisted steering, a manual sunroof and an intermittent wash-wipe system. All three S-specification models – 2300S, 2400SD Turbo and 2600S – gained Shadowstripe and Plain Velvet upholstery plus electric sunroofs as standard. The 2000 and 2300 now had Plain Velvet upholstery (1984's Shetland Tweed had always seemed rather utilitarian for a Rover) and Box and Plain Velvet became standard for the two Vanden Plas models, while leather was relegated to an extra-cost option. The Raschelle fabric available as a Vanden Plas option for the 1984 model year had not proved very popular and now disappeared. Every model from the 2000 upwards now came with electrically adjusted and heated door mirrors, plus headlamps wired through the ignition circuit so that they could not be left on by mistake when the car was parked.

Less visibly, the 1985 petrol models in the mainstream range all came with SU HIF44E carburettors that incorporated an electronic mixture control system to improve fuel economy.

1986 Models

With everything on course for the new Rover 800 range to be announced in July 1986, SD1 had just one more year to go when the 1986-model revisions were announced in July 1985. There were four new paint colours, but these were not extended to the full model range, and the only other real change was that radio aerials disappeared as the tail window demister element was wired in to replace them. At Motor Show time in October, the 2000 was mildly upgraded with a three-band stereo radio cassette head unit as standard. There was then a final change in January 1986, when all models were given repeater turn indicators in the front wings.

The SD1 range gradually ceased production during the 1986 model year, although residual stocks remained in the showrooms until well into 1987. In the UK, the 2400SD Turbo was the first to disappear from the catalogues, and was not advertised after July 1985, although examples remained available overseas until later. The first models to go out of production were the 2400SD Turbo and the 2000, followed by the 2300S and 2600S and then the V8 cars, including the Vanden Plas EFi. Just the 2300, 2600 Vanden Plas and Vitesse were left by the early summer, the Vitesse remaining in plentiful supply because large numbers were built towards the end of production to satisfy racing homologation requirements.

The last UK cars attracted the E-prefix registrations introduced in August 1987, and among them were a number that were sold to police forces in the UK. These were probably treated as unwanted stock and it appears that they were resprayed white in November 1987 before sale. The cars were mostly 2300 and 2600 Vanden Plas types, and London's Metropolitan Police was among the forces that removed the Vanden Plas badges before the cars entered service, not wanting the public to believe that policemen rode around in luxurious patrol cars!

PAINT AND TRIM OPTIONS – 1982–1986 MODELS

February 1982 to June 1983

There were eleven paint options, all of them new for the facelifted SD1 range. Black was still an extra-cost option, and metallic paints cost extra on all models.

As before, there were four different upholstery types, with the same four colour choices. However, the matching of paint and upholstery options was more complex; in addition, Vitesse models from October 1982 came only with one type of upholstery, which combined Flint sculpted velvet with Osprey plain velvet.

In the table below, PV is the Plain Velvet used on 2000 and 2300 models; P&P is the Plain & Pinstripe Velvet used on the 2300S and 2600S; HV is the Hairline Velvet standard on the 3500SE and optional on the Vanden Plas; and L is the Leather that was standard on the Vanden Plas.

Colour name	***Description***	***Interior options***
Black	Black (BLVC 90)	PV: Oatmeal P&P: Caviar or Oatmeal HV: Caviar or Oatmeal L: Caviar or Oatmeal
Cashmere Gold	Mid-gold metallic (BLVC 422)	PV: Caviar P&P: Caviar or Oatmeal HV: Caviar or Oatmeal L: Caviar or Oatmeal
Champagne Beige	Beige (BLVC 248)	PV: Oatmeal P&P: Bayleaf or Oatmeal HV: Bayleaf or Oatmeal L: Oatmeal
Clove Brown	Dark brown (BLVC 398)	PV: Oatmeal P&P: Oatmeal HV: Oatmeal L: Oatmeal
Ermine White	White (BLVC 243)	PV: Caviar P&P: Bayleaf or Caviar HV: Bayleaf or Caviar L: Caviar
Monza Red	Mid-red (BLVC 457)	PV: Oatmeal P&P: Caviar or Oatmeal HV: Caviar or Oatmeal L: Caviar or Oatmeal
Moonraker Blue	Mid-blue metallic (BLVC 424)	PV: Oatmeal P&P: Oatmeal or Prussian HV: Oatmeal or Prussian L: Oatmeal
Opaline Green	Light green metallic (BLVC 423)	PV: Caviar P&P: Bayleaf or Caviar HV: Bayleaf or Caviar L: Caviar
Oporto Red	Dark red metallic (BLVC 425)	PV: Oatmeal P&P: Caviar or Oatmeal HV: Caviar or Oatmeal L: Caviar or Oatmeal
Silver Leaf	Silver metallic (BLVC 421)	PV: Caviar P&P: Caviar or Prussian HV: Caviar or Prussian L: Caviar
Zircon Blue	Light blue metallic (BLVC 471)	PV: Oatmeal P&P: Oatmeal or Prussi HV: Oatmeal or Prussia L: Oatmeal

July 1983 to October 1984

There were again eleven paint options in this period of SD1 production, of which two were new in July 1983. Black was a r option on Vanden Plas models but cost extra elsewhere; Silve was a no-cost option on the Vanden Plas and Vitesse but cost elsewhere.

The Vitesse again came only with one type of upholstery, th combined Flint/Osprey Sculptured and Plain Velvet. On the ot models, there were now five different upholstery types, with new colour choices (Bounty Blue, Brushwood, Claret, Osprey Sandpiper). The matching of paint and upholstery options rem complex, and when a Brushwood interior was specified on a 2 or 3500SE, it came with Sandpiper seat trim.

In the table below, ST is the Shetland Tweed used on 2000 2300 models; P&P is the Plain & Pinstripe Velvet used on the 2400SD and 2600S; HV is the Hairline Velvet standard on the and 3500SE; R is the Raschelle knitted fabric optional on the Plas; and L is the Leather that was standard on the Vanden Pla

Colour name	***Description***	***Interior options***
Arum White	White (BLVC 449)	ST: Brushwood P&P: Brushwood or Cl HV: Brushwood or Cla R: Brushwood or Clar L: Brushwood or Ospr
Black	Black (BLVC 90)	ST: Osprey P&P: Osprey or Claret HV: Osprey or Claret R: Osprey or Claret L: Brushwood or Ospr
Cashmere Gold	Mid-gold metallic (BLVC 422)	ST: Brushwood P&P: Brushwood or Sa HV: Brushwood or Sa R: Brushwood or Sand L: Brushwood

rown	Mid-brown (BLVC 398)	ST: Sandpiper P&P: Brushwood or Sandpiper HV: Brushwood or Sandpiper R: Brushwood or Sandpiper L: Brushwood
Blue	Dark blue (BLVC 459)	ST: Bounty Blue P&P: Bounty Blue or Osprey HV: Bounty Blue or Osprey R: Bounty Blue or Osprey L: Osprey
Red	Mid-red (BLVC 457)	ST: Sandpiper P&P: Sandpiper or Osprey HV: Sandpiper or Osprey R: Sandpiper or Osprey L: Brushwood or Osprey
ker Blue	Mid-blue metallic (BLVC 424)	ST: Bounty Blue P&P: Bounty Blue or Osprey HV: Bounty Blue or Osprey R: Bounty Blue or Osprey L: Osprey
Green	Light green metallic (BLVC 423)	ST: Brushwood P&P: Brushwood or Osprey HV: Brushwood or Osprey R: Brushwood or Osprey L: Brushwood or Osprey
Red	Dark red metallic (BLVC 425)	ST: Sandpiper P&P: Claret or Sandpiper HV: Claret or Sandpiper R: Claret or Sandpiper L: Brushwood or Osprey
af	Silver metallic (BLVC 421)	ST: Osprey P&P: Claret or Osprey HV: Claret or Osprey R: Claret or Osprey L: Brushwood or Osprey
lue	Light blue metallic (BLVC 471)	ST: Bounty Blue P&P: Bounty Blue or Osprey HV: Bounty Blue or Osprey R: Bounty Blue or Osprey L: Brushwood or Osprey

ber 1984 to October 1985

re twelve paint options for the SD1 in this period: Monza deleted and Champagne Beige and Targa Red were both new. all metallic paints were a no-cost option on the Vanden Plas ost extra on all other models. The Vitesse was available in colours: Black, Moonraker Blue, Silver Leaf and Targa Red. tery came in eight different colours, although the grey Flint/ ombination was used only on the Vitesse, which continued nique combination of Sculptured and Plain Velvet. There other upholstery types: Plain Velvet (PV) on 2000 and 2300 models; Shadowstripe and Plain Velvet (SPV) on 2300S, 2400SD and 2600S; Box and Plain Velvet (BPV) was standard on the 2600 Vanden Plas and 3500 Vanden Plas, and was a no-cost option on the Vanden Plas EFi; and Leather (L) was standard on the Vanden Plas EFi and an extra-cost option on all other models except the Vitesse.

Bitter Chocolate was dark brown; Caramel was mid-brown; Claret was deep red; Flint was grey; Ice Blue was light blue; Osprey was grey (leather only); Prussian Blue was dark blue.

Colour name	***Description***	***Interior options***
Arum White	White (BLVC 449)	PV: Bitter Chocolate SPV: Bitter Chocolate or Claret BPV: Bitter Chocolate or Claret L: Bitter Chocolate or Caramel
Black	Black (BLVC 90)	PV: Caramel SPV: Caramel or Claret BPV: Caramel or Claret L: Caramel or Osprey
Cashmere Gold	Mid-gold metallic (BLVC 422)	PV: Bitter Chocolate SPV: Bitter Chocolate BPV: Bitter Chocolate L: Bitter Chocolate
Champagne Beige	Beige (BLVC 248)	PV: Bitter Chocolate SPV: Bitter Chocolate BPV: Bitter Chocolate L: Bitter Chocolate
Clove Brown	Mid-brown (BLVC 398)	PV: Caramel SPV: Caramel BPV: Caramel L: Caramel
Eclipse Blue	Dark blue (BLVC 459)	PV: Prussian Blue SPV: Prussian Blue or Flint BPV: Ice Blue or Flint L: Osprey
Moonraker Blue	Mid-blue metallic (BLVC 424)	PV: Prussian Blue SPV: Prussian Blue or Flint BPV: Ice Blue or Flint L: Osprey
Opaline Green	Light green metallic (BLVC 423)	PV: Flint SPV: Bitter Chocolate or Flint BPV: Bitter Chocolate or Flint L: Bitter Chocolate or Osprey
Oporto Red	Dark red metallic (BLVC 425)	PV: Caramel SPV: Bitter Chocolate or Caramel BPV: Bitter Chocolate or Caramel

(continued overleaf...)

Paint and Trim Options – 1982–1986 Models *(continued)*

		L: Bitter Chocolate or Caramel
Silver Leaf	Silver metallic (BLVC 421)	PV: Flint SPV: Flint or Claret BPV: Flint or Claret L: Osprey
Targa Red	Bright red (BLVC 641)	PV: Flint SPV: Caramel or Flint BPV: Caramel or Flint L: Caramel or Osprey
Zircon Blue	Light blue metallic (BLVC 471)	PV: Prussian Blue SPV: Prussian Blue or Flint BPV: Flint L: Osprey

November 1985 to July 1986

There were again twelve paint options in this last period of SD1 production, of which four were new in November 1985. The four new colours (Azure Blue, Nightwatch Blue, Silk Green and White Diamond) were not available on 2000 and 3500 Vanden Plas models.

Black and all metallic paints were a no-cost option on the Vanden Plas EFi but cost extra on all other models. The Vitesse was available in only four colours: Black, Moonraker Blue, Silver Leaf and Targa Red.

Upholstery came in eight different colours, although the grey Flint/Osprey combination was used only on the Vitesse and, as before, had a unique materials combination of Sculptured and Plain Velvet. There were four other upholstery types: Plain Velvet (PV) on 2000 and 2300 models; Chalkstripe and Plain Velvet (CPV) on 2300S, 2400SD and 2600S; Box and Plain Velvet (BPV) was standard on the 2600 Vanden Plas and 3500 Vanden Plas and was a no-cost option on the Vanden Plas EFi; and Leather (L) was standard on the Vanden Plas EFi and an extra-cost option on all other models except the Vitesse.

Bitter Chocolate was dark brown; Caramel was mid-brown; Claret was deep red; Flint was grey; Ice Blue was light blue; Osprey was grey (leather only); Prussian Blue was dark blue.

Colour name	*Description*	*Interior options*
Azure Blue	Light blue metallic (BLVC 639)	PV: Prussian Blue CPV: (Not available) BPV: Ice Blue or Flint L: (Not available)
Black	Black (BLVC 90)	PV: Caramel CPV: Caramel or Claret BPV: Caramel or Claret L: Caramel or Osprey
Cashmere Gold	Mid-gold metallic (BLVC 422)	PV: Bitter Chocolate CPV: Bitter Chocolate BPV: Bitter Chocolate L: Bitter Chocolate
Champagne Beige	Beige (BLVC 248)	PV: Bitter Chocolate CPV: Bitter Chocolate BPV: Bitter Chocolate L: Bitter Chocolate
Clove Brown	Mid-brown (BLVC 398)	PV: Bitter Chocolate CPV: Bitter Chocolate BPV: Bitter Chocolate L: Bitter Chocolate
Moonraker Blue	Mid-blue metallic (BLVC 424)	PV: Prussian Blue CPV: Prussian Blue or Flint BPV: Ice Blue or Flint L: Osprey
Nightwatch Blue	Very dark blue (BLVC 629)	PV: Prussian Blue CPV: (Not available) BPV: Ice Blue or Flint L: (Not available)
Oporto Red	Dark red metallic (BLVC 425)	PV: Caramel CPV: Bitter Chocolate or Caramel BPV: Bitter Chocolate or Caramel L: Bitter Chocolate or Caramel
Silk Green	Light green metallic (BLVC 901)	PV: Flint CPV: (Not available) BPV: Bitter Chocolate or Flint Leather: (Not available)
Silver Leaf	Silver metallic (BLVC 421)	PV: Flint CPV: Flint or Claret BPV: Flint or Claret L: Osprey
Targa Red	Bright red (BLVC 641)	PV: Flint CPV: Caramel or Flint BPV: Caramel or Flint L: Caramel or Osprey
White Diamond	White (BLVC 854)	PV: Bitter Chocolate CPV: (Not available) BPV: Bitter Chocolate Claret: L: (Not available)

TECHNICAL SPECIFICATIONS – ROVER SDI, 1982–1986 (EXCEPT VITESSE AND VANDEN PLAS EFI)

Engines

2000
4-cylinder O-series petrol
1994cc (84.45 x 71.1mm)
Single overhead camshaft, belt-driven
Five-bearing crankshaft
Compression ratio 9.0:1
Two SU HIF44 carburettors (1982–84); two SU HIF44E carburettors with electronic mixture control (1984–86)
101bhp at 5,250rpm
120lb ft at 3,250rpm

2300
Type PE 146 6-cylinder petrol
2350cc (81 x 76mm)
Single overhead camshaft
Four-bearing crankshaft
Compression ratio 9.25:1
Two SU HIF44 carburettors (1982–84); two HIF44E carburettors with electronic mixture control (1984–86)
123bhp at 5,000rpm
134lb ft at 4,000rpm

2400 diesel
4-cylinder VM HR492 diesel
2393cc (92 x 90mm)
Overhead valves
Five-bearing crankshaft
Compression ratio 9.21:1
Indirect injection with KKK turbocharger
90bhp at 4,000rpm
142lb ft at 2,350rpm

2600
Type PE 166 6-cylinder petrol
2597cc (81 x 84mm)
Single overhead camshaft
Four-bearing crankshaft
Compression ratio 9.25:1
Two SU HIF44 carburettors (1982–84); two HIF44E carburettors with electronic mixture control (1984–86)
136bhp at 5,000rpm
152lb ft at 3,750rpm

3500
V8-cylinder petrol
3528cc (88.9 x 71.1mm)
Single overhead camshaft
Five-bearing crankshaft
Compression ratio 9.35:1
Two Solex 175 CDEF carburettors (1982–84); two SU HIF44E carburettors with electronic mixture control (1984–86)
155bhp at 5,250rpm
198lb ft at 2,500rpm

Transmission
Five-speed manual gearbox standard on all models
Ratios 3.32:1, 2.08:1, 1.39:1, 1.00:1, 0.79:1; reverse 3.43:1 (0.77:1 fifth gear on 2400SD Turbo models)
Three-speed Borg Warner type 66 automatic gearbox optional, 1982
Ratios 2.39:1, 1.45:1, 1.00:1; reverse 1.92:1
Three-speed GM automatic gearbox optional, from 1983, and standard on 2600 and 3500 from May 1984
Ratios 2.40:1, 1.48:1, 1.00:1; reverse 1.92:1

Axle ratio

2000	3.9:1
2300	3.45:1
2400	3.9:1
2600	3.45:1
3500	3.08:1

Suspension, steering and brakes
Front suspension with MacPherson struts, lower links and anti-roll bar
Rear axle with torque tube, trailing arms, Watt's linkage and coil springs; self-energizing ride-levelling struts on all models except 2000 and 2300
Rack-and-pinion steering; power assistance optional
Disc brakes at front with 10.5in diameter; drum brakes at rear with 9.0in diameter; vacuum servo assistance standard

Dimensions

Overall length	186in (4,724mm) standard 187in (4,750mm) with headlamp washers
Overall width	70in (1,778mm)
Overall height	55in (1,397mm)
Wheelbase	110.8in (2,814mm)
Front track	59.1in (1500mm) with steel wheels; 59.3in (1506mm) with alloy wheels
Rear track	59.1in (1500mm) with steel wheels; 59.3in (1506mm) with alloy wheels

Wheels and tyres
14in five-bolt steel wheels with 5.5in rims (2000, 2300, 2300S, 2400SD and 2600S); 14in five-bolt alloy wheels with 6in rims standard on 3500SE and Vanden Plas, and optional on others
Steel wheels with 175 HR 14 tyres; alloy wheels with 195/70 HR 14 tyres

Unladen weights

2,888 lb (1,310kg)	2000
3,018 lb (1,369kg)	2300, 2300S
3056 lb (1386kg)	2600S automatic
3062 lb (1389kg)	2600S manual
3050 lb (1387kg)	3500SE automatic
3080 lb (1397kg)	3500SE manual
3095 lb (1404kg)	Vanden Plas automatic (V8)
3117 lb (1414kg)	Vanden Plas manual (V8)
3252 lb (1475kg)	2600 Vanden Plas
3366 lb (1527kg)	2400SD Turbo

CHAPTER SIX

INJECTED AND EXCLUSIVE – VITESSE AND VANDEN PLAS EFi

The idea of a high-performance derivative of the SD1 had been around for some time before such a car ever reached the showrooms. Spen King had been one of those who believed that a 'halo' model would have a beneficial effect on the sales of all SD1s, and of course the success of Janspeed and others with their high-performance aftermarket conversions (*see* Chapter 10) made quite clear that a small but certainly not negligible market existed. In the early 1980s, these thoughts came together with the plan to put the SD1 into saloon car racing, and by the autumn of 1982 what was then Austin Rover had a production car ready.

However, it is important to recognize that this production car – brought to market as the Rover Vitesse – was very much a 'homologation special'. That is, it was a derivative built to enable the car to go racing. As Ian Elliott purs it:

> *Without the impetus of competition, I very much doubt if the production car would have gained fuel injection in the days when it was normally only specified for emission-control reasons – as per Australian SD1 3500. The Vitesse didn't fit into the normal pattern of production car development and retailing.*

Inspiration and Prototype

The road to building the Vitesse had been an interesting one. An important part in the story was played by the tuned 3500 that was owned by David Clarke in the marketing department. This car had been modified largely by David Price Racing, who also built the first race-spec car for BL Motorsport

ABOVE AND OPPOSITE, TOP: XON 742T was the first styling prototype for the Rover Rapide. It was photographed in the styling studio on 11 November 1980.

The Rapide prototype was fitted with high-back seats and a US-specification three-spoke steering wheel.

(see Chapter 9), and it had 200bhp from an engine fed by twin-choke Weber carburettors. With lowered suspension and Minilite wheels, it was very much a road-racer, but word about it got around the company and eventually even Harold Musgrove is said to have borrowed it. Musgrove said that he would like to see a 200bhp Rover SD1 in production, but that it would have to be much more refined and suitable for everyday use than Clarke's car.

In the meantime, David Bache's styling department had been looking at options for what was by now known as the VHPD version of the SD1; the letters simply stood for Very High Performance Derivative. The styling was developed on an actual car rather than a studio mock-up, and that car was registered as XON 742T, which suggests it was a 1979 model. This was in fact almost certainly the David Clarke car – although Clarke's car is remembered to have been green in the beginning, and by the time it was photographed in November 1980, the styling car was black.

Bache's team added 1981-model cosmetic details to the exterior, fitting rubber-faced bumpers and the latest Viking ship badge; the car also had the latest front panel with additional air intake, although that could have been fitted from new. At the front, it had an early version of the chin spoiler planned for the 1982 facelift, and at the rear it had a spoiler on the trailing edge of the tailgate. Bache applied a graduated shade effect to the rearmost side windows (he had something similar on his own SD1 at the time, which also had the chin spoiler), and the rear badge plinths were painted matt black to carry the name of Rover Rapide in red script. Red coachlines and a twin-exhaust tailpipe added to the effect.

More than one option was examined for the interior, which was essentially to 1981 specification. Recaro front seats were tried, and so was a North American-specification three-spoke steering wheel. The gear lever (this was a five-speed car) was replaced by one with with a wood finish item with a deep leather gaiter. Also tried were a 1982-specification instrument panel and steering wheel, the former looking rather incongruous with its digital clock in addition to the analogue clock in the centre of the original dash.

The author saw this very car on the M4 motorway near London one morning, but the Minilite wheels seemed to suggest that it was an aftermarket confection and not a fac-

Just over a year later, styling studio ideas had progressed to this stage. Photographed on 12 November 1981, the Rapide styling prototype now carried the planned facelift features, styled wheels that did not make production, and side graphics.

tory prototype. The Rover Rapide badges also suggested that this car was the result of an enthusiast spending more money than was sensible on modifying a two-year-old SD1.

The name Rover Rapide certainly sounded right and gained some acceptance within JRT. It was used on a styling mock-up car completed in November 1981 on which the word 'Rapide' was emblazoned on each side as a graphic – clearly anticipating the eventual production style for the car. However, the model name was registered to Aston Martin Lagonda, who had last used it on a rather unsuccessful model called the Lagonda Rapide between 1961 and 1964. When they proved unwilling to release it, JRT had to look elsewhere.

The marketing department now put forward the name of Vitesse, which actually belonged to Triumph, who had first used it in the 1930s and more recently on a 2-litre derivative of their Herald saloon that had gone out of production in 1971. Nevertheless, Rover Vitesse sounded good as a name, and was highly appropriate for the new high-performance SD1 because 'vitesse' is French for 'speed'. So it became the favoured choice.

The heart of the Vitesse was its 190bhp injected version of the V8 engine. The cast plenum of this version was quite different from the flat black type used on the emissions-controlled V8s for Australia and the USA.

Engine Development

Quite obviously, a more powerful version of the V8 engine had to be central to the new high-performance SD1. One way forward could have been to increase the swept volume, but that would have required new tooling and would have been relatively expensive. Much more affordable and, in the long run, beneficial was to develop the existing 3.5-litre engine by using fuel injection to deliver extra power and torque. It would be a continuation of work that had already been done with fuel injection for overseas markets with tight exhaust-emissions regulations, and the work might also have other applications in the future. As things were to turn out, although this was not envisaged at the time, the injected V8 engine became vital to the further development of the Range Rover, which took on a lower-powered version from mid-1984 and would use that same engine when it was launched into the USA in 1987.

By this stage, reorganizations within British Leyland had left both manufacture and development of the V8 engine in the hands of Land Rover Ltd, whose home was the Solihull site that had once belonged to Rover. So the engine was redeveloped by Land Rover engineers – although in practice most of these were the same people who had worked on it in Rover days. Among them was Richard Twist, who redesigned the inlet manifold for the Vitesse engine to incorporate eight separate inlet tracts, each of which ended in a flared tubular steel 'trumpet' inside a cast plenum mounted on top of the engine. This feature gave the engine a quite different appearance from the earlier injected Rover V8s, and a ribbed top face on the plenum was a neat visual touch. At the side of the plenum was a single throttle butterfly.

Breathing was improved slightly over the standard engine by machining both inlet and exhaust valves just behind their heads to give better gas flow, but neither the cylinder heads nor the camshaft were changed. The standard SD1 V8 exhaust manifolds were retained, too, but they fed into an exhaust system with a 60mm bore instead of the 54mm bore of the standard type. This helped to give the Vitesse a more sonorous exhaust note, as well as aiding the flow of exhaust gases. Then the compression ratio was raised to 9.75:1 from the 9.35:1 of the carburettor engines by fitting pistons with a shallower depression in their crowns. As for the injection system itself, the Lucas type was retained, but with a few alterations. These included a new air flow meter and a recalibrated ECU with a different ignition curve for the distributor. The cooling system was also uprated to cope with the additional stresses on the engine.

As the Vitesse was conceived as a performance car, a manual gearbox was planned as the only type available. So the five-speed 77mm type was specified, but in stronger form than the version used in mainstream SD1 models. It had shot-peened gears and stronger bearings like the version used in Jaguar XJ6 models with that company's 4.2-litre engine. The Jaguar engine put out 200bhp and 236lb ft of torque; the Rover engine, with 190bhp at 5,280rpm and 220lb ft at 4,000rpm, was well within those limits.

The Early Vitesse

The Vitesse was introduced at the Motor Show in October 1982 alongside another 'VHPD' model from Austin Rover, in this case the MG Metro Turbo. From a marketing point of view, it made good sense to introduce these two new cars back to back because the two cars together were likely to attract more media attention than just one on its own. There was also good sense in keeping the arrival of the Vitesse separate from that of the facelifted cars in January 1982; it meant that each would get separate coverage in the media. However, the car's very special nature was confirmed by the fact that it was not offered through all Austin Rover dealers; only selected dealers had it, and their staff received special training in sales and service of the model.

The Vitesse had been prepared by the styling department under David Bache, and it certainly looked the part. The bodyshell was unaltered but carried large 'Vitesse' decals along the lower flanks and a black polyurethane spoiler on the bottom of the hatchback. There were black polyurethane aerodynamic fairings ahead of the rear wheel arches, and the rear badge plinth was in black rather than the silver of the mainstream SD1 range. The Vitesse also sat an inch lower on its suspension than other SD1s, and was shod with low-profile 205/60 VR 15 Pirelli P6 tyres on special spoked alloy wheels. The lowered suspension and additional spoilers lowered the drag coefficient from 0.395 on the standard cars to a useful 0.36 – not class-leading, but a very worthwhile improvement.

Inside the passenger cabin, the upholstery was in dark and light grey velour (which Rover called velvet) with all colours, a choice made partly to keep manufacturing costs down. 'Sculptured and Plain Velvet' panels provided an attractive visual contrast. Special 'sports' front seats meanwhile gave better lateral location than the standard seats. The wood trim was satin-finish walnut, and both a trip computer and a four-speaker stereo radio cassette unit were standard. Rear seat belts came as standard. There was a zone-tinted windscreen, and air conditioning was available as an extra-

Pictured outside the old main office block at Rover's Solihull works, this silver Vitesse shows clearly the side graphics, cross-spoke wheels and rear spoiler characteristic of the early cars. This one, photographed by Craig Pusey, is ROE 973Y, one of the press-launch cars.

Austin Rover's press-release photos for the Vitesse showed a car with darker paintwork – probably red – which did not show the side graphics so clearly. Perhaps this was deliberate; Rover may have been concerned about an adverse reaction to the graphics.

Spoiler and tail badging are clear in this photo from the 1982 press release.

cost option. The Vitesse also came with a Vanden Plas-style headlamp power wash, electrically adjusted and heated door mirrors and a manually operated sunroof – electric operation cost extra.

Suspension, brakes and steering were all uprated to cope with the car's higher performance. Spring and damper rates were increased by around 20 per cent front and rear and the Vitesse had uprated self-levelling struts fitted in tandem with variable-rate coil springs; the Boge struts were used with linear-rate coil springs on other SD1s. Stiffer bushes on the Watt's linkage gave firmer axle location to improve high-speed stability. Although the rear brakes remained unchanged, the front brakes were swapped for four-piston AP calipers with 10.15in ventilated discs. These were the same brakes that had been developed for the SD1s used by the Metropolitan Police (see Chapter 7) and were subsequently fitted to the motor sport cars as well (see Chapter 9). As for the steering, a different pump reduced the amount of power assistance provided at speed, although the actual steering ratio remained unchanged.

With a UK price of £14,950, the Vitesse immediately became the most expensive model in the SD1 range, and

The interior of the Vitesse was special, the grey seats having contrasting dark and light grey velvet sections and the wood trim having a straight grain. The buttons for the trip computer can be seen clearly below the heater control panel.

The dashboard of the production cars was very much the standard item, but note the Vitesse name on the steering wheel of this 1984 automatic model.

The side graphics were decals. The edges of the panels can just be seen in this close-up picture.

that gave it a certain prestige. However, as first introduced, it could be had in only three colours from the standard range – solid Monza Red and metallic Moonraker Blue or Silver Leaf. This was not to be a permanent state of affairs, but was done to minimize production costs while the car gained customer acceptance. It soon became clear that Austin Rover had got the specification pretty well right – with a couple of exceptions – and that the Vitesse had found a ready market. Black was subsequently added to the range of colours available, but the Vitesse was never offered with all the paint options used on the rest of the SD1 range.

Production Changes to the Vitesse

Two features of the Vitesse did not meet universal customer approval. One was the large black side decals, which many customers found too garish, so from early 1983 it became possible to order the car without them. The other was that the car could be had only with a manual gearbox.

Demand for an automatic alternative took the marketing team at Austin Rover by surprise. In fact, one enquiry for an automatic Vitesse came from Frank Williams, head of the Williams Formula 1 racing organization. As Ian Elliott remembers:

> *We had connections with Williams F1 through the work that Patrick Head and his team did on the Metro 6R4 rally car, and ended up with a deal that put the 'Austin' and 'Rover' legends on each side of the F1 cars, in exchange for us providing Williams team with a small fleet of cars. (By megabuck F1 sponsorship standards, this was a very good deal for us!) Frank wanted a Vitesse, but also wanted an automatic. It wasn't, in the earlier stages, homologated with automatic transmission. The only way we could comply was to build a one-off and register it as a prototype!*

Frank Williams was certainly not alone in wanting such a car, though. Demand was persistent enough to persuade Austin Rover to get an automatic Vitesse homologated for production and to offer it as a no-cost option to the standard manual model from January 1984. No fewer than 363 cars were supplied in automatic form before the option was withdrawn a year later. What the exercise had made clear was that there was a demand for an SD1 with every available option – luxury as well as performance – and that the Vanden Plas EFi model introduced in May 1984 was more than capable of catering for this on its own. May 1984 also brought a minor change for the Vitesse, when burr walnut replaced the straight-grain walnut facia and door trim pieces. Clearly, customer demand for more luxury had not fallen on deaf ears.

The next production changes for the Vitesse came in October 1984 on the 1985-model cars. Again, there were just four paint options, now with Targa Red in place of the earlier Monza Red. Electric sunroof operation, formerly

On the later cars, like this 1984 model, burr walnut wood trim replaced the original straight-grain type.

an extra-cost option, now became standard. These later cars lost the large decals altogether, together with the rear wheel arch fairings, and instead took on Vanden Plas-style side bump rubbers. They also gained a new front spoiler, designed originally to improve the performance of the 'works' competition cars and now added to the showroom models for homologation reasons – the works cars were not allowed to run with an item that was so radically different from the standard production type, so the production type had to be altered to suit.

Ian Elliott remembers that the new spoiler was

> *a pure aerodynamic design by the in-house BL Motorsport aerodynamicist . . . [and it] was signed off for production even though it wouldn't pass the normal ramp clearance stipulations. It was needed for racing – at circuits like Brno, speeds reached around 180mph and the new spoiler reduced front-end lift by the weight of an engine!*

This new chin spoiler left no room for the fog lamps that had previously been standard, and so these were simply deleted from the specification.

The side graphics were not universally liked. It soon became possible to have them deleted, and by the time of the 1985 cars they were no longer standard. This car has the deeper front air dam introduced that year so that it could be homologated for racing.

The 1986 Model and Twin Plenum Vitesses

From October 1985, the Vitesse had its radio aerial embedded in the glass of its hatchback and so, like the other SD1s then in production, it was no longer fitted with a radio aerial for the 1986 model year. However, the major change for the 1986 Vitesse was a modified engine that was once again associated with racing homologation requirements. This engine has always been known as the Twin Plenum type, and an absence of documentation has prompted a great deal of inaccurate speculation about it.

The background to the story is that Austin Rover Motorsport wanted to get more power out of the Vitesse engines for racing in the 1986 season. Although the cars were being developed and run by TWR (see Chapter 9), the basic hardware, including engines, had to come from Austin Rover itself. So the Motorsport division worked with Lotus to develop a modified injection system that used not one but two throttle butterflies. Although these fed into a common plenum, and the system was properly known as a 'twin-throttle plenum' type, the inaccurate name of Twin Plenum became popular as a kind of shorthand for it.

The Group A racing regulations in force at the time required 5,000 production examples of a car to be made, and Rover probably made up the 5,000 that enabled the fuel-injected Vitesse to go racing from 1983 by adding together all the injected cars built for Australia (*see* Chapter 8) and North America (*see* Chapter 4) plus a small number of Vitesse models built in 1982. However, the twin-plenum system was a major modification that required additional homologation during 1985, and this required a further 10 per cent or 500 more cars to be built with it.

The evidence strongly suggests that Rover did achieve this figure – even though, in the mid-1980s, manufacturers' teams honoured the racing homologation rules in the breach as often as in the observance. In the absence of clear factory records or documentation, determined research by the Rover SD1 Club has uncovered much of the story. It is clear that the Twin Plenum cars were built in two batches and that all of them had right-hand drive. The Twin Plenum specification was standard for the UK and other right-hand-drive markets for 1986, although left-hand-drive markets continued to take Vitesse models with the standard single-throttle injection system.

The first batch of Twin Plenum cars was built between June and August 1985, with engines numbered between 30A-0003109 and 30A-0003239. The cars were built at Cowley and were then shipped by road – in transporter loads of five or six at a time – to the Lotus works at Hethel to have the twin-plenum systems fitted. Either 55 or 56 cars were so

Again produced for homologation reasons, this was the 'twin-plenum' engine available on the last Vitesse models. The different plenum casting with two inlets is the obvious recognition feature.

treated; the engine number sequence covers 131 cars, which makes clear that it included standard Vitesse engines as well. The second batch was built between November 1985 and July 1986, with engines numbered from approximately 30A-0003401 to 30A-0003897 (which was the last Vitesse engine of all). The cars in this much larger batch were assembled with twin-plenum injection systems on the lines at Cowley and did not go to Lotus at Hethel. Once again, there were some engines within this second number sequence (which totals 497) that had the standard injection system.

The twin-plenum racing engines used in the 1986 season (*see* Chapter 9) developed over 300bhp, and roadgoing versions of the engine were expected to make 220bhp. However, the special WL9 racing camshaft made the cars less tractable and, as racing regulations permitted modified camshafts, it was omitted from the production specification. Nevertheless, the roadgoing twin-plenum engines did have the stronger forged-steel rockers that were used on the racing engines, with the racing adjustment screw welded in place on them; again, homologation requirements were the reason.

There is still some speculation over the exact outputs of the engines in the roadgoing Twin Plenum cars. Rover made no claims about additional performance for them, and the truth seems to be that the benefits of the twin-plenum system were minimal without the special racing camshaft designed to go with them. None of that has prevented the cars from attracting a special status and generally higher prices than their standard counterparts – nor has it prevented enthusiastic owners from fitting twin-plenum systems to cars that did not originally have them.

Both standard and Twin Plenum Vitesse cars built from January 1986 had the same wing-mounted turn-indicator repeaters as other SD1s of the time. The very last SD1 built on the production lines in the UK was a Vitesse. Built in July and painted in Silver Leaf, it was road-registered as D537 PUK and was handed over to the collection at the Heritage Motor Centre in Gaydon.

Vitesse Specials

Although the Twin Plenum model quickly became the legend of the Vitesse range, it was certainly not the fastest of the road-going versions from Austin Rover. Special customers were able to order special cars, and towards the end of the Vitesse's production run a number of special cars were assembled with 3.9-litre engines built by Andy Rouse Engineering in Coventry. (Rouse won the 1984 British Touring Car Championship in a Vitesse and had established his own workshop, which continued to provide high-performance versions of the Rover V8.)

Some of these special cars went to VIPs, and among those was TV personality Noel Edmonds. Edmonds featured in Austin Rover advertising at the time and had an ARG 'fleet' as part of his deal. In addition, remembers Ian Elliott, one or two 3.9-litre cars 'appeared in the senior management car parks around ARG'.

It is worth noting that the 3.9-litre engine later developed for Range Rovers was not around at this stage. All V8 engine production and development, including that for Rover cars, was handled within Land Rover after 1982 and it was not until February 1987 that the first 3.9-litre blocks were ordered to build prototype engines.

The Vitesse and the Press

Although the Vitesse had been announced in autumn 1982 and some magazines had published initial impressions, the first full evaluations did not appear until early the following year.

The *Autocar* test was published on 12 February 1983. Although they felt it lacked the sophistication of some of its peers (Audi 200T, BMW 735i, Jaguar XJ6, Mercedes 380SE and Opel Monza S were considered), they 'ended up liking the car for almost this very reason. It has a distinctly 'animal' character all of its own.'

The magazine could not match the factory's claim of 0–60mph in 7.1sec and 135mph (217km/h) maximum, but did manage 7.6sec and 130mph (209km/h) – and achieved an overall figure of 21.8mpg (13ltr/100km), 'the best overall fuel consumption we have seen for an SD1 V8 on road test'. By way of compensation, 'the slightly disappointing maximum speed was balanced by the Vitesse's deliciously torquey mid-range 'go' and excellent flexibility'. When fully exploited, the car 'becomes eager and effortlessly swift, eating up the road ahead, to the accompaniment of a delightfully purposeful growl on wide open throttle'.

As with other SD1s the magazine had tested, 'wind noise intrusion is rather worse than average, particularly for this class of car', becoming 'the most obvious source of noise when travelling much above 80mph'. The low-profile tyres did roar on coarse surfaces and thumped over potholes. The

The Vitesse had grown out of the racing programme, and Craig Pusey's press-launch car is seen here in an appropriate setting.

spoilers seemed to make the car more stable in a straight line, but the revised suspension gave a disappointing ride while permitting very little cornering roll: 'Enthusiastic drivers are likely to relish the fairly stiffly sprung Rover's handling and acceleration response, if not some slightly agricultural aspects of its ride.'

The seats offered 'rather better sideways location' than in other SD1s, and *Autocar* found their two-tone grey cloth 'attractive'. Brakes performed very well, but the gearchange was 'disappointingly stiff and notchy', and both second and third gear whined. The clutch, too, was 'fairly heavy'.

What Car? in May 1983 pitted the Vitesse against two of its key rivals, the BMW 528i and the Saab 900 APC Turbo SE, both admittedly cheaper than the Rover. The BMW came out on top when individual scores were added up,

> *but for us the BMW is not the winner.... for sheer excitement there is nothing to touch the Vitesse. It is a thrilling high-speed racer, a magnificent long-distance mile-eater and a sensibly predictable handler. It has its faults – that steering wheel would be destined for the dustbin, for a start – but in the face of such fabulous flexibility and such spectacular performance no genuine enthusiast need look anywhere else.*

Motor Sport tried a Vitesse for its issue of August 1983, and joined the list of those who disliked the quartic steering wheel. They did like the car's flexibility in high gears, and achieved an overall average of 22.5mpg (12.6ltr/100km) for the test period which 'by any standards is extremely acceptable for a car with this sort of performance'. That performance put the car among the very fastest luxury saloons, 'but it has to be said that the big Rover V8 saloon, for all its on-paper excellence, has never managed to assume the quality cachet associated with its rivals'. It also looked too much like other, cheaper, Rovers, and

> *although some people will relish its rugged character, it is competing in a market sector where buyers expect just a little more style, refinement and general 'pizzazz' than the Rover Vitesse can really offer.*

Motor magazine ran a Vitesse as a long-term test car. The car they had was the red 1985 model that had been on the Austin Rover stand at the 1984 NEC Motor Show, now registered as B28 OAC. Reporting on 24,000 miles (38,500km) with it in the magazine's issue of 29 March 1986, Daniel Ward admitted that the standard quartic steering wheel had been replaced with a round one from a US-specification SD1.

The Rover had a bout of electrical problems early on and was generally far from trouble-free. Oil and coolant systems, and the power steering, all leaked; the engine was prone to pinking and would idle high after a motorway run. Lent to a second driver, the engine 'still sounded wonderful when revved hard, but the mid-range was flaccid to say the least'. Following variable service attention from two separate dealers, the Vitesse was returned to Austin Rover, and only then did it achieve the sort of acceleration expected, although a certain amount of lag on part throttle remained. There was also an unpleasant brake action, with a long travel followed by sharp braking.

Overall, though, Ward and his colleague John Simister loved the car. *Motor*'s conclusion read:

> *If you get a good Vitesse, you have not only a bargain but an excellent, fast car with an individual character few cars can match for the money. It's British and distinctive, and better for it. Get an unreliable example and you will doubtless wonder why a model which has not, after all, just arrived on the market has so many faults which should have been de-bugged. Find a good dealer and it is easier to keep faith with the Vitesse; the incapable could lead you to despair.*

THE VANDEN PLAS EFi

Austin Rover probably anticipated that there might be demand for a car that combined the performance of the Vitesse with the luxury equipment of the Vanden Plas models, and it seems that company chairman Harold Musgrove was driving around in such a car by the beginning of 1983. However, there was clearly some hesitation on the marketing side about whether this was what customers really wanted, and to some extent that explains why an automatic Vitesse was made available as an interim option in January 1984.

Nevertheless, the new top-model Rover arrived in May 1984, badged as a Vanden Plas EFi. Those letters stood for Electronic Fuel Injection, the lower-case 'i' probably being inspired by the success of the Volkswagen Golf GTi. The Vanden Plas EFi combined the 190bhp fuel-injected V8 of the Vitesse with the three-speed GM 180 automatic gearbox, and no manual alternative was available. The cross-spoke alloy wheels, low-profile tyres and four-piston front brakes with ventilated discs all came from the Vitesse, but the ride height remained standard. As for badges, the rear plinth proclaimed that the car was a Rover Vanden Plas EFi, and there was a small '3500' badge low down on each front wing.

The body and equipment were not quite to pure Vanden Plas specification. Where leather upholstery had been relegated to an extra-cost option on the 2600 and 3500 Vanden Plas models, it was standard on the Vanden Plas EFi. Box Velvet was the optional alternative. However, the new model was so fully equipped that the only other option available for it was air conditioning. Not surprisingly, its cost price was at the same elevated level as its specification, and it was always a low-volume variant built to special order.

Like other SD1 models, the Vanden Plas EFi cars built after October 1985 had no radio aerial but used the demister elements of the rear window as a 'diversity' aerial. However, none of them ever had the deeper front air dam introduced on the Vitesse for the 1986 model year, and of course none of them ever had either a rear spoiler or the twin-plenum version of the injected engine.

Production of the Vanden Plas EFi finished towards the end of 1985, and no further models appear to have been built in 1986. Nevertheless, some of the last cars did have the additional side turn signal repeaters introduced on other SD1s from January 1986. The last examples of just 1113 cars built in rather less than two years of production had reached their owners well in advance of the arrival of the Rover 825 Sterling model that replaced them from July that year.

The Vanden Plas EFi and the Press

Assessing a Vanden Plas EFi in its October 1984 issue, *What Car?* was rather disappointed:

Mix 3500 Vanden Plas with the injected engine and Vitesse wheels, make automatic transmission standard, and you have the 1984 Vanden Plas EFi. The car had neither side graphics nor rear spoiler and shared its wing-mounted '3500' badge with the carburettor models. The badge on the rear plinth was, of course, unique to the model.

PAINT AND TRIM OPTIONS – VITESSE AND VANDEN PLAS EFi

All paint and trim options for these two models are listed in the main paint and trim tables for 1982–1986, see Chapter 5.

Note that there were some special orders, particularly for the Vitesse. Some cars were supplied in white (a non-standard colour) for police use, and at least one Twin Plenum car was built with Diamond White paint for the top man at a Rover dealership.

> *The Vanden Plas EFi is not as happy a blend of qualities as we had hoped. And it is not such an appealing package as its five-speed Vitesse stablemate which costs only a few hundred pounds less. . . It is fast, of course . . . but it does not have the easy, relaxed and fabulously flexible feel of the manually geared Vitesse. . . . the fussy nature of the three-speed automatic fails to allow the engine to operate in its favourite speed range, slogging lazily but with tremendous torque and flexibility at very low revs.*

Motor nevertheless liked the car when it published a test on 15 December 1984. 'From the outside, the eight-year-old SD1 shape still looks modern – confirming that it was well ahead of its time when launched.' Though it was slower than a Vitesse,

> *once on the move, the lusty power spread of the big V8 shows and the acceleration times are comfortably better than anything else in this class. [Admittedly] it is not the last word in sophisticated engineering, and it is certainly flawed in a number of important areas. But it also has some very positive attributes. . . . Ultimately, it is still a prestige car with character – and one that offers more performance than anything at a cheaper level than the V12 Jaguar. As a value-for-money executive express, it will be a hard act for Austin Rover to follow.*

TECHNICAL SPECIFICATIONS – ROVER VITESSE AND VANDEN PLAS EFi

Engine
V8-cylinder petrol
3528cc (88.9 x 71.1mm)
Single overhead camshaft
Five-bearing crankshaft
Compression ratio 9.75:1
Lucas air flow meter fuel injection
190bhp at 5,280rpm
220lb ft at 4,000rpm
Power and torque figures for 1986-model twin-throttle plenum engine were never published, although they are unlikely to be very different from those for the standard engine.

Transmission
Five-speed manual gearbox standard on Vitesse but not available on Vanden Plas Efi
Ratios 3.32:1, 2.08:1, 1.39:1, 1.00:1, 0.79:1; reverse 3.43:1
Three-speed GM 180 automatic gearbox standard on Vanden Plas EFi and optional on Vitesse during 1984 only
Ratios 2.40:1, 1.48:1, 1.00:1; reverse 1.92:1

Axle ratio
3.08:1

Suspension, steering and brakes
Front suspension with MacPherson struts, lower links and anti-roll bar
Rear axle with torque tube, trailing arms, Watt's linkage, coil springs and self-energizing ride-levelling struts
Rack-and-pinion steering with power assistance as standard
Ventilated disc brakes at front with 10.15in diameter and four-piston calipers; drum brakes at rear with 9.0in diameter; vacuum servo assistance standard

Dimensions

Overall length	187in (4,750mm)
Overall width	70in (1,778mm)
Overall height	55in (1,397mm)
Wheelbase	110.8in (2,814mm)
Front track	59.3in (1506mm)
Rear track	59.3in (1506mm)

Wheels and tyres
15in five-bolt alloy wheels
205/60 VR 15 tyres (Pirelli P6 as optional extra on the Vitesse)

Kerb weight

3173 lb (1439kg)	Vitesse

CHAPTER SEVEN

THE SDI IN POLICE SERVICE

The Rover P6B 3500, which would be one of the cars replaced by the SDI, had been much liked by UK police forces as a motorway patrol car despite its relative lack of space for emergency equipment. So Rover planned early on to build a police-specification SDI in order to retain this valuable market. They were very successful, too: police SDIs remained a familiar sight on motorway patrol duties right through the production run of the car and into the later 1980s. However, not all forces found the SDI to their liking. Some probably had bad experiences with early cars that suffered from poor build quality, and these forces typically switched to the Ford Granada or Vauxhall Senator; some forces took examples of all three cars for in-service comparison.

By April 1976, work was under way at Rover on a police-specification interior. Although the police-specification cars would most naturally have V8 engines to deliver the necessary performance, this early work was done around a 'Low-Line' or 2300 instrument panel with its single large dial. A rev counter occupied this position, and there was no speedometer in the main instrument panel. Instead, there was a calibrated electronic speedometer in its own pod, mounted roughly on the centre line of the car where it could be seen by both driver and observer. Although the calibrated speedometer became part of the standard police specification, it is not clear whether the 'Low-Line' instrument panel was ever ordered.

A police demonstrator became available early on. Registered MOC 393P, it may have been built before the full specification had been developed. Build records show that the first proper 'police-specification' car was no. 8807, which was not built until December 1976 and would therefore have attracted an R-suffix registration.

Orders for the 3500 flowed in from police forces, and the 2600 also attracted many police customers when it was released in 1977. Although no full list of those forces that bought SDIs is available, the records of the Police Vehicle Enthusiasts' Club show that examples of the pre-facelift cars were delivered to the following eleven forces:

Avon & Somerset Constabulary
Central Scotland Police
Cheshire Police
Dumfries & Galloway Police
Hertfordshire Police

MOC 393P was given a generic police livery and became the first demonstrator.

The Kent Constabulary was one of the earliest users of the SD1. SKL 473R, pictured here by the force's own photographer, was one of a small batch with consecutive registration numbers.

An early SD1 with the Avon & Somerset Constabulary, apparently just about to undertake convoy escort duties. It comes from the Matt Holmes Collection, which now belongs to the Police Vehicle Enthusiasts' Club.

In a posed official photograph, Thames Valley's RWL 963X is a late pre-facelift car. Note the rather vulnerable mounting of the loudhailer, below the front bumper.

CYW 575V belonged to London's Metropolitan Police, who fitted Minilite wheels to provide extra ventilation for the brakes.

- Kent County Constabulary
- Lothian & Borders Police
- Metropolitan Police
- Thames Valley Police
- Warwickshire Police
- West Yorkshire Police

There were special police-specification manual gearboxes for both the 2600 and the 3500, and these were fitted to the majority of cars. However, some automatic 2600s were also supplied, and these had another special-specification gearbox. To improve the stopping ability of the police models, an uprated braking system was developed and was in production by about 1980. This employed four-piston front brakes (made by AP) in place of the standard two-piston type.

UK police interest remained high after the facelifted cars became available in 1982. Both 3500 and 2600 models were popular, and a small number of forces also took on examples

This Thames Valley motorway car is visually typical of the facelifted models in police service.

The same car, pictured from the rear, shows its 3500SE badges. Note the lack of brightwork on the bumpers.

of the Vitesse. The known users of 'facelift' models, again based on the records of the Police Vehicle Enthusiasts' Club, were the following thirteen forces:

Avon & Somerset Constabulary
Central Scotland Police
Dumfries & Galloway Police
Fife Constabulary
Grampian Police
Kent County Constabulary
Lancashire Constabulary
Metropolitan Police
South Wales Police
Sussex Police
Thames Valley Police
West Midlands Police
West Yorkshire Police

Note that the standard police specification for these cars dispensed with bright trim for the bumpers. C356 YST, one of the Grampian cars, was a Vitesse that was supposedly specially uprated by BL Motorsport so that the police could catch speeding drivers on a particular section of motorway. It was based at Stonehaven.

Some late 2300 and 2600 Vanden Plas models that had not found buyers were resprayed white and were sold to police forces in or around November 1987 (see Chapter 5).

This was how many people remember the SDI police cars. This is a Thames Valley example, waiting for a call on a special raised area alongside the M4 motorway.

This was clearly a specially posed photograph, as Lancashire's D347 SHG is facing the wrong way for rapid pursuit on the motorway!

This less commonly seen view shows the inside of a Thames Valley car. Note the calibrated speedometer and police radio mounted in front of the instrument panel.

B413 LYJ was an exception among police SD1s. Not only was this Sussex car a Vitesse model, but it also retained the bright bumper trims of the standard cars. The force had more than one car with this specification.

At least two Scottish police forces used these ventilated aftermarket wheels, presumably to improve brake cooling. This car belonged to the Lothian & Borders Police; the other known user was the Fife Constabulary.

CHAPTER EIGHT

THE SDI OVERSEAS

The SDI build records show that the first cars for overseas markets were built in December 1976, although there had been cars with left-hand-drive built from very early in production in order to provide test samples. The earliest export cars were built for France, Holland, Belgium and Switzerland (the Swiss being allocated a relatively large number by comparison with other export markets), and cars for Austria followed after Christmas 1976. In January 1977, cars for Eire (with right-hand drive) and West Germany began to come off the lines as well. Despite high hopes, sales in Europe would nevertheless prove disappointing, and figures quoted by Chris Cowin (in his book *Export Drive*) show that only 30,000 SDIs were sold in Europe between 1977 and 1981. Not surprisingly, the arrival of the diesel-engined 2400SD Turbo improved the position, boosting sales in France, Italy and Holland.

Most SDIs for sale outside the UK were assembled at Solihull, but there were also two overseas assembly operations. These were in New Zealand and South Africa, and each one produced cars that had interesting differences from those built at Solihull. In addition, the SDI was built in India for a time by the Standard Motor Company, using tooling exported from the UK and a number of locally sourced components.

The notes which follow do not claim to be comprehensive, and in some cases are based on incomplete records, but they are intended to give an idea of the SDI's record outside the UK.

Australia

The SDI (all V8-engined models) was sold in Australia between August 1978 and early 1987. Few cars were sold before the start of the 1979 calendar year. These first Australian SDIs had a 'detoxed' engine to meet Australian emissions regulations. The V8 had an 8.13:1 compression ratio

Early Australian SDIs were visually identical to those in the UK market. This is the cover of a March 1980 sales brochure, showing a 1980 model with the intake slot for the factory-supplied air-conditioning system.

The 1981 models became known in Australia as 'Series 1½' cars. Just visible above the V8 badge on the wing of this one is the small 'Fuel Injection' badge.

This 3500SE was photographed in March 1981 at the Melbourne Motor Show on the Jaguar Rover Australia stand. Alongside the SD1 are Land Rovers and Range Rovers also sold by that company.

and an air-injection pump that was driven by an auxiliary belt, an exhaust gas recirculation valve, and an evaporative emissions-control system with a charcoal canister that prevented petrol vapour from the carburettor float chambers and the fuel tank from escaping into the atmosphere. The engines had twin Zenith-Stromberg 175CD-SET carburettors, giving maximum power of 136bhp. These carburettors had automatic chokes, some four years before the Solex automatic choke was fitted to V8 engines for the UK market.

All the early Australian SD1s had automatic gearboxes, alloy wheels with 195/70 HR 14 tyres and electric windows. They also had an oil pressure gauge that was marked in bars rather than in pounds per square inch. Many, quite probably all, were fitted by Leyland Australia with an Alpinair air-conditioning system. The controls and air ducts for this were mounted on a raised panel in the centre of the facia; additional ducting caused the removal of the glovebox light on the passenger's side. Leyland Australia also added side intrusion bars into the doors to meet local regulations, and split the brake warning light into separate handbrake and fluid level warning lights. Most of the 1979-model SD1s sold in Australia had an AWA Clarion stereo radio-cassette player.

A small number of five-speed cars were imported from late 1979 to stimulate customer interest. These were essentially 1980 models like those for other markets, with the revised rear, front wing and bonnet badges, and the 1980-pattern front panel air intake slot. They were mechanically similar to the 1979-model Australian cars, with the 136bhp carburettor engine, but they now had the factory-fitted SU-Butec air-conditioning system that had become available in mid-1979.

The revised 1981-season SD1s did not reach Australia until mid-1981, and these are generally now known as the 'Series 1½' cars although they were not sold under that name. They carried 3500SE badges but now came with the fuel-injected engine developed for North America that developed 142bhp. 'Fuel Injection' badges were added to the front wings just above the standard V8 badges. The automatic gearbox was still standard, although ten cars were imported with five-speed gearboxes. These had the lower 3.45:1 final drive from the 2600 models in order to improve acceleration. The factory-installed SU-Butec air-conditioning system was standard, and the in-car entertainment (ICE) system was a Pioneer KE 1000 stereo radio cassette player with four speakers.

An unknown quantity of the 'Series 1½' cars seem to have been painted in the colours that would be introduced for the facelifted cars in February 1982. One known example was a late-1981 build finished in Opaline Green with VIN SAR-RRFWV3BA-191793.

This late 1982 'Series 1½' model was painted in Opaline Green, one of the colours associated with the facelifted 'Series 2' cars. Neither the dark tinted glass nor the side bump-strip were standard features.

This was the special wing badge used on the 'Series 1½' cars.

Before the facelifted SD1s were introduced, Leyland Australia undertook a major re-evaluation exercise of the car, focusing particularly on the quality of materials used for the interior. One result of this was that some items of trim on the facelifted cars had a specifically Australian configuration, probably mainly to improve their resistance to the hot Australian climate. Wood trim was one item that was specific to the Australian cars, and the version thus fitted was identified on the back with a kangaroo stamp.

The facelifted second-series 3500SE appeared in 1982 at about the same time as its home-market counterpart, and was supplemented by the Vanden Plas model in 1983. Both cars had fuel-injected engines, which enthusiasts describe as more powerful and smoother than the earlier types – although Leyland Australia did not admit to any differences, the low compression ratio of 8.13:1 was unchanged, and the injection system was visually the same as on the earlier cars. The majority had automatic gearboxes, although once again a small number of five-speed cars were imported between 1982 and 1984, again with the 3.45:1 axle ratio to improve acceleration. Cruise control was standard on the Vanden Plas and was also fitted to some 3500SE models. Both models had electrically adjustable door mirrors as standard, and the standard ICE head unit was a digital AWA Clarion stereo radio cassette player.

All the Australian injected cars had a version of the injection system developed for the USA. It is seen here on a 1984 Vanden Plas model.

The later cars were marketed as Series 2 types in Australia, as this March 1983 sales brochure confirms.

Although the SE specification was discontinued for 1985 in the UK, it remained available in Australia. Some of the last 3500SE models came with the wood trim on the facia that was otherwise associated only with the Vanden Plas models, and most 1985 cars seem to have had the headlamp washers that had earlier been an option on the 3500SE.

The last cars exported to Australia were 1985-built models, which exempted them from the tighter emissions-control requirement introduced in January 1986. Nevertheless, the final examples appear not to have been sold until early 1987. The SDI was replaced in Australia by the Rover 825i and Rover Sterling saloons during 1987.

All Australian-market cars carried an Australian compliance plate, which was riveted to the scuttle panel close to the stamped VIN. These plates were normally attached to the cars by Leyland Australia or, later, JRA Limited (Jaguar Rover Australia) when they were sent to the dealers. The compliance plates stated that 'This car was manufactured by Leyland Motor Corporation of Australia Ltd' or 'This car was manufactured by JRA Limited', even though all Australian market SDIs were imported in fully built form from the UK.

There were three types of plate:

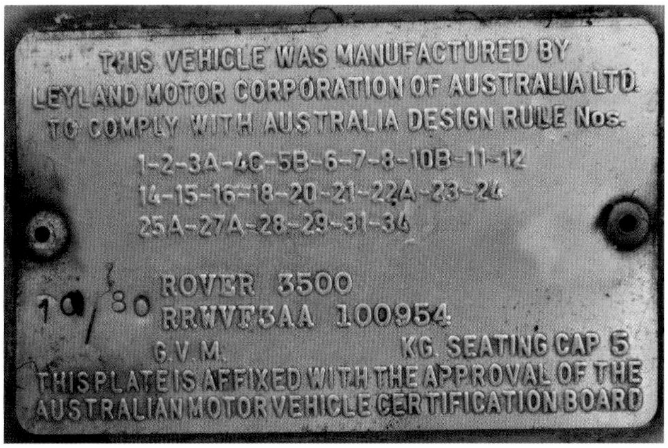

The compliance plates read as if the cars had been built in Australia, but they were all exported in fully built condition from the UK. Note the manufacturing date (10/80) on this one.

- Series I cars (1979–80 model years) had a single compliance plate with a hand-stamped month and year date that represented the date when the car was sent to a dealer.
- 'Series 1½' Fuel Injection cars (1981 model year) also had one compliance plate with the month and year in the same machine-stamped font as the rest of the plate.
- Series 2 cars (1982 onwards) had two plates, one being the Australian compliance plate, the second showing the actual Solihull or Cowley manufacturing date. These

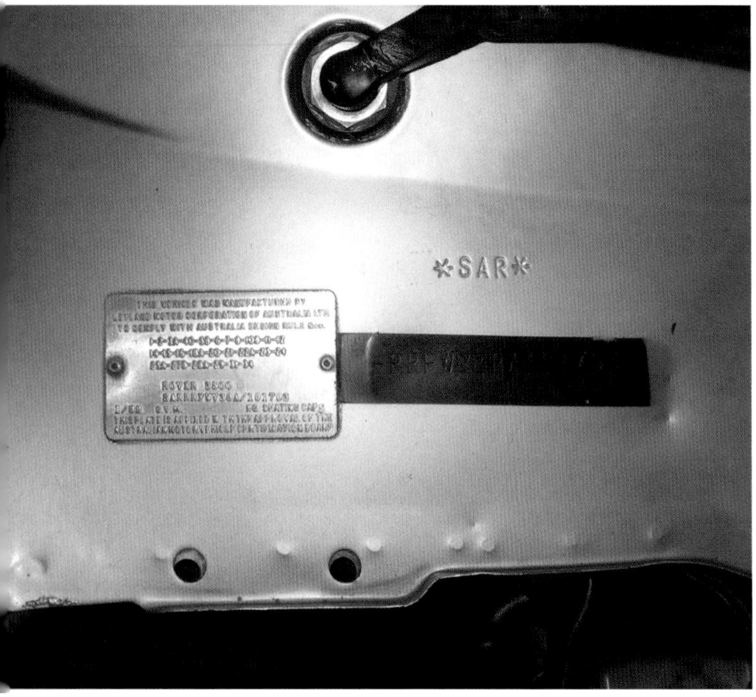

On the 'Series 1½' cars, the compliance plate was mounted alongside a black strip that contained the VIN. This one dates from January 1982.

This was the arrangement on the late models. Note that although the compliance plate gives a date of 7/84, which would have been the date of certification, an additional plate alongside gives the date of build as May 1984.

two plates were mounted side-by-side, and there was no apparent consistency to the order of the two plates.

(The above notes are based on work done by Rob Turner and others for the website https://roversd1australia.wordpress.com which is a valuable resource for those with an interest in the Australian models.)

Canada

The original plan was to introduce the SD1 in Canada before it reached the USA, and the build ledgers show that the earliest cars were in fact destined for Canada. In the event, however, the cars were introduced in both countries at the same time. The Canadian cars had the same specification as those for the USA, with the addition of daytime running lights and the option of a cylinder block heater. There was also a special sales brochure for the Canadian market. No sales figures are available for Canada, but the totals were included in those for the US-specification cars.

The Canadian market had its own sales brochure for the North American specification SD1.

Denmark

The SD1 reached Denmark as a 1979 model in approximately July 1978, when the first road test reports appeared. In the beginning, only the 3500 model was available, but this was joined by the 2600 in March 1979. Both models could be had with a choice of manual or automatic gearboxes. The national importer for British Leyland was DOMI A/S of Glostrup.

Sales of all British Leyland cars were dropping alarmingly in Denmark in this period, and DOMI was forced to take on new franchises to maintain its business. During 1979, for example, it took on the Renault franchise for Denmark. Despite slow sales, the company nevertheless persevered with the SD1, which remained available as a 2600S and 3500 Vanden Plas into the post-1982 facelift era, again with a choice of manual or automatic gearbox on each model.

In Denmark, sales of cars from Austin Rover had dropped alarmingly by the early 1980s. Long-standing importer DOMI A/S was clearly unwilling to spend very much on the sales brochure for the 1983 SD1s, even using black-and-white photographs showing UK-market cars.

France

The 2600 was launched in France in late 1978 and, according to the December 1978/January 1979 issue of *Specialist Car* magazine, a Jaguar Rover Triumph internal publication, attracted 400 orders within two weeks. As the French taxation system penalized petrol engines larger than 2.8 litres, the 3500 was always going to be a slower seller, but it had become available by February 1979. Both cars were available with a choice of manual or automatic gearboxes.

France had a quite comprehensive range of SD1s by the end of production, although most sales probably went to the 2000S and the two variants of the diesel model. This was the sales brochure for the 1985 season, which shared its design with those for other European markets and was actually printed in Britain.

The facelifted cars were also sold in France, and the 1983 range consisted of no fewer than seven models. These were the 2000, 2300S and 2400SD Turbo, all with manual gearboxes, and the 2600S and 3500 Vanden Plas, each with a choice of manual or automatic gearboxes. The introduction of the diesel-engined 2400SD Turbo provided the expected improvement in sales, although the cars were never very common in France.

There was a slightly modified line-up for the 1985 model year. The SD1s available were the 2000S (with alloy wheels now standard), 2400SD Turbo, 2400SDL Turbo, 2600S, 2600 Vanden Plas, 3500 Vanden Plas and 3500 Vitesse. The precise specification of the 2400SDL model is not clear, but it appears to have included items that were not part of the basic 2400SD specification.

Germany

At this stage, Germany was still divided and the SD1 was sold only in West Germany. Only 2.6-litre 6-cylinder and 3.5-litre V8 models were available, beginning in 1978, and it appears that around 2,000 cars were sold during 1979. Both models were available with a choice of manual or automatic gearbox.

Germany continued to take the cars in facelifted form from 1982. Once again, there were 2.6-litre and 3.5-litre models with a choice of manual or automatic gearbox in each case. However, Germany took the best-equipped versions, and the model range consisted of 2600S and 3500 Vanden Plas, which were joined later by the Vitesse.

India

The SD1 was never sold in India as a Rover, but the design and tooling were sold to Standard Motor Products of Madras in the mid-1980s and a locally made version of the car called the Standard 2000 was available between April 1985 and 1988. This was sold only on the Indian market but was not a great success because of its high purchase price.

Rover's German importers issued a series of sales brochures with shaped cutaway tops, like this one for the 2600 models in June 1979. The slogan translates as 'Superior technology from a proven manufacturer'.

Although the Madras factory had a theoretical capacity of around 4,000 cars a year, production of the Standard 2000 never attained this level – an educated guess is that no more than 8,000 or so were built in the three years of production.

For many years, Indian government policy was to support local assembly of cars designed overseas, with gradually increasing levels of local content. The various companies involved were made responsible for different market sectors and vehicle sizes, with the result that there was no competition and therefore no real spur to improve the products. High taxes on imported cars also ensured that most Indians who could afford a car at all bought Indian-built models. Then a relaxation of government policy in the early 1980s saw Japanese makers moving into the Indian market with small and medium-sized cars, leaving a gap for a larger and more expensive car at the top end of the market.

Standard Motors determined to fill that gap. In 1983 they opened discussions with a number of companies about building an existing design in India. One of those companies was Austin Rover, and by March 1984 managing director C V Karthik Narayanan had concluded a deal. This called for Austin Rover to supply 12,000 sets of SD1 body panels to Standard, who would assemble them into complete cars that would be powered by Indian-built engines. There would also be some minor engineering and

The Indian-built Standard 2000 looked much like a UK-built Rover 2000 from the outside, although powertrain and interior were very different.

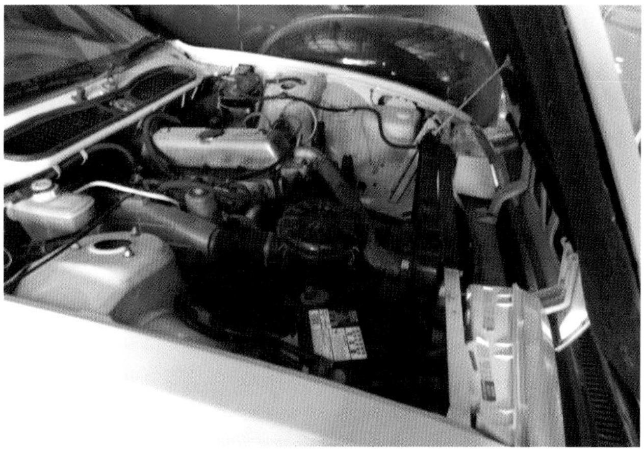

The elderly 4-cylinder engine in the Standard 2000 put out just 83bhp.

This was a sales brochure for the Standard 2000. Note that the logo here carries the name 'Stampro'.

equipment changes to make the car more suitable for Indian conditions.

The original plan was to use Standard's 2-litre petrol and 2.5-litre diesel engines, although the diesel model never materialized. The 1991cc (83mm bore x 92mm stroke) petrol engine was a direct descendant of the Standard-Triumph 4-cylinder engine of the same capacity that had been introduced for the Vanguard saloon in 1948 and had subsequently powered Triumph sports cars up to and including the TR4. A special new version was created for the Standard 2000, with twin carburettors and redesigned combustion chambers that used a Heron-head design. With an 8.0:1 compression ratio, it produced 83bhp at 4,250rpm – considerably less than any engine used in Rover versions of the car.

Unsurprisingly, performance was poor, with a top speed of around 91mph (146km/h) thanks to low gearing of 14mph (23km/h) per 1,000rpm in the top ratio of the locally designed four-speed gearbox. Skinny 175 SR 14 tyres on 5J steel wheels and a ride height raised by an inch (achieved by inserting alloy blocks between the springs and the body mounts) in deference to India's poorly made roads can have done little to help the handling.

Nevertheless, when motoring writer Graham Robson sampled a Standard 2000 for *Autocar* magazine of 18 February 1987, he was favourably impressed:

> *The car I drove in India was not only being used as VIP-transport for FISA officials on the Himalayan Rally, which gave it a very hard life over a ten-day period, but it was the very first Standard 2000 ever built in India. After two years, not only as a demonstrator, but as an engineering development car, it was still impressively free of rattles, and completely dust-proof. . . . at the speeds possible around New Delhi, the ride and handling feel the same as those of the European versions.*

The Standard 2000 was priced at 212,000 rupees (about £12,000), which restricted sales to wealthy businessmen, but it appears that many were also bought by government bodies and large businesses. The car came as standard with luxury features such as electric windows and air conditioning, but it did not show up well against the imported luxury cars available on the black market in India. Nevertheless, there were hopes of export sales as well, and two cars were exported to Australia for evaluation, although nothing came of this venture.

In its first two years, more than 2,500 examples of the Standard 2000 were delivered, and by early 1987 production had reached twelve cars a day, or a theoretical 3,000 a year. Some sources claim that the Madras plant was making its own panels by that stage, using tooling that had been shipped out to India from the UK after SDI production had ended in summer 1986. However, other sources claim that the tooling never reached India, but was on the dockside in the UK awaiting shipment when Standard Motors stopped production in 1988.

The end came for the Standard 2000 when its manufacturers were accused of falsifying fuel consumption claims for the car. (The official figures appear to have been 22–35.7mpg (8–13ltr/100km)). A long legal enquiry resulted, and eventually the factory was simply closed down. After production ended in Madras, most of the remaining UK-made SDI parts that had been shipped to India were purchased by British classic car parts specialists Rimmer Brothers and were shipped to Britain.

Italy

The SDI became available in Italy in October 1977, initially in 3500 form although the 2300 and 2600 were added to the range later in the 1978 model year. The V8-S was made available during the 1980 model year – those for the Italian market had a wing-mounted repeater lamp (as required by local traffic regulations) but appear not to have had the gold-coloured alloy wheels.

The facelifted SDIs became available in Italy during 1982. Marketed as 'Serie 82' models, the range initially appears to have consisted of the 2000, 2600S and 3500 Vanden Plas. The arrival of the 2400SD Turbo boosted sales as Italy was already a strong market for diesel passenger cars. It became the best-selling model. The four-model range of 2000, 2400SD Turbo, 2600S and 3500 Vanden Plas continued into 1984 and possibly beyond.

Japan

The SDI was introduced to Japan in left-hand-drive 3500 form in autumn 1979. Although Japan is a right-hand-drive country, left-hand-drive models have a certain cachet and it seems likely that the plan was to give the SDI an aura

Italy took V8-S models for the 1980 model year. The front wing on this one has the small round repeater indicator required by Italian regulations.

Tax on cars with petrol engines larger than 2 litres was heavy in Italy, so the Rover 2000 was expected to do well. It came with alloy wheels as standard by the time of this May 1983 sales brochure.

Powered by an Italian-made diesel engine, the 2400SD Turbo quickly became the best-selling SDI in Italy.

of exclusivity by offering only left-hand-drive models in the beginning. The cars had carburettor engines with an 8.13:1 compression, Stromberg carburettors, an air pump and an EGR valve, and a non-return catalytic converter. All of them had automatic gearboxes and came with Alpinair air conditioning as standard.

Right-hand-drive 3500 models for Japan were due to follow in spring 1980, but it is not clear whether they ever did so. These cars were planned to have SU-Butec air conditioning, injected engines with an 8.13:1 compression ratio, and air conditioning and automatic transmission as standard. If the cars ever were sent to Japan, they were not available after mid-1981.

Netherlands

The Dutch market proved to be a strong one for the SD1, as it had been for earlier Rovers. The 3500 became available early in 1977 and the 2300 and 2600 followed as soon as they were available. The post-1982 facelifted models came as a 2000, a 2300S or a 2400SD Turbo, all with manual transmission; the 2600S was available with either manual or automatic gearboxes, as was the 3500 Vanden Plas. The diesel-engined 2400SD Turbo gave a welcome boost to sales, and some examples of the Vitesse were also imported.

This early 3500 was photographed in a Dutch setting for the European launch that was scheduled for early spring 1977. Unfortunately, the specification was subsequently changed and the coachlines were deleted, no doubt to save costs. As a result, all the carefully taken photographs had to be scrapped. Note the Dutch-pattern '19-BL-76' number plate.

'Pure class in duplicate' reads the strapline on this Dutch sales brochure for the early models. The two models available were the 3500 and 2600.

For the facelift models, BL Nederland clearly thought that a picture of the new front end allied to a statement of the price range was enough for the cover of the sales brochure. Those prices were shown in Dutch florins.

By way of proof that the Vitesse was sold in left-hand-drive form, this is a Dutch-registered example.

New Zealand

Assembly of British Leyland models in New Zealand during the 1970s was carried out by the New Zealand Motor Corporation (NZMC), which had been formed in 1971 by combining all the former BMC and British Leyland operations in New Zealand. So the initial study into the feasibility of building SD1 in New Zealand was carried out during 1977 by NZMC's Plant Operations Divisional Office (PODO) in Petone, Wellington.

It became clear that the wheel trims could not be manufactured locally, and that the huge front and rear screens were also beyond the capabilities of the local Pilkingtons branch. This later led to an unusual and unexplained delivery situation, where the rear window would reach New Zealand from Solihull in the CKD packs, while the windscreen was supplied by Pilkington in the UK to their New Zealand branch, who in turn supplied it to the NZMC assembly plant.

Many other items were either beyond local manufacturing capabilities or would be uneconomic to manufacture in New Zealand. So the SD1 would have a lower than usual local content. All this was taken into consideration in a provisional costing study based on assembly of 500 vehicles a year at the Petone plant. A memo dated 15 February 1978 from the Divisional Engineering Office (which had succeeded PODO) then confirmed that the SD1 would be built in New Zealand, but at the Nelson plant rather than in Petone.

At that stage, the Nelson plant was assembling Land Rovers, the BL Princess 1800, the Triumph 2000 and 2500, and the Jaguar XJ6. Up to October 1976, it had also assembled Rover 3500 (P6B) models for the Australian market. Jaguar assembly would end in December 1978, and the car would not be directly replaced; Triumph assembly would end in March 1979; and the new 2000 version of the Princess would

The New Zealand-assembled Rovers had their own paint colours. This is Astral Blue metallic, and the car is the fourth one to leave the Nelson assembly line in 1979. It is parked next to one of its ancestors – a Rover P4 110 dating from 1964.

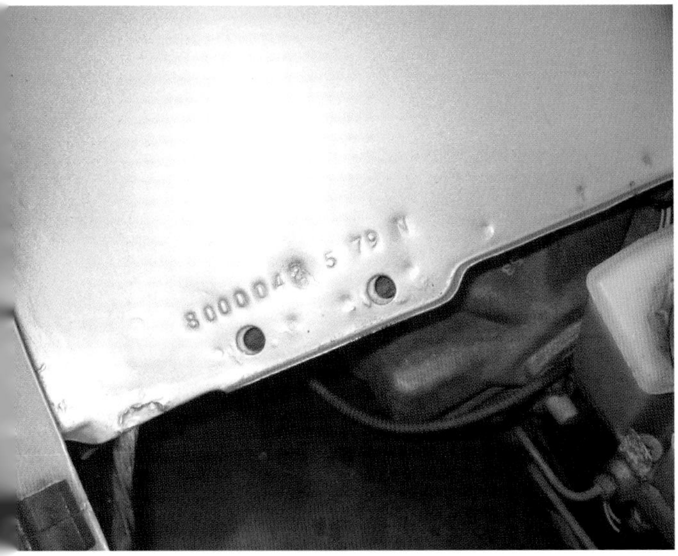

The New Zealand cars had their own identification numbers, as well as a date of build stamp – which in this case is showing May 1979.

This number stencilled on the front suspension turret may have been some kind of body number; nobody is quite sure now.

replace the 1800 version from August 1979. NZMC seem to have hoped that the Rover SDI would replace the Triumph 2500 and, to a degree, the Jaguar, while the Triumph 2000 would be replaced by the bigger-engined version of the Princess. The Rover's direct competitors on price were large Australian Fords, Holdens and some imported makes.

Surviving documents show that NZMC anticipated annual SDI build figures of between 600 and 1,000 cars. Meeting minutes from the SDI launch planning group dated 19 September 1978 break this down into 400 of the 3500 automatic, 300 of the 2600 manual and 300 of the 2600 automatic. In practice, build volumes only just attained the lower end of NZMC's expectations. In the twenty-one months from April 1979 to December 1981, fewer than 1,100 SDIs were actually built, the monthly average working out at just over 50 and the annual average at just over 600.

The preparations for local assembly began during 1978, and John Miller (in *From Cotton to Cars*) recalls that one Richelieu Red 'pilot' car was repeatedly assembled, dismantled and reassembled between late 1978 and approximately March 1979 in order to prove the fit and function of components, jigs and fixtures, and to test assembly methods. NZMC also had a Caribbean Blue pilot car, an automatic like the other one, and on brief loan there was also a Brazilia car with manual gearbox that had been privately imported from the UK. It was also during 1978 that NZMC examined the South African CKD specification, taking particular interest in the different seat construction used in that country. In the end, the decision was taken to go with the UK version, using the new specification introduced at the same time as New Zealand assembly began.

Assembly actually began in April 1979 with 3500 automatic models, which replaced the Triumph 2000 and 2500 models on the lines at Nelson. Assembly of 2600 models in both manual and automatic form followed from August 1979. The SDIs were assembled on the same line as Austin Princess models with the 2-litre O-series engine.

The SDI was announced in New Zealand in June 1979 but, like the contemporary Princess assembled at Nelson, it proved a slow seller. Many examples of both cars were stockpiled in fields around the assembly plant on completion and, despite special precautions to protect the interiors from sun damage, this probably did nothing for the eventual longevity of the cars. When assembly of the 'Series 1' cars ended in December 1981, there was a pause in assembly until the facelifted 'Series 2' models entered production in August 1983.

Series 2 assembly was very limited, and this time only two derivatives were built rather than three. These were 2600S models with a manual gearbox and 3500SE models in automatic form. New Zealand assembly of SDIs ceased in May 1984 after just 312 cars had been built in nine months, the

The apparent informality of the New Zealand production line was quite different from the way things were at Solihull. This photograph was taken in 1979 when Spen King, on the right of the picture, visited the newly opened assembly operation. To his right, standing against the car, is Roger Harding, manager of the Nelson assembly plant and a long-standing Rover stalwart.

Final set-up checks at the end of the Nelson line. The car is in Amarillo paint, subtly different from the Turmeric Yellow used in the UK.

Sales of the SD1 were slower than anticipated, and unsold cars were stored in the open around the assembly plant at Nelson. This picture was taken in June 1980; also visible are the Austin Princess and Land Rover models assembled at Nelson.

monthly average being even lower than before at just under 35 cars. Subsequent cars for New Zealand were shipped in fully built form from the UK.

The cars assembled in New Zealand had their own identification numbering system, and used some paint colours not found on UK-built cars. As in the UK, a left-hand door mirror was always an extra-cost option, although it became a standard fitting with the Series 2 models from August 1983. In theory, the first 312 examples of the 3500 had steel wheels, while later examples all came with alloy wheels to distinguish them from the 2600, which was introduced in August 1979; however, some early cars exist with alloys, which may have been fitted retrospectively. It may be that the 2600 models had steel trims rather than the polycarbonate type used on UK-built cars. Most of the 1980-model 3500 cars with alloy wheels also had a visual specification similar to the V8-S, with body side mouldings, V8 badges on the front wings, the coloured Rover bonnet badge and a left-hand door mirror.

Paint colours were mostly similar to those used on UK-built cars, but had their own names. The SD1 was the first car from the Nelson plant to have metallic paint options, and the main trim colour for Series 1 cars was Nutmeg for the hard trim with Coriander (coded ACH) for the seat facings. These were made of a cropped polyester fabric in New Zealand by NZ Fabrics and had a Scotchguard coating, and the SD1 application was the first use of a new product that had fortuitously been developed just in time for the beginning of the car's assembly at Nelson. The nine known Series 1 paint options were:

- Amarillo (bright yellow)
- Arctic (or Crystal) White
- Astral Blue metallic
- Gilt metallic (i.e. gold)
- Nordic Bronze (brown metallic)
- Paprika metallic
- Sandglow (this colour was a little richer than its UK equivalent)
- Spanish Olive
- Signal Red

All the Series 2 cars had blue upholstery, and there were more metallic paints among the options. These included Quartz Blue and Silver, and there was also a gunmetal-style grey whose name is not known.

The official figures for New Zealand SD1 assembly were in some ways a 'best guess' effort created by staff in 1998 before the plant closed. They are reproduced below. John Miller points out that as the CKD packs always consisted of 24 cars each, some of these figures are hard to believe. He thinks it is more likely that the Series 1 2600 figures were actually 288 for the automatic models (12 packs of 24) and 264 for the manual models (11 packs of 24). However, there is no reason to doubt the overall totals.

3500 automatic	April 1979 to December 1981	504
2600 automatic	August 1979 to December 1981	280
2600 manual	August 1979 to June 1981	272
Series 1 total		**1,056**
2600 manual	August 1983 to April 1984	120
3500 automatic	September 1983 to May 1984	192
Series 2 total		**312**
Overall total		**1,368**

Portugal

SD1 exports to Portugal appear to have begun with the facelifted models in 1982 or 1983. Four different left-hand-drive models were available, and probably around 200 cars were sold in all – a substantial quantity for a country like Portugal at the time. The models available were the 2000 and 2400SD Turbo with manual gearboxes, and the 2600 and 3500 with automatic gearboxes.

(Special thanks to João Peres and José Almeida for researching the Portuguese SD1 story.)

South Africa

In British Leyland's South African line-up, the SD1 replaced the Triumph Chicane, a locally built version of the 2.5-litre 'Innsbruck' saloon. Leykor, the South African Leyland operation, invested about £10 million to permit local manufacture of the Rover at the Blackheath plant in Elsies River, a suburb of Cape Town where there had been car assembly plants since the 1920s. A high degree of local content (around 60 per cent) was achieved, and about 14,400 cars are thought to have been assembled between 1978 and 1983, when car manufacture at the Blackheath plant ended altogether.

There was a brief pause in production during 1979; a plan to move SD1 assembly to Silverton in Pretoria was abandoned at the last minute when an amalgamation of British Leyland's assembly operations with those of the Sigma Motor Corporation fell through. Sigma was an assembler of cars for the French (Citroën and Peugeot) and the Japanese (Mazda and Mitsubishi).

According to the Jaguar Rover Triumph in-house magazine *Specialist Car*, South African assembly of SD1s began in March 1978. However, the car did not become available through showrooms until October 1978, when the first road tests appeared. South Africans were eventually offered six different models of SD1. The base model was called a Rover SD 2600, and came with five-speed manual or three-speed automatic gearboxes; next up came the Rover SDX 2600, again with five-speed or automatic gearboxes; above that were models with the 3.5-litre V8 engine, known as the SDE 3500 when fitted with automatic transmission and the SDS 3500 when fitted with the five-speed manual. The 'E' was probably intended to stand for 'Executive', and the 'S' for 'Sport'.

The early South African cars all had black tail badges. The left-hand badge showed the trim level . . .

. . . while the right-hand badge revealed what type of engine and gearbox were fitted.

This slightly later car had the black bumpers associated with the 1981 models.

Although the V8 engines were shipped out from the UK, that 60 per cent local content was achieved partly by local assembly of the bodyshell, partly by local manufacture of the 6-cylinder engine in the 2600 models. This was not the Triumph PE166 engine used in UK-built cars but a totally different engine of similar capacity whose design had originated in Australia. There, it had been developed as a 2.2-litre 6-cylinder version of the E-series 4-cylinder (used in the Austin Maxi and Morris Marina) to power models such as the Australian-built Austin Tasman and Kimberley, and then as a 2.6-litre for the Leyland P76 saloons. The South Africans knew the engine as the R6, and also used it in a locally assembled version of the Land Rover known as the Series IIIS type. Though slightly less powerful than the Triumph engine used in UK-built 2600 models, this twin-carburettor engine earned a good reputation for smoothness and longevity.

All these South African-built cars came with a number of unique features. All had forward-facing reflector discs bolted below the front bumper ends to meet South African traffic regulations, and the bumpers themselves were chromed steel rather than the stainless steel used on UK-built cars. The front seats were similar to UK production items but the rear seats incorporated extensions intended to act as head restraints. Upholstery on top models was in hard-wearing velour cloth and, on the SDX models at least, could have a special striped cloth finish that contrasted with vinyl-covered bolsters and armrests. Air conditioning seems to have been standard, and there was a raised panel for the air outlets on the dashboard. The cars had special rear badges in silver on black, and manual examples were labelled '5-spd' on the right-hand badge with the engine size.

Assembly of the early models continued into 1983, but only some of the 1981 changes made their way to South Africa, such as black bumpers. From later in 1983, the facelifted models then became available. Once again assembled in Cape Town, these cars were distinguished by chromed steel bumpers and the absence of the front apron spoiler from all models. There were again six different models, the line-up consisting of SD 2600 manual, SDX 2600 automatic, SDS 3500 manual, SDE 3500 automatic and Vanden Plas models in both manual and automatic forms.

THE SOUTH AFRICAN R6 ENGINE

The R6 engine used in South African-built 2600 models of the SD1 could trace its origins to the 4-cylinder E-series overhead-camshaft engine designed in the UK as a replacement for the transverse BMC A-series and B-series engines. That engine first appeared in the Austin Maxi for 1969.

From the beginning, the E-series was drawn up so that both 4-cylinder and 6-cylinder derivatives could be made on the same tooling. The 6-cylinder derivative was first seen in the Austin and Morris 2200 models in 1972. Both this and the 4-cylinder had been designed for overseas manufacture as well, and the 6-cylinder ('E6' engine) was also used for the Austin Tasman and Kimberley models built in Australia.

All these engines were mounted transversely. However, when Leyland Australia wanted a big 6-cylinder engine for north-south mounting in its P76 saloon model, it turned to the E6. A long-stroke 2623cc version was created by using the 95.75mm stroke of the 1750cc 4-cylinder E-series, and other modifications were made to make the engine fit for its north-south orientation. In this guise, the 2.6-litre E6 delivered 121bhp and 165lb ft of torque. Just over 7,000 examples of the 6-cylinder P76 were built before Leyland Australia ceased operations in late 1974.

This left the engine tooling and assembly lines going begging, and in the event both were transferred to Leyland South Africa, which needed an engine of this size to increase local content in its CKD Rover SD1

This cutaway model of the R6 engine shows its essential features. Unlike the UK-built 6-cylinder engines, its overhead camshaft was driven by a roller chain.

saloons and Land Rover Series III models. The engine was mildly reworked for South African production, with a different camshaft and an uprated cooling system. Power and torque were both reduced from the Australian version, and noise levels on the South African engine were also said to be lower than on its Australian parent. The actual figures for the South African version were 110bhp at 4,750rpm with 148lb ft of torque at 2,500rpm, with two SU HIF6 carburettors and an 8.75:1 compression ratio.

In South Africa, the 2.6-litre engine was always known as an R6 type ('Rover 6-cylinder'). It had no relationship of any kind to the later R-series 4-cylinder engine introduced in the 1983 Austin Maestro.

The South African-built 6-cylinder engine was a neat fit under the bonnet of the SD1.

These cars all had South African identity numbers which are totally different from the VINs used on UK-built SDI models. Generally speaking, their durability seems to have been better than that of UK-built cars, although tales of quality-control problems at the South African assembly plant are also legendary. Nevertheless, Austin Rover in the UK had a high respect for the South African operation.

In *Rover SDI: The Complete Story*, Karen Pender claims that when South African assembly ended, John Bacchus (Austin Rover's director of business and product strategy) was keen to import the body dies to the UK because they were of better quality than the ones that Pressed Steel were then using.

The seats were designed in South Africa. The external reclining mechanism is clear on these front seats; this was the velour upholstery option.

Hard-wearing striped fabric with vinyl-covered bolsters was an alternative upholstery option on the early cars. Note how the gearshift pattern is indicated next to the cigarette lighter, not on the dash as on UK-built cars. The bright metal knob behind it appears to be a radio speaker balance control and was not a standard feature.

The rear seats on early cars were also unique, with taller backrests that provided built-in head restraints. The tailgate window has been fitted with louvres to protect against glare from the sun; this was a very necessary accessory in South Africa.

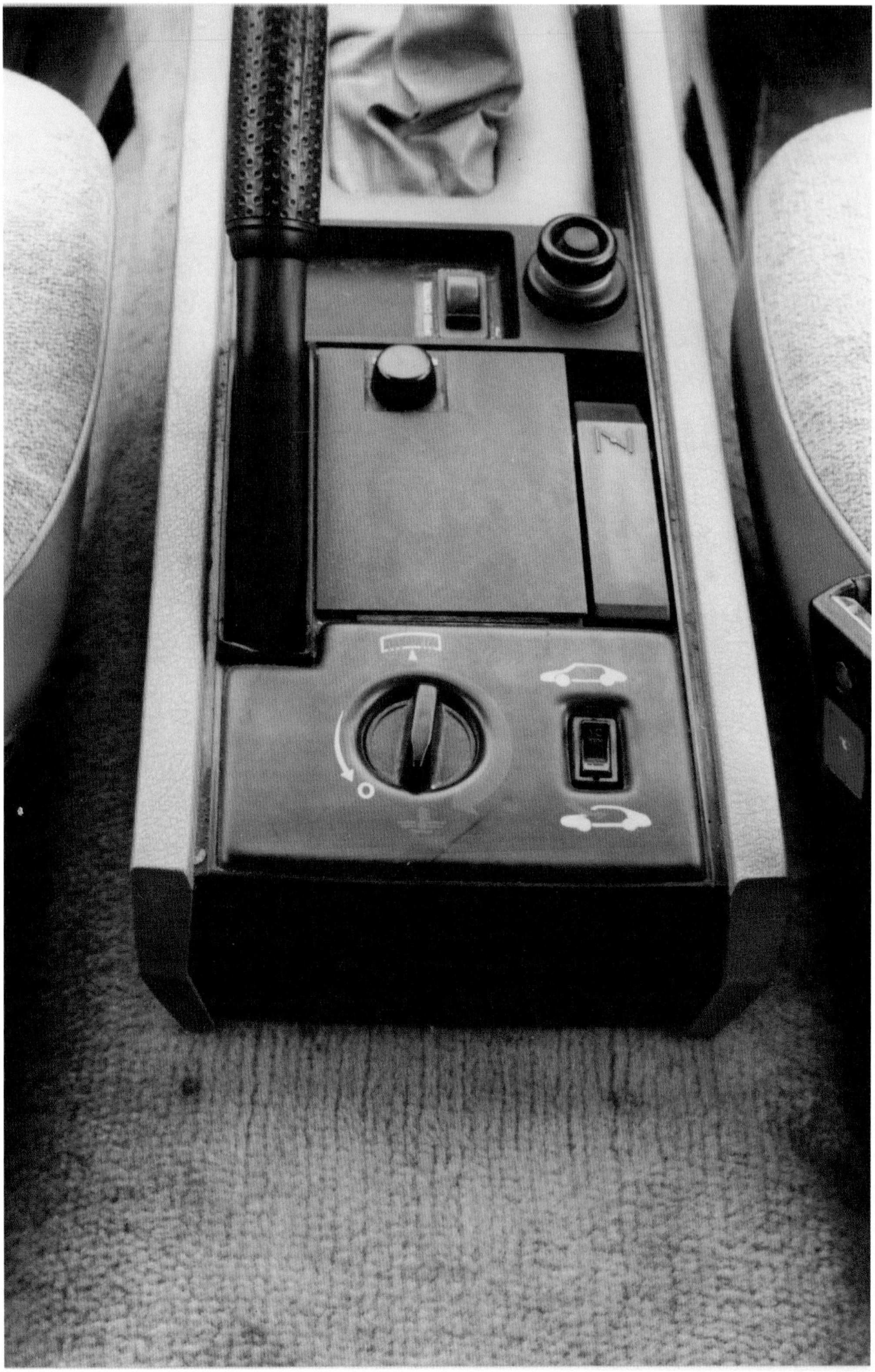

The controls on the rear of the tunnel console were for the optional air-conditioning system.

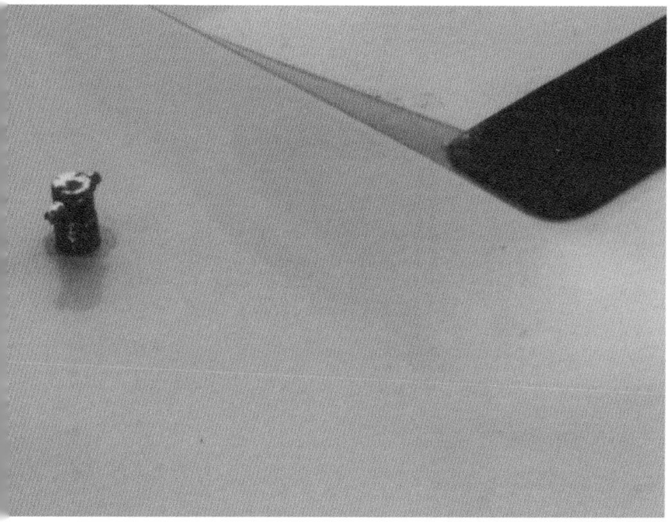

Detail differences: the South African cars had different washer jets from the UK-built models.

The South African identification numbers were quite different from UK types. This identification plate for car number 5004566 is quite different from . . .

. . . this identification plate, for an apparently later car numbered 5010550.

Sweden

The SDI in 3500 form gained Swedish type approval in May 1977, and imports began in June for a September start to sales. All the Swedish SDIs had automatic transmission.

Although the cars sold quite well, British Leyland (Sweden) had only a small and scattered service organization. The Swedish press quite rightly questioned the wisdom of buying a Leyland product when it might be necessary to travel a long distance for service and parts support. The last SDIs exported to Sweden were 1980 models, and these were probably all versions of the V8-S, with a 135bhp engine. This had an 8.13:1 compression, Stromberg carburettors, an air pump and an EGR valve. The Swedish cars had neither a sunroof nor air conditioning.

Switzerland

The early history of the SD1 in Switzerland is unclear, although the car was available from early on because it was thought to have strong appeal to Swiss buyers. Rover importers Emil Frey AG of Streag had despaired of the poor quality of cars coming from the British Leyland companies, and in the early to mid-1970s put all freshly imported BL cars through a careful 110-point 'Swiss Finish' inspection programme, which sometimes went as far as partial rebuilding to remove faults. Cars thus treated were given a special three-year guarantee and the programme was heavily publicized, but it is not clear if the SD1 was among the cars that benefited from it.

From approximately February 1980, Switzlerand took a version of the V8-S that retained those badges but was marketed as a 3500S and sometimes as a 3500S Executive. It differed from the UK-specification cars by having stand-

In Switzerland, the V8-S model was marketed as the 3500S. Although badges were unchanged, it did not have the gold-finished wheels of the UK cars. Note the headlamp wash-wipe units on this car.

The facelifted cars had no significant differences from those sold in the UK. This is a 2600S.

ard alloy wheels instead of the special gold-finished type. By February 1981 the SD1 was available either as a 2600S or a V8-engined Vanden Plas, and by March 1982 both models could be had with either manual or automatic gearboxes. The diesel 2400SD Turbo was not made available as there was no price advantage to buying diesel fuel in Switzerland.

The Vitesse was introduced as a new top model, probably late in 1982 or early in 1983. A delay in homologating the injected engine for the Swiss market meant that the car was initially available only with the carburettor engine, with power quoted at 154PS. The injected engine (with 195PS) was then homologated for 1984; for a while, examples of both types were available through the showrooms until the last of the old stock had been cleared. The 1984 range in fact consisted of three models: the Vitesse, the 2600 Vanden Plas with automatic gearbox and the 2600SE with manual gearbox.

USA

The development of the North American cars (for Canada and the USA) was closely intertwined with the overall development of the SD1, and is explained in Chapter 4. Briefly, the cars were all 3500 models with emissions-controlled engines and special impact bumpers. Just 1,254 cars were sold, predominantly in the USA, between their introduction in summer 1980 and their ignominious withdrawal from the market in summer 1981. There is some unconfirmed evidence that a few 1981-specification cars were built for North America.

CHAPTER NINE

THE SD1 IN MOTOR SPORT

Between 1980 and 1986, British Leyland and its Austin Rover successor ran SD1s in both track events and rally events. They were not alone: a number of privateers and private teams also saw the motor sport potential of the big Rovers, and some enjoyed spectacular successes. From the manufacturer's point of view, the motor sport programmes were intended to gather positive publicity for the SD1 and enhance sales. As a result, the cars were not run as full 'works' entries in the early days, so that failure would not have an adverse publicity effect. Nevertheless, the race-going public knew exactly what was going on and the SD1s became a much-loved sight in British and some European events in the first half of the 1980s.

THE SD1 ON THE TRACKS

The event that brought the Rover SD1 into motor sport was a change in the regulations of Group 1 British Saloon Car Championship racing for 1980. The BSCC at the time used its own version of the international FIA regulations, and announced in 1979 that the capacity limit for its Class A events would be raised from the existing 3000cc to 3500cc.

The BL Motorsport division already had a version of the 3.5-litre Rover engine that was doing well in its TR7 V8 rally cars, and it now made sense to explore the possibility of entering a V8-engined Rover SD1 for the Group 1 BSCC championship. A plan came together. Basic development of the car and engine would be down to BL Motorsport, then based at the MG works in Abingdon and run by John Davenport. However, team management and detail preparation of the cars would be entrusted to David Price Racing of Twickenham, who had prepared the March F3 Dolomites for British Leyland in 1978–79.

Sponsors materialized in the shape of Triplex, who made the Ten-Twenty windscreen for the Rover; Esso, who were to provide fuel and oils; and *Motor* magazine. The *Motor* deal was an inspired one, because it would allow maximum publicity from the events. Rex Greenslade, *Motor*'s technical editor and a semi-professional racing driver, would drive one of the cars and would provide a behind-the-scenes look at events when he wrote about them. Lead driver was to be saloon car racer Jeff Allam. As Greenslade explained in *Motor*'s 22 March 1980 issue:

> *Although the Triplex/Esso/*Motor *effort isn't one that carries official factory status, it most definitely carries factory approval and co-operation – from the boardroom right down to the shop-floor.*

The SD1s first went racing in 1980, with sponsorship by Triplex, Esso and *Motor* magazine.

The Group I racing Rover first ran in prototype form at the Gaydon test track in October 1979. The plan was to field two cars and to build a third as a spare. Engine development was led by David Wood at BL Motorsport, but the Group I regulations meant that many of the special features developed for the Group 4 rallying TR7 V8 engines could not be used. The Group I regulations also insisted on that 3500cc size ceiling, so the V8 engine was given a special short-stroke crankshaft, the new stroke dimension of 70.35mm reducing the swept volume to 3495cc.

1980 BSCC Season

By the start of the ten-round championship in March 1980, the Rover engine was producing about 250bhp at 6,800rpm and 235lb ft at 3,500rpm, with more than 200lb ft of torque available all the way up to 6,250rpm. The compression ratio was between 10.5:1 and 11.0:1, the camshaft was a specially homologated design, and – according to *Motor* magazine in their 22 March 1980 issue – there were twin SU HIF7 carburettors with 1.875in chokes. Everybody knew this would be a shake-down season, and engine reliability issues were acknowledged to be inevitable because of the high proportion of production components that were required under the Group I regulations.

The racing Rovers retained the five-speed 77mm gearbox but with close ratios as permitted by the Group I regulations and a slightly higher third gear than was used in the TR7 rally cars' version of the gearbox. Rear axle gearing was altered, and the cars would usually run with a 4.55:1 ratio although a 4.30:1 was available for circuits where it was considered appropriate. In both cases, a Salisbury limited-slip differential was fitted.

The suspension used metal spherical joints where rubber was used on production cars, and the braking system was uprated. The racers had AP four-piston front calipers, as available for UK police cars and on some vehicles for the armed forces, and these were served by twin master cylinders. There was a balance-bar pedal box, and an adjustable brake bias valve in the rear hydraulic circuit. In most events, the cars would run with 15in wheels made by Ronel, with a 7in rim width. A Minilite wheel option was also available.

Weight was pared to get the cars down to the regulation limit of 1,130kg (2,492lb) and in fact the SDIs were light enough in stripped-out racing form to need 30–40lb of lead ballast in order not to be lighter than the prescribed limit. As Rex Greenslade wrote in *Motor* magazine of 22 March 1980:

> *There are no passenger seats, carpets or sound deadening material inside. The fuel tank has been replaced by a properly vented single-seater bag-type tank (behind a carefully engineered fire-wall) and there is a sturdy roll-cage for accident protection. Other obvious changes include the very special Recaro driver's seat (that has shoulder support to help the driver counteract the 1.0g cornering loads that modern Group I cars can generate) and a six-point Willans full harness seat belt.*

Thus prepared, the racing Rovers entered the first round of the 1980 Tricentrol BSCC season at Mallory Park on 23 March. The results were mixed: Rex Greenslade finished fifth in class (which was dominated by Ford's well-developed 3-litre Capris) but Jeff Allam was unable to finish because of engine failure. There were then no good results from the next four rounds. It was all very frustrating, not least for those who were following the progress of 'Rex's racing Rover' through reports in *Motor* – which were conspicuously absent from issues of the magazine in this period.

Meanwhile, the cars had been developed in the light of experience. After Easter 1980, they switched to a twin-choke Weber carburettor (the Group I regulations allowed only two chokes in all, so it had to be a single carburettor). This raised power to 275bhp at 7,000rpm and added valuable torque for accelerating out of slow corners. Then came a mid-season rule change, which enabled the team to use an American Huffaker manifold and a two-barrel Holley carburettor. Power went up again, this time to around 280bhp, although torque dropped slightly.

At Brands Hatch on 13 July, where the Group I BSCC race supported the main event of the British Grand Prix, the Rovers' luck seemed to have changed. Jeff Allam led the field almost immediately and never looked like being caught. He won, and Rex Greenslade in the number two car came sixth overall. More mixed fortunes followed, and engine weaknesses began to show up in a big way. In all, Rover had wrecked no fewer than twenty-six race engines during the season – a wholly unacceptable figure. The blow-ups were mainly due to catastrophic bearing lubrication and con-rod failures.

There had been talk within British Leyland of withdrawing the cars – but a solution presented itself mid-season. That solution was an offer from Tom Walkinshaw Racing to take over management of the cars for the 1981 season, and it was backed up by development work that showed the Walkinshaw magic might just do the trick. So when the racing Rovers appeared at a motor sport event at Donington over the weekend of 25–26 October, they had a future – although it remained a closely guarded secret at that stage. For completeness, the record has it that one car appeared in the Eaton Vale Rallysprint on 25 October, with world champion Alan Jones at the wheel. On 26 October, both cars appeared in the thirty-lap SMMT Motor Show Trophy race, driven by Jones and Jeff Allam.

Enter TWR

Tom Walkinshaw Racing (TWR) appeared on the SDI scene around the middle of the 1980 racing season. The company already had a strong track record in preparing racing BMW saloons and Mazda RX-7 coupés, and was looking to expand its business.

TWR was based at Kidlington in Oxfordshire, not far from BL Motorsport, which moved from Abingdon to Cowley at the end of 1980. Its involvement in the SDI motor sport programme was initially kept secret. Walkinshaw had approached BL Motorsport's John Davenport, and had been allowed to test one of the BL Motorsport cars. The deal was that there would be no payment until certain agreed improvements in lap times were achieved. TWR knew that the Rovers' biggest problem was engine unreliability, but the company also suggested some suspension changes which made an improvement.

At an early stage in the project, four Group I full race engines were delivered to Kidlington from BL Motorsport, where development work had been continuing on the racing V8. According to Allan Scott, whose book *TWR and Rover's SDI* provides fascinating and detailed insight into TWR's involvement in the SDI racing programme, the engines at this stage were typically delivering around 260bhp at 6,500rpm and 228lb ft at 5,500rpm. There was work to be done.

HOW FAST? THE 1980-SEASON CARS

At the end of the 1980 BSCC season, *Motor* magazine tested one of the racing SDIs to provide some performance figures. The results were published in its issue dated 18 October 1980, and showed:

0–60mph in 5.3sec
0–100mph in 14.3sec
Standing quarter-mile in 14.0sec

The car was estimated to be capable of around 150mph (241km/h) with the right gearing, and at this stage the engine was developing around 280bhp at 7,000rpm.

1981 BSCC Season

The 1981 season once again saw just two teams in the BSCC fielding Rovers. This time, Tom Walkinshaw racing was running the 'semi-works' cars, with sponsorship from the *Daily Express* newspaper and a new livery to match. Patrick Motorsport, who had run a car in the 1980 season, this time entered a two-car team.

The TWR-prepared cars started the season slowly, but by Round 6 at Silverstone in June had become a serious challenge to the dominant Capris. Drivers Peter Lovett (car no. 10) and Jeff Allam (no. 9) piled on the pressure, and Lovett won his class at Silverstone in June, at Silverstone again the following month and at Donington Park in August. Jeff Allam won the final three rounds, at Brands Hatch in August, Thruxton in September and Silverstone in October. Lovett was declared the series' Class D winner with Allam the runner-up.

1982 BSCC Season

The 1982 season was again contested by two teams fielding SDIs, running in Class A of the FIA Appendix J Group I. The 'works supported' cars were Team Sanyo Racing with Esso Hepolite Glacier Racing (and the same team also fielded a Metro 1300 driven by Steve Soper), while Patrick Motorsport ran two cars with sponsorship from Duckhams Oil and ICI Petrol. The rival Ford Capris were faster than ever and the competition closer still, but Jeff Allam just managed to amass enough points to carry off a class win for Team Sanyo.

There was sponsorship from Sanyo and Esso in the 1982 season, when pre-facelift cars were still being used.

Allam drove the no. 1 car in all eleven rounds of the BTCC, and he was joined on Team Sanyo by Frank Sytner, who drove the no. 2 car in the first four rounds. Tom Walkinshaw drove the spare team car in Round 4 at Thruxton. Allam took four class wins: in Round 1 at Silverstone on 20 March, in Round 2 at Mallory Park on 28 March, in Round 6 at Silverstone again on 13 June and in Round 9 at Donington Park on 15 August. He was forced to retire in Round 5 at Thruxton. Frank Sytner's season was altogether less successful, with a retirement from Round 1, a poor finish in Round 2, a non-start in Round 3 at Oulton Park and another retirement in Round 4.

1983 BSCC Season

Two major changes affected Rover's 1983 racing season. One was that Ford's 3-litre Capri was no longer in production and was therefore no longer eligible to race. The other was that John Davenport's BL Competitions Department (by this stage known as Austin Rover Motorsport) had asked for a 'homologation special' version of the SD1 and had been granted it in the shape of the Vitesse, which had reached showrooms in autumn 1982.

The 1983 Trimoco RAC British Saloon Car Championship was the first one to be run under the European Group A rules, which allowed much more freedom for suspension, braking and wheel modifications than Group 1, but actually allowed less freedom for engine modifications. The 1983 season was also the first one for the TWR-prepared Vitesse cars, which went on to win eleven out of eleven rounds in the hands of Steve Soper, Pete Lovett and Jeff Allam. However, as *Motor* put it on 24 March 1984, the 1983 season...

> *... produced some of the worst bickering and post-race squabbling known in British racing history, all of which recently culminated with two expensive weeks in London's High Court.*

The saga began when Frank Sytner, running the 6 Series coupés in the championship for BMW, protested about the legality of a modification to the TWR-prepared Rovers whereby the rear wheel arches were widened inwards to accommodate wider tyres. This protest was supplemented by one about the adjustable rocker arms used on the TWR-prepared Vitesse engines. A long-running battle ensued and

Steve Soper should have won the 1983 BSCC in this Hepolite-Glacier Vitesse, but the result was challenged and eventually the title was awarded elsewhere.

was not resolved until July 1984, when the verdict went against Austin Rover. In the meantime, the company had lost patience with the whole issue and in June had withdrawn its Vitesses and its MG Metro Turbos from the 1984 championship, at the same time renouncing its claim to the 1983 title. The whole thing was little short of a farce.

None of that prevented the action on the tracks in 1983 from being exciting. The 'semi-works' Rover Vitesse cars were developing a claimed 280bhp at 6,800rpm at the start of the season, going on to around 300bhp before the end. All of them had Getrag five-speed gearboxes and disc brakes all round, both of which were modifications permitted under the Group A regulations. The racing weight at the start of the season was 1,125kg (2,480lb), and there were two separate sponsors: the no. 2 car (for Jeff Allam) and the no. 3 car (for Peter Lovett) were run with the blue livery of Team Sanyo Racing with Esso, while the no. 4 car (for Steve Soper) ran in the yellow and red livery of sponsors Hepolite-Glacier and Esso. The Hepolite car, incidentally, also won the ETCC Tourist Trophy race at Silverstone in September 1983.

1984 BSCC Season

When the 1984 BSCC opened in March, the issue of who had won the 1983 event was still unresolved. Nevertheless, TWR once again fielded a 'semi-works' team of three cars. Car no. 1, with Team Sanyo and Esso sponsorship, was for Tony Pond; car no. 2, wearing Austin Rover Group col-

The Andy Rouse-prepared Industrial Control Services car made a welcome appearance at Goodwood in 2014.

EUROPEAN MOTOR SPORT EVENTS

When the Rover works team pulled out of the BSCC in 1984, it was by no means burning its boats in the racing world. The SD1 was already established as a force in racing on the European continent, and Austin Rover simply refocused its efforts on that.

French saloon car racer René Metge had taken over one of the 1980 'works' cars prepared by David Price Racing, and he raced this in the 1981 French Production Championship. The French Group 1 was run under different rules from those used in Britain, and DPR prepared the car with a four-carburettor set-up. Metge raced with Marlboro (cigarettes) sponsorship, and his greatest success in 1981 was first place in the Group 1 event supporting the French Grand Prix on 5 July. In 1982, he won the French Championship outright.

In 1983, two of the Metge cars found their way to Portugal, one going to José Peres and the other to Pedro Meireles. Both initially had right-hand drive, but for the 1984 season they were converted to left-hand drive. Although both drivers anticipated use of the latest TWR-developed injection system, that did not reach them and so the cars were slower than expected in their first season. The Meireles car raced in red with Traffic sponsorship between 1983 and 1985, and in the latter season was sometimes used by Ni Amorim. The Peres car went to Artur Mendes, who used it in the 1984 Iniciados Championship for new drivers; in 1985 Helder Oliveira used it in the same series and in 1986 it was José Nelson Graça, who went on to use the car in the 1987 National Championship.

The first 'works' Rovers appeared in European competition during 1983, when TWR-prepared Vitesses were entered for the national championships in Belgium (one in Hepolite-Glacier colours and one with Austin Rover and Barclay colours), France (with Marlboro sponsorship) and the Netherlands (again with Austin Rover and Barclay colours). At the same time, Armin Hahne entered the German national championship in a locally prepared Vitesse, and won the final round. On a grander scale, TWR ran four cars in the European Touring Car Championship (ETCC), two sponsored by Sanyo, one by

Hepolite-Glacier, and one by Austin Rover with Barclay.

While the 'works' cars focused on the ETCC in 1984, Austin Rover Deutschland sponsored entries in the new DPM (German Production Car Championship) events. Olaf Manthey and Jörg van Ommen were signed as drivers, but Van Ommen had several crashes and was later replaced by Dieter Selzer; Manthey finished second overall. Meanwhile, a single TWR car ran in Marlboro colours in the 1984 French national series.

For 1985, Austin Rover Deutschland again sponsored entries in the German national championship. Walter Mertes drove in a few races but the main focus was on Olaf Manthey, who again finished the season second overall. For 1986, as the German championship became the DTM (Deutsche Tourenwagen Meisterschaft), the SDI interest focused on Autotechnik Nickel, who prepared a Vitesse as a private entry for Kurt Thiim. It is rumoured that the engine in this car came from TWR. Wearing Toshiba sponsorship, the car took the title for Thiim that year. It also raced in a few rounds of the 1987 championship before the Nickel team switched to an Alfa Romeo 75.

This TWR car was sponsored by Marlboro and Hepolite.

The SDI became a successful racer on the European continent, too. This left-hand-drive Vitesse was pictured in German hands.

Kurt Thiim took the Toshiba-sponsored Vitesse to victory in the 1986 German Touring Car Championship.

ours, was for Steve Soper; and car no. 4 was in Team Sanyo colours for Peter Lovett. Pond's car ran as no 11 in some events, and Lovett's car as no. 2.

The big challenge to the 'works' Rovers this year came from Andy Rouse, driving a Vitesse that his own company had prepared. Otherwise, the main challenge came from the BMW 635 CSi coupés prepared by Frank Sytner. It soon became clear that the BMWs were simply outclassed; at Thruxton in May, the 'works' Rovers took first, third and fourth places, and Andy Rouse's car came in second. But the Silverstone round in June, which fell to Rouse's Rover, would be the last appearance of the 'semi-works' Vitesses that year. Disgusted by the long process of appeal and counter-appeal about the result of the 1983 series, Austin Rover withdrew all of their cars from the championship.

1985 ETCC Season

When the Rover works team returned to racing for the 1985 season, it was not to the British championship. Instead, this year's focus was on the European Touring Car Championship. Still prepared by TWR, the Vitesse racers were sponsored by the Belgian cigarette company Bastos and by the oil company Texaco, and raced in a distinctive white and red livery. They also benefited from a much-improved electronic engine management system that TWR had developed.

This year, the big challenge was from the tubocharged Volvos. The season began well for the Rovers, with a 1-2-3 finish at Monza in March for the cars of Walkinshaw, Jean-Louis Schlesser and Allam. At Donington in May, it was a 1-2-3 finish for the Rovers again, with the Walkinshaw/Percy car finishing ahead of Soper and Thibaut's car no. 6 and the Allam/Hahne car in third place.

Then things started to go wrong. At the Swedish Anderstorp event in May, at Brno in June and at Zeltweg later that month, there arose problem after problem. Salzburg in June brought a second place for Walkinshaw and Percy, and there was another second for Joosen and Soper at the Nürburgring in July. Spa in July saw all three Rovers retire with the same problem of a failed distributor shaft. However, back on home turf at Silverstone in September after six races without victory, the TWR cars were back on form with first and second places. Nogaro in September gave the Rovers a 1-2-3 victory, but the rest of the season produced mixed results and the 1985 ETCC title went to Volvo.

Car no. 1 was driven by Tom Walkinshaw and Win Percy in several 1985 events.

There were minor variations in the livery from one event to the next. This is again one of the TWR-Texaco-Bastos cars.

Walkinshaw and Percy crewed car no 1 to victory at the Vallelunga ETCC race held on 21 April 1985.

THE TWR-PREPARED CARS

It is notoriously difficult to establish the precise history of a competition car, but the task of identifying the cars prepared by TWR has been greatly aided by Allan Scott's excellent book, *TWR and Rover's SD1*. Scott was a member of the TWR team, and his book goes into minute detail that will fascinate any enthusiast of the racing and rallying SD1s. Much of the information presented in this table is based on his work, and is used with grateful acknowledgement. Additional material is based on further research by Dave Puzey of the Rover SD1 Club.

A total of eighteen cars were built over a four-year period. These were built from the start for competition work, and were based on bodyshells taken from the assembly lines. As a result, they did not carry standard SD1 VINs. Each car had its own individual number, stamped on a small aluminium plate attached by self-tapping screws to the bodyshell just above the right-hand headlamp. They were numbered from TWR 001 to TWR 020.

Although twenty numbers were allocated, car 007 was rebuilt into car 012 and no car was built with no. 013, making that a total of eighteen. Car numbers TWR 001 to TWR 012 had steel roll cages made by Safety Devices to a TWR design, and modified front strut mount panels. Their interiors were painted black. Car numbers TWR 014 to TWR 020 had alloy roll cages made by Matter in Germany, again to a TWR design. Their interiors were painted white.

1983 cars

TWR 001 Prepared for the French Production Championship and ran in Marlboro colours. In 1983 it was driven by René Metge and in 1984 by Jean-Louis Schlesser.

TWR 002 Prepared for the BSCC and ran in Hepolite-Glacier colours. Driven by Steve Soper in 1983. Also ran in the 1983 Belgian Saloon Car Championship, again with Soper driving, and in the 1983 ETCC, with Soper and Jeff Allam, or Soper and Metge, or Soper, Allam and Metge driving.

TWR 003 Prepared for the BSCC and ran in Sanyo colours. Driven by Peter Lovett in 1983; in the 1984 BSCC it was driven by both Lovett and Jean-Louis Schlesser (on one occasion by Schlesser with Tony Pond). For 1985 it was converted into a rally car with registration number B565 AOX.

TWR 004 Prepared for the BSCC and ran in Sanyo colours. Driven by Jeff Allam in 1983 and by Tony Pond in 1984. It also ran in one round of the 1983 ETCC, driven by Allam, Lovett and Soper. In 1984 it ran in the Bathurst 1000 Race in Australia, driven by Jeff Allam and Armin Hanhe.

TWR 005 Prepared for European events in 1983 and

Pictured at the Motor 100 event at Silverstone in 1985, this was one of the TWR-Texaco-Bastos cars. Its exact identity is unclear.

The sponsorship decals on this car are for Austin Rover Finance and British Car Rentals; the name on the driver's helmet is that of Jeff Allam.

built with left-hand drive. The car wore Austin Rover-Barclay colours. It was driven by Eddy Joosen in the Belgian Saloon Car Championship and the Netherlands Touring Car Championship, and by Joosen with René Metge or Peter Lovett (and once by all three) in the ETCC. For 1984 it was converted to right-hand drive and wore Marlboro colours in the French Production Championship. It was normally driven by Marc Duez and on one occasion by Claude Ballot-Léna.

TWR 006 Built as a rally car and competed in the British, Belgian and European championships in 1983 and 1984. In 1983 it ran in Herbie Clips colours; in the 1984 Belgian championship it was sponsored by Herbie Clips, the *Daily Mirror* and Marlboro; in the 1984 British championship the sponsor was initially Herbie Clips and later the *Daily Mirror*. Drivers were Tom Walkinshaw and John Davenport (1983 and 1984), Tony Pond and Rob Arthur (1983 and 1984), Marc Duez and Willy Lux (1984), and Tom Walkinshaw and Rob Arthur (1984) The car wore four different registration numbers (see below).

1984 cars

TWR 007 Prepared for the 1984 ETCC and ran in Gitanes colours. Drivers were Eddy Joosen with Tony Pond or Joosen with Pond and Jean-Pierre Jabouille. The car was given an updated specification and renumbered as TWR 012 for the 1985 season.

TWR 008 Prepared for the 1984 BSCC and ETCC and ran in Austin Rover Fleet colours. For 1985, it ran in the ETCC with Bastos colours. The car had a variety of drivers: Martin Brundle, Marc Duez, Armin Hahne, Eddy Joosen, Jean-Louis Schlesser, Steve Soper, Pierre Alain Thibaut and Tom Walkinshaw all had a turn at the wheel. In 1986, it went to New Zealand for the Nissan-Mobil Series and ran in Whittaker Peanut Slab colours, driven by Walkinshaw with Win Percy.

TWR 009 Prepared as a rally car and ran in Computervision colours during 1985 in the British International Championships. Drivers were Tony Pond with Rob Arthur.

TWR 010 Prepared for the 1984 ETCC and ran in Austin Rover Fleet colours. Driven variously by Steve Soper with Jeff Allam, Allam with Eddy Joosen, Allam with Marc Duez, and Duez with Jean-Louis Schlesser and Peter Lovett.

TWR 011 Prepared for the 1984 Bathurst 1000 race in Australia, with Mobil colours. Ran in the Nissan-Mobil Series in New Zealand in 1985 with More magazine colours. The 1984 drivers were Steve Soper with Ron Dickson; the 1985 drivers were Tom Walkinshaw and Ron Dickson.

1985 cars

TWR 012 Renumbered from TWR 007. Prepared for the 1985 ETCC and ran in Bastos colours. In 1986 it ran in the Nissan-Mobil Series in New Zealand wearing Whittaker Peanut Slab colours, and in 1986 returned to the ETCC, again in Bastos colours. Drivers were Jean-Louis Schlesser with Pierre Alain Thibaut or Steve Soper (1985), Armin Hahne with Ron Dickson (1986 New Zealand), and Jeff Allam with Suguru Akaike (1986 ETCC).

TWR 014 Prepared for the 1985 French Production Championship in Marlboro colours and driven by Jean-Louis Schlesser. For 1986 it was repainted in Bastos colours for the ETCC, where it was driven by Jeff Allam with Eddy Joosen or Gianfranco Brancatelli. In 1986 it also ran in South Pacific Racing colours and in Istel colours, in both cases driven by Allam and Denny Hulme. It appeared in Herbie Clips colours for one round of the 1986 BSCC, driven by Allam, and then in Watsons colours at the Guia Race supporting the Macau Grand Prix, driven by Brancatelli.

TWR 015 Prepared for the 1985 ETCC season in Bastos colours. It was driven by Jeff Allam with Armin Hahne, and they were joined by Jean-Louis Schlesser for the 24-hour Spa race.

TWR 016 Prepared for the 1985 ETCC in Bastos colours. Driven by Tom Walkinshaw with Win Percy, plus Hans Heyer in the 24-hour Spa race. Walkinshaw also drove it in one round of the 1985 BTCC.

TWR 017 Prepared for the 1985 ETCC in Bastos colours. Driven by Tom Walkinshaw and Win Percy in two rounds after their regular car (TWR 016) was damaged. It was subsequently damaged itself and written off.

1986 cars

TWR 018 Prepared for the 1986 ETCC in Bastos colours. Driven by Armin Hahne with Jean-Louis Schlesser in most rounds; Jeff Allam, Gianfranco Brancatelli and Win Percy all took turns as Hahne's co-driver, and Hahne and Allam were joined by Denny Hulme for the Spa 24-hour race.

TWR 019 Prepared for the 1986 ETCC in Bastos colours. Driven by Tom Walkinshaw with Win Percy, plus Eddy Joosen in the Spa 24-hour race. This car was subsequently purchased by JD Classics and at the time of writing made regular appearances in historic racing events.

TWR 020 Prepared for the 1986 ETCC in South Pacific Racing colours. Driven by Ron Dickson and Neville Crichton, plus Denny Hulme at Misano. Also ran in Herbie Clips colours in one BSCC round, driven by Jean-Louis Schlesser, and at the Guia Race supporting the Macau Grand Prix in Watsons colours and driven by Tom Walkinshaw.

Steve Soper at the wheel of one of the Austin Rover Fleet cars.

THE NON-WORKS RACING ROVERS

The 'works' Rovers were certainly not the only examples of the SDI to enter national and international saloon car racing events in the first half of the 1980s. The list below does not claim to be exhaustive.

Patrick Motorsport

The Patrick Motorsport Group (an arm of the Birmingham dealership chain Patrick Motors Ltd) entered a single car in the 1980 BTCC events, beginning in mid-season in July. The car was shared by Australian Brian Muir and teammate Terry Watts, who had a somewhat mixed season.

PMS fielded a team of two cars in the 1981 series, with sponsorship from Duckhams, ICI Petrol and *Motor* magazine. With *Motor*'s support came driver Rex Greenslade, who had been Jeff Allam's teammate in the 1980 season with David Price Racing. The 1981-season PMS cars were prepared by Martin Thomas at SRG Racing in Biggleswade, with full technical assistance from BL Motorsport even though they were strictly private entries. Engines were prepared by a newly established company called RS Race Engineering, based in Cambridge. Reports from Rex Greenslade were to appear in *Motor*, but he had a frustrating and disappointing season, finishing only once in the points. There were correspondingly few reports in *Motor*.

In the 1982 BSCC races, PMS ran two cars with the same sponsorship as in 1981. Drivers Rad Dougall and Brian Muir consistently finished at the back of their class. Nevertheless, the PMS team had set its sights on the European Touring Car Championship for 1983, and entered a car prepared to the Group A specifications for the Tourist Trophy event that was one of the last in the 1982 season. It was an auspicious start, too: the car looked for a time as if it might finish in second place but ran out of fuel with just six laps to go.

Dennis Leech

Privateer Dennis Leech entered the BSCC with a Rover during 1982, driving car no. 12 in Round 1, Rounds 3–8 and Round 11. However, he did not show well in the early rounds and then had three retirements. Undeterred, he entered again in 1983 and in every subsequent year up to and including 1988. His car was painted in black with dayglo orange stripes, and in later years carried Demon Tweeks sponsorship decals. Leech won a round of the BSCC at Thruxton with the Rover in 1987.

Charles Sawyer-Hoare

Charles Sawyer-Hoare switched from a Ford Capri 3-litre in the 1982 BSCC to a Rover Vitesse for 1983. The car ran in red Equipe Esso colours with sponsorship from the *Daily Mirror* and was back again for the 1984 season but without notable success. During 1984 the car was prepared by Andy Rouse.

Neil McGrath

Saloon car racer Neil McGrath ran a Vitesse in the BSCC between 1984 and 1986. His car was the former Spice Racing car that was still run by Martin Thomas in 1984, and that year wore Linden Racing livery. In 1985 it was in green and wore Castrol Sport Racing with Connells Estate Agents decals. The livery changed to white in 1985, and McGrath again entered for Linden Racing. That year, he finished seventh overall in the BSCC and third in Class A.

Andy Rouse

Andy Rouse had been both driver and racing development engineer for the Broadspeed team in the 1970s. In 1981 he set up his own engineering company, Andy Rouse Engineering. His personal involvement with the Rover Vitesse lasted a single season, and was hugely successful. In 1984, Rouse drove car no. 7 to victory in the BSCC series, with sponsorship from Industrial Control Services.

Rouse Engineering also prepared Charles Sawyer-Hoare's Vitesse in the 1984 season. In 1985, again running with sponsorship from Industrial Control Services, a Rouse-prepared car was driven by Pete Hall and, on occasion, by Phil Dowsett.

Old racers go on for ever..... this was one of the 1980 Patrick Motorsport cars, still competitive in 2014 when it won the Gerry Marshall Trophy at Goodwood. It was then owned by JD Classics.

1986 ETCC Season

For the 1986 ETCC season, Rover again fielded three cars, although only two ran in some rounds. The cars were now making some 340bhp, thanks mainly to a new twin-throttle plenum injection system. The Bastos-Texaco sponsorship remained intact, although for some races one of the cars was attributed to TWR – South Pacific Racing, and its crew was made up of Australian and New Zealand drivers, among them former world champion Denny Hulme. However, car no. 9 had a new collection of sponsors for the Silverstone round in September, and was entered by TWR with Istel, Austin Rover Finance and British Car Auctions logos.

Even though this would be the Rovers' last ETCC season because the cars were about to go out of production, they remained surprisingly competitive. The competition for the driver's title soon boiled down to just two drivers – Win Percy on the Rover team and Roberto Ravaglia driving for BMW. For a time, it looked as if Percy would win, but right at the end of the season the championship organizers remembered their January 1986 ruling that a driver's five worst results (it had been four in 1985) would not count towards his points total. So the driver's title went to Ravaglia.

THE SDI IN RALLIES

Rover burst onto the rallying scene with a completely unexpected appearance by a works-prepared SDI in the Pace Rallysprint at Esgair Dafydd in mid-Wales on 27 April 1982. Driven by Tony Pond, who had been the lead driver during British Leyland's TR7 V8 rally programme, the car performed extremely well, and could well have finished in second place behind an Audi Quattro but for a gearchange problem late in the event. Either Pond missed a gear or third gear seized, depending on who tells the story, but the result was that the SDI actually finished in seventh place.

The secrecy surrounding the SDI rallying project had been total. It had actually started some time around Christmas 1981, and the prototype rally car first ran in February 1982. According to *Cars and Car Conversions* magazine for September 1982, there had been thoughts about entering the car for the Peking–Paris long-distance rally in 1982 – an event that did not come to fruition. The car itself, which carried registration number GJW 584W and wore Unipart sponsor's livery, had originally been planned as a successor to the Group 2 Rover that had run just once – in the Silverstone TT race – but the project had been mothballed when BL Motorsport moved from Abingdon to become AR Motorsport at Cowley and its staff was drastically reduced.

Not surprisingly, the rally-car project picked up on the work done for the earlier TR7 V8 rally cars. That programme had been ended during 1980 as part of BL's desperate drive to save money so that it could fund essential new showroom products, but the expertise remained. In fact, engineer Richard Hurdwell had worked on the TR7 V8 cars, and had now been put in charge of the rallying SDI development project. Initial gravel testing of the prototype car was entrusted to veteran rally driver Colin Malkin, until the car was ready for Tony Pond to take over for fine-tuning.

This first development car used the same engine, gearbox and rear axle as the later TR7 V8 cars. The engine had been developed by Don Moore, the Cambridge specialist, and developed 300bhp at 7,500rpm with four Weber 48DCOE carburettors. There was a dry-sump lubrication system, for which the oil tank was mounted inside the boot. Maximum speed was claimed as 132mph (212km/h), with the 0–60mph sprint taking just 4.9sec. Those 300bhp were right on the limit of usable power with two-wheel drive, but there were plans to reduce the maximum power to around 250bhp in the interests of longevity and fuel economy.

The gearbox was a five-speed type modified by specialists Jack Knight, and the rear axle was a Salisbury 4HA type as used in Jaguars. This allowed for a much larger than standard crown wheel and pinion, and a 5.3:1 final drive was fitted to give the right low-down acceleration characteristics for a rally car. The Salisbury axle lacked the torque tube used on production SDIs so the car was fitted with a modified split propshaft from a Jaguar XJ12. Axle location was completely different from the production SDI type and used four long, adjustable parallel links with rose joints, plus a Panhard rod. There were twin coil-and-damper units on each rear wheel, too, mounted in fabricated turrets. Meanwhile, the main fuel tank was relocated and this, together with an auxiliary tank, give a total fuel capacity of around 40gal (182ltr). The windows, as on most rally cars, were made of plastic. Overall weight was nearly 2,866lb (1,300kg) with 100lb (45kg) of ballast bolted to the floor to meet the regulations then current.

That first appearance at the Pace Rallysprint proved to be a big help in developing the car further, and GJW made a few more appearances on minor events to test ideas. At this stage, the rallying SDI programme was focusing on long-distance events, so its main aim was to achieve reliability. However, GJW had outlived its usefulness as a development car by late 1982, and a new purpose-built rally car was built to take the programme forwards.

GJW was meanwhile sold to rally driver Ken Wood at the end of the year, deliberately disguised with the new registration number OOC 272X. Wood, who had been the 1982 Scottish Rally champion in a TR7 V8, campaigned it in the 1983 Esso Scottish Rally Championship. Wearing Golden Wonder (potato crisps) livery, the car took some time to become reliable, but won the Border Counties Rally in July and was doing well on the Arnold Clark Scottish International Rally before the engine blew up. Wood and his co-driver Peter Brown continued to campaign it in 1984 and 1985 events.

'Works' Rally Cars

Unlike the racing SDIs, the rally cars had to wear registration numbers, and those associated with the factory all did so. However, these numbers were not an infallible guide to a car's identity: the TWR-prepared cars 'borrowed' numbers from other cars and went through several different identities.

Note also that there were a few privateer SDI rally entries in this period; for example, Andrew Smalley and Martin Dixon entered the 1983 RAC Rally in a car sponsored by bread makers Warburton's.

Austin Rover Motorsport Cars

When the Austin Rover SDI rally programme began in earnest, the plan was to enter SDIs in the 1983 Paris–Peking long-distance endurance rally. Three cars were built to Group 2 specification, and they wore the registration numbers A683 AJO, A377 VUK and A379 VUK (there was no rally car registered A378 VUK). The registration number A379 VUK was at one point 'borrowed' by TWR for one of their rally cars (TWR-006).

Disappointingly, the 1983 Paris–Peking rally was cancelled. The two A-VUK cars were nevertheless not wasted. In October 1983, A377 VUK and A379 VUK both ran in the Trophée Jean Francois Piot at Sarlat in France. However, only A377 VUK (driven by Tony Pond) was the original AR Motorsport car, and the registration A379 VUK was used on a TWR-prepared car driven by Tom Walkinshaw. Both were probably painted white with Austin Rover sponsorship decals. Walkinshaw also drove 379 (the TWR car) on the National Breakdown Rally in February 1984 but without success.

Both 377 and 379 (the latter number now on the original AR Motorsport car) appeared at the Austin Rover Rallysprint event held at Donington at the start of November 1983. This colourful event pitted established rally drivers against Grand Prix drivers in short-distance rally stages, and Austin Rover fielded examples of the MG Maestro as well as the SDI. That year's celebrity grid consisted of Penti Arikkala, Stig Blomqvist, Nigel Mansell, Jimmy McRae, Tony Pond, Danny Sullivan, Derek Warwick and John Watson.

There was also a third AR Motorsport rally car and this was based, like the two VUK cars, on a 3500 rather than a Vitesse. The third car was built at Cowley in 1984, wore the registration number A683 NJO, and was entered for the 1984 Middle East Rally Championship. Note that the number A684 NJO was used on one of the TWR rally cars.

The A-VUK cars were replaced for the 1984 season by three new ones, registered as A478 WOE to A480 WOE and prepared by AR Motorsport. Tony Pond drove 478 on that year's Lombard RAC Rally but hit a tree on the first stage. All three of the WOE cars were present at the Austin Rover Rallysprint at Donington in October, where they were driven by eight celebrity drivers, this year's list being Martin Brundle, Marc Duez, Per Eklund, Colin McRae, Nigel Mansell, Michele Mouton, Keke Rosberg and John Watson. 480 was later used by Russell Gooding on the 1985 FIA European Group A Challenge.

TWR Rally Cars

There were only ever three TWR-prepared rally cars, although their identities changed from time to time. As Allan Scott has explained, the rally programme was so low-key in its early days that Austin Rover did not have the necessary paperwork in place. As a result, three of the rally cars carried number plates and tax discs 'borrowed' from Austin Rover company cars: FJO 450Y came from John Davenport's company road car, A379 VUK came from an Austin Rover Motorsport Group 2 rally SDI (see above) and A684 NJO was borrowed from an Austin Rover Cowley pool car.

The three cars were:

TWR 003 Ran as a racer in 1983 and the early part of 1984. Subsequently converted to rally specification

THE ARG RALLY CARS

The list of the ARG rally cars that follows has been prepared with the kind assistance of Ian Elliott and of a number of former Austin Rover Motorsport people. The first four cars were based on Rover 3500 models:

Prototype	GJW 584W, later OOC 272X	Built at Abingdon and Cowley in 1982, this was the Austin Rover rally car prototype. It was based on a 3500 model and appeared in 1982 at the Rallysprint event at Esgair Dafydd. From 1983, the car carried registration number OOC 272X. At the end of the test programme the car was allocated to Ken Wood and Peter Brown, to compete with during the 1983, 1984 and 1985 rally seasons, when it wore Golden Wonder Crisps sponsorship colours.
001	A377 VUK	Long-distance specification rally car, built at Cowley in 1983. Appeared in the 1983 Rallysprint event at Donington Park.
002	A379 VUK	Long-distance specification rally car, built at Cowley in 1983. Appeared in the 1983 Rallysprint event at Donington Park.
003	A683 NJO	Long-distance specification rally car, built at Cowley in 1984. Entered for the 1984 Middle East Rally Championship; did not compete in any ARG Rallysprint events.

The final three cars were based on Rover Vitesse models:

001	A478 WOE	Built at Cowley in 1984. Appeared in the 1984 Rallysprint event at Donington Park.
002	A479 WOE	Built at Cowley in 1984. Appeared in the 1984 Rallysprint event at Donington Park.
003	A480 WOE	Built at Cowley in 1984. Appeared in the 1984 Rallysprint event at Donington Park.

Goodwood, 2014: the car is A480 WOE, one of the three 1984 AR Motorsport rally machines. Note the US-specification headlamps, which were more or less universal on the rally cars.

and registered as B565 AOX.

TWR 006 Built as a rally car. Ran during 1983 and 1984 as FJO 450Y, A379 YUK and A684 NJO, finally becoming B564 AOX in August 1984.

TWR 009 Built as a rally car in 1984 and registered as B563 AOX in August that year.

TWR's initial rally car was built from their bodyshell TWR 006 and was theoretically a Vitesse. It initially carried the registration number FJO 450Y. The car was painted in white with blue stripes and carried TWR and Motul identification decals; it also featured the centre-lock wheels of the racing TWR Vitesse cars.

FJO 450Y was initially sponsored by Herbie Clips, makers of plastic hose clips. It was given a try-out at the Criterium Lucien Bianchi rally in Belgium on 2–4 September 1983. The drivers were Tom Walkinshaw and John Davenport – the latter no doubt keen to compare the TWR rallying SD1 with those prepared by AR Motorsport – but the car did not finish. Walkinshaw was driving and was lying eighth when he crashed. The rear axle was ripped off and the bodyshell was severely damaged.

Nevertheless, a car wearing the registration plates FJO 450Y appeared just a couple of weeks later with Tony Pond at the wheel in the 1983 Rothman's Manx International Rally. The full story is still not clear, but it seems almost certain that the mortal remains of the original car had been rebuilt into a new bodyshell. On this occasion, the car also failed to finish, being put out of the running when a half-shaft failed. TWR 006 then appeared in February 1984 as A379 VUK, driven by Tom Walkinshaw and Rob Arthur in the British Open Rally Championship. In March, it became A684 NJO, and subsequently appeared in the Belgian Rally Championship, driven by Marc Duez and Willy Lux, and in the British National Rally Championship, driven by Tom Walkinshaw and John Davenport. However, its multiple iterations had done their work in the development programme, and now TWR turned to building its definitive rally cars.

There were three of these, registered B563 AOX to B565 AOX. B563 AOX and B565 AOX ran in blue and white livery with Computervision sponsorship in the 1985 season. However, not one of the three was a new car: B565 AOX was converted to rally specification from a race car (it was TWR 003, Peter Lovett's mount in the 1983 season); B564

This was B565 AOX as prepared for Tony Pond to drive in rallies.

Pictured on display at the Silverstone 100 event in 1985, B565 AOX was the best-known of the Computervision-sponsored rally cars.

Brian Goff and Mike Stuart crewed B565 AOX in the Tudor Webasto Manx Rally. Note the differences of livery, headlights and wheels from the car photographed at Silverstone in summer 1985.

B565 AOX again, this time driven by Tony Pond with Mike Aitken.

AOX was TWR 006, had started life as FJO 450Y, and had subsequently carried registration numbers A684 NJO and A379 VUK; and B563 AOX was TWR 009.

What is clear is that B563 AOX and B565 AOX were built for Tony Pond to campaign seriously in the 1985 British Open Rally Championship. Although these were not good years for British rally drivers, the cars were quite successful, winning their class in four rounds with top-ten finishes overall. TWR 003 (confusingly registered as B564 AOX) finished third overall on the 1984 Manx Rally driven by Tony Pond and Rob Arthur. However, Austin Rover's rally focus was already shifting from the big and heavy SDI to the small and nimble four-wheel-drive Metro 6R4. B565 AOX was also driven by Marc Duez and Mike Stuart. The AOX cars also appeared at the Austin Rover Rallysprint event, this time held at Donington at the end of November. The celebrity drivers were Stig Blomqvist, Thierry Boutsen, Martin Brundle, Kalle Grundel, Juha Kankkunen, Nigel Mansell, John Watson and Malcolm Wilson.

CHAPTER TEN

THE SDI AFTERMARKET

Aftermarket accessories and conversions were not something that the Rover marque had ever had to contend with very seriously before the introduction of the SDI. However, the 1970s were a time when aftermarket conversions of all kinds were becoming increasingly popular, driven to some extent by the demand for customized vehicles from the newly oil-rich Middle East. Many people also felt that the SDI, at least in its early form, lacked the luxury appointments that a car of its type deserved. Then there was the fact that the V8 engine had already become a favourite with aftermarket performance specialists, who were only too pleased to find an additional market for their products on a road-going car.

For the most part, the specialists held off for a couple of years against the possibility that Rover might introduce a more up-market model that would nullify their efforts. But by 1979 no such car had reached the market, and the SDI had sold in large enough numbers to provide a pool of potential customers for improvements and upgrades.

The Carawagon Limousine prototype was based on a black V8-S model. This press picture was issued by JRT's Rover Triumph division in 1979.

These pictures show the inside of the Carawagon car. The front head restraints have been removed to give adequate clearance for the division, and rear legroom was probably only barely adequate for a car with limousine pretensions.

Carawagon

Carawagon Coachbuilders Ltd of Sunbury-on-Thames grew out of R. J. Searle Ltd, a Land Rover dealer who specialized in camping and caravan conversions. These took on the Carawagon brand name in the early 1970s, and the name was subsequently adopted by the company's coachbuilding division.

It was probably Carawagon's links with Rover through its Land Rover business that led to it creating a limousine conversion of the SDI. The prototype car seems to have been a black V8-S model registered HRW 266V, and this registration number suggests that it was a Rover-owned car that was supplied to Carawagon for conversion.

The car was given a limousine division trimmed in Draylon fabric to match the interior lining. The division was sloped in order to reduce intrusion into rear-seat legroom. Its top section was made of two sliding panes of safety glass. Built into the lower section were a pair of folding hardwood tables that flanked a central cabinet with a fold-down door that acted as a drinks tray. A bottle compartment and glasses were part of the standard equipment; alternatively, the cabinet could be adapted to contain a tape recorder, radio telephone or other business aids. Optional extras included reading lights, a digital clock, sheepskin rugs, a radio-telephone and a radio cassette player for the rear compartment.

That Rover took an interest in this conversion seems to be confirmed by the fact that Rover Triumph issued two publicity photographs of it in the late summer of 1979, describing it simply as a 'Chauffeur driven Rover' and not mentioning the Carawagon connection. Carawagon also issued their own sales flyer for it, picturing what was almost certainly the same car and noting that the conversion was available for 2300 and 2600 models as well. However, take-up seems to have been very small, and in fact no cars other than the prototype are known to have been completed.

Care le Gant

Care le Gant was a London company that specialized in upmarket add-on accessories in the early 1980s. It introduced a body kit for the facelifted SDI range some time around 1984, with modified front- and rear-end details and oversills with flared flank panels. This kit seems not to have attracted buyers in any quantity.

Care le Gant offered this body kit for the later cars. Note how the rear bumper section obscured the badging. The car pictured was probably a 3500SE model.

This was the Care le Gant logo.

Cartel

Cartel were based at Woking in Surrey and produced body kits for several cars from around 1983, particularly Ford Escorts and Capris. They also manufactured one for the facelifted SD1, which was exhibited at Motorfair in 1983. Made from GRP, the kit was designed to be bonded to the bodywork rather than screwed to it. It consisted of flared front and rear aprons, flared wings and flared sill panels, together with a rear wing spoiler. There were also fairings for the door mirrors and motorized headlamp covers.

The basic kit was priced at £399 plus VAT in January 1984, although the rear panel (with slits cut out to accommodate the tail lights), tail spoiler, mirror fairings and headlamp covers all cost extra, as did fitting.

Ron Haynes Enigma

High Wycombe motor sport specialists Ron Haynes developed a conversion for the V8-engined SD1 called the Enigma, which they made available in summer 1984. For £600, they would raise the power to close on 200bhp; a further

Body kits in the early 1980s were expected to include front spoilers and bumper extensions, wider wheel arches, side sills and rear spoilers with an apron. The Cartel kit for the SDI did not disappoint.

£500 brought new wheels and tyres; £700 was the cost of a high-quality hi-fi system; and a body kit added a further £1,200 to the cost. The full conversion took between two and three weeks, but customers could have part or all of the work carried out on either a new or used SD1. It is not clear how many took up the option.

Janspeed

Janspeed Engineering built up an excellent reputation for its work with turbocharging in the 1970s and by mid-1979 had developed turbocharger conversions for both the 2600 and 3500 models of the SD1. The company was also able to supply uprated wheels, tyres, brakes and sus-

Although wearing what appear to be Vitesse wheels, this is actually a Series I car, fitted with a Janspeed Turbo conversion. The side decals on the demonstrator were an optional extra on customers' cars.

This is the Janspeed twin-turbo conversion on a V8 engine. Note how the carburettors have been relocated from their standard positions.

pension components to match the improved performance of the turbocharged cars.

On the 2600 engine, Janspeed provided a compression plate to reduce the compression ratio in order to prevent misfiring. This was accompanied by an extra-long timing belt so that the standard timing installation could be used. There was a fabricated exhaust manifold that carried a single Roto-Master Turbosonic turbocharger with a Roto-Master wastegate. To enable the correct fuel-air ratio to be maintained when the engine was running on boost, there was a fuel enrichment valve actuated by a pressure-sensitive switch. The twin carburettors of the original engine were also replaced by a single SU, and a boost gauge could be fitted to the dashboard. Janspeed claimed that their turbocharged 2600 was 'very nearly as quick and flexible as the turbocharged 3500 vee-eight while offering a significant saving in initial cost'.

The 3500 conversion cost £1,022.45 before fitting in mid-1979. It depended on twin Roto-Master Turbosonic turbochargers mounted on special cast-iron exhaust manifolds, with wastegates limiting boost pressure to 7psi. The standard carburettors were retained, along with the standard compression ratio. Modified front exhaust pipes and an oil cooler were fitted. The kit also came with a boost gauge. Janspeed claimed a 0–60mph time of 6.6sec, a top speed of 138mph (222km/h) in fifth gear and very much improved mid-range acceleration at all speeds. In July 1979, *Autosport* recorded 7.5sec and 131mph (211km/h), commenting:

> *The surge of power, anywhere between 2,000 and 5,000rpm, was enormous, and it was delivered with complete smoothness. Between 5,000 and 6,000rpm, the power unit began to run out of puff and I obtained the best acceleration figures without ever going above 5,500rpm.*

Janspeed also offered an extractor manifold kit for non-turbocharged 3500 models, which they claimed gave a power increase of around 15 per cent.

In later years, the Janspeed conversion for the 3500 was further upgraded. First came a blow-through conversion using a single Weber carburettor in place of the twin Strombergs that supposedly made the conversion more tractable than the earlier iteration. Later still, an intercooler was added, and these final versions retained the twin carburettors of the factory-built engine.

Kat Designs

Kat Designs were run by professional stylist Simon Saunders, who had worked with both Vauxhall and Aston Martin Tickford. Based at Hanslope in Buckinghamshire, the company had developed and marketed a body kit for the Ford Escort before turning to the Rover. By December 1983, they had a Rover body kit for sale, bearing a strong resemblance to the one they had done for the Escort. The kit consisted of a front dam, two side skirts and a tailgate spoiler, all made of GRP and designed to be easy to fit and easy to remove as well, in case the owner wanted to return the car to standard. The parts could be purchased individually or as a complete kit. The full kit cost £449 plus VAT, or Kat Designs would fit it and paint it as necessary for an all-in cost of £1,095.

Kat Designs also offered interior retrims and, in conjunction with Turbo Technics of nearby Northampton, a high-performance conversion as well. A partial retrim with leather seats and door cards cost £1,195; a full retrim with a redesigned full-width dashboard faced with wood, Wilton carpets, a new headlining and leather over all visible plastic interior elements cost £2,495.

The performance package cost a further £2,900 and brought twin turbochargers with an intercooler for the V8 engine, giving more than 300bhp. Clutch and transmis-

Oselli was one of several companies whose SD1 work focused on performance and handling. This demonstrator appears to have been based on a late-model Vitesse, although the leather upholstery and wing badge suggest it may have started life as a 3500 Vanden Plas.

sion were also uprated, and the car was given Koni dampers and four-caliper front brakes. Wheels were available to suit the customer's taste, but the prototype was fitted with British-made Compomotive items. Kat Designs claimed that their prototype car had been tested to just over 150mph (241km/h), that 0–60mph took about 6sec and that 0–100mph took 15sec.

David Price Racing

David Price Racing had prepared the 'semi-works' SD1s for track racing during 1980 (see Chapter 9) and they put the knowledge gained from that to good use. From March 1981, they offered a high-performance conversion of the SD1 as a dual-purpose track and road car.

David Price Racing focused on performance conversions of the SD1, although customers could specify whatever else they wanted on their cars. This one, photographed in 1981 when fairly recently converted, has aftermarket front and rear spoilers and the Viking badge conversion (see below), as well as an attractive use of contrasting paint for the crease along the side of the body.

The SMC Cabriolet

SMC Engineering was a Bristol company founded in 1982 that specialized in aftermarket conversions and also built prototype and pre-production cars for mainstream manufacturers. The company is probably best known for its conversions of Land Rovers and Range Rovers, but it was also responsible for a single cabriolet version of the SD1.

The cabriolet was built as the prototype for a volume production run – SMC hoped to sell the car in the USA and possibly on the European continent, although there were no plans for UK sales. The basic design was done by Peter Jones, SMC's managing director.

SMC began by buying a second-hand gold 3500 (probably a 1979 car) from Garage Vermeulen, in the Borgerhout district of Antwerp. The tail section and most of the roof were removed, and a Webasto-type fabric sunroof and folding fabric rear section containing the rear window were added. The rear end was neatly redesigned with an enclosed boot, and the fabric roof sections were designed to fold down into a well in front of this.

The Kat body kit was used to give SMC's cabriolet conversion additional presence.

VIKING BADGE

On the early cars, the skeletal Rover badge proved a source of annoyance to many customers and an aftermarket alternative became available by 1980 or 1981. Apparently moulded from resin, this was essentially a Viking's head motif (similar to that on the Rover P4 models) on a plinth that was shaped to fit the curved nose of the SD1's bonnet. The new badge had an all-over gunmetal finish. Although there was an initial flurry of interest when it appeared, it seems not to have been widely adopted and appears to have been available only by mail order from the manufacturer.

This was the replacement Viking's head bonnet badge available from an unidentified aftermarket supplier.

SMC wanted the car to be 'loud' for the US market, as Peter Jones explained it, so they added a KAT body kit of front spoiler, side sills, rear apron and rear spoiler. Wide wheels and tyres were fitted, and the whole car was painted white with red highlights and coachline. According to Jones, British Leyland were aware of the project but declined to become involved; he suspected that money was too tight at the time for them to take more of an interest.

The car was first shown in public in Brussels, for a BL dealer, and soon afterwards was shipped to New York. By this time, BL's own sales of the SD1 had long since ceased, and the specialist importer who intended to handle sales ran

This was the SMC cabriolet as originally built, although the car was looking a little tired in this photograph, dating from late 1993 or early 1994.

This more recent picture shows the SMC car as it survives today. Note the shape of the special boot, and how the side window sections remain in place when the roof is open.

into financial difficulties, partly because of the cost of getting the design certificated for US sales.

The prototype was eventually shipped back to SMC in the UK, and was registered to Peter Jones himself on 23 May 1984. He ran it for a while with the registration plate OD 1. It was subsequently sold on, having two UK owners and then going to a Belgian enthusiast in January 1994. The car still exists, and at the time of writing was in the Netherlands, having lost its KAT body kit but retaining the original cabriolet configuration.

Another recent picture, taken shortly after the car had been fitted with a new roof, shows the two fabric sections clearly.

Wood & Pickett

Wood & Pickett was an established specialist in coachwork modifications. Although founded in 1947, it had come to public attention in the 1960s with upgraded Minis that were much liked by celebrities of the time. From 1978, the company had offered a series of upgrades for the Range Rover, and by 1980 they had decided to turn their attention to the Rover SDI. They marketed their conversions as the Rover Prestige, although each car would have been individually created from a menu of options.

The Wood & Pickett demonstrator car was registered as 99 EFC, although the car went through several changes and the number may well have been transferred from one car to another. In early guise, it was a silver car with a red side decal and aftermarket styled alloy wheels. In later guise, and as tested by *Autocar* magazine for its issue of 4 October 1980, it was a two-tone black and silver car with chromed wire wheels.

No doubt the company would have performed its upgrades on any SDI that a customer had brought to them,

The Wood & Pickett demonstrator, 99 EFC, started life looking more like a performance car than a luxury conversion. Note the aftermarket Viking badge, and the front spoiler, both of which are also seen on the David Price Racing conversion shown earlier.

ABOVE AND BELOW: This was the later incarnation of 99 EFC, now in black and silver and with wire wheels and other obvious modifications. The left-hand rear badge reads 'Rover Prestige'; the badge on the right reads 'Wood & Pickett of London'.

Wood & Pickett were noted for their high-quality interior work, seen here on the later version of 99 EFC. Note the built-up dashboard with its polished wood facing, the wooden door cappings, and the electrically adjustable Recaro seats.

but the demonstrator in October 1980 was based on a 2600 automatic. The total cost of the upgrades to this car was £9,377.03, which was more than the cost price of the basic car (£8,637.98), making the whole package cost a huge £18,015.01, inclusive of VAT. According to the *Autocar* article:

> *Wood and Pickett point out that their primary objective was to take the modern Rover and restore some of the feel of luxury exuded by its illustrious predecessors. The restoration of walnut veneer to the interior is the focal point of the plan, and the rest are optional extras, enabling an owner to spend £500 or £5,000 or more.'*

The Rover Prestige added a built-up dashboard extension that ran the full width of the standard facia and was faced with burr walnut. The standard instruments were retained, and there was an additional glovebox on the passenger's side. This was accompanied by matching wooden door cappings. A wood-rimmed or black leather-trimmed steering wheel was available, and Recaro sports front seats with multi-way electric adjustment were a further option; when these were ordered, the entire interior was retrimmed in Draylon cloth, which was fashionable at the time. Stereo speakers could be incorporated in the head restraints at extra cost, and an electric glass sunroof could be ordered as well.

On the outside, a functional front air dam with inset fog lights could be matched by a spoiler at the bottom of the tailgate. Paint details and finelining were to the customer's choice, and priced accordingly, and the chromed wire wheels were designed to take 185/70 VR 14 tyres that, on the demonstrator, were by Dunlop.

Further options were a digital keyless entry system, operated by a keypad located on the driver's side B-pillar, an onboard fuel and speed computer, and an electronic cruise control. To improve performance, Wood & Pickett fitted a Janspeed turbocharger conversion.

There seems to be absolutely no information about how many of these conversions were built. However, the Rover Prestige certainly remained rare.

CHAPTER ELEVEN

BUYING AND OWNING AN SDI

The poor build quality of the early SDIs and the general taint of unreliability that affected all British Leyland cars of the 1970s and 1980s meant that large numbers of viable cars were scrapped quite early in their lives. The thirst of the V8 engine was another factor that persuaded owners not to persevere with these cars as they became older and began to need work. Values fell and a number of otherwise quite reasonable examples were bought cheaply to be turned into customized cars.

As a result, relatively few have survived to the present day in original condition. Values of all but the very best have remained low, with a gradual upward trend led by the Vitesse. However, the good news is that there is no real shortage of parts or expertise for these models, and that ownership can be an enjoyable experience. An SDI is a strikingly good-looking car, with strong performance from the more powerful versions, a comfortable ride and good handling for such a large car. Refinement is surprisingly high, and both everyday maintenance and many restoration jobs are straightforward. However, major restoration is likely to be both difficult and costly, so buying a cheap and rough car at a time when prices of good ones are relatively low is likely to prove a false economy. Generally, it is best not to buy a car that has been neglected, at any price.

As for parts and expertise, it is worth remembering that Rimmer Brothers (www.rimmerbros.co.uk) have become the world's leading parts specialists for the SDI, and that the Rover SDI Club (www.roversdIclub.net) is home to a

There was a wide choice of SDI models, although the actual choice on the market today has been reduced by a high rate of attrition. This is a 1976 model; registered on 31 July 1976, the first day the cars went on sale in the UK, it was the 803rd car built.

At the other end of the production run, this is a late-model Vitesse from 1986. The survival rate of the Vitesse models is much higher than that of the earlier cars.

number of experts or at least experienced owners who can usually help if problems arise. There are also many aftermarket specialists, especially for the V8 engine, who can offer ways of improving the performance of these cars.

All SD1s share a common structure, so these notes of advice on buying begin with the problems that may be encountered in that, and then go on to look at the different interiors, engines, gearboxes, and so on.

Body Structure

Early SD1 bodyshells were notorious for paint problems. Gas trapped underneath the paint caused blistering which promoted rust in the metal underneath. Almost every early car will by now have had some attention to its paintwork for this very reason. The problem was not really eradicated until the start of the 1980 season. The facelifted cars introduced in 1982 were generally free from problems of this sort, although that does not make them immune to either cosmetic or rust problems.

The pressure-ventilation system has kept the sills of most SD1s free from the terminal rust that attacked the sills of many of their contemporaries. However, the outer sills may well show signs of rust, typically caused when paint has been damaged by stones thrown up from the road. With luck, this rust will be fairly superficial, but in bad cases it will penetrate right through the outer sill panel – in which case moisture may well have got into the sill cavity and caused more extensive damage.

Wheel arch edges can also rust, especially if they have been damaged and cheaply repaired and, of course, especially on pre-1980 cars. Both front and rear arches may be affected. The bottoms of the doors may also rust through, partly again after paint damage caused by gravel or stones thrown up from the road, but partly because water may gather inside the doors if the drain holes have become blocked. New door skins are available and will rectify prob-

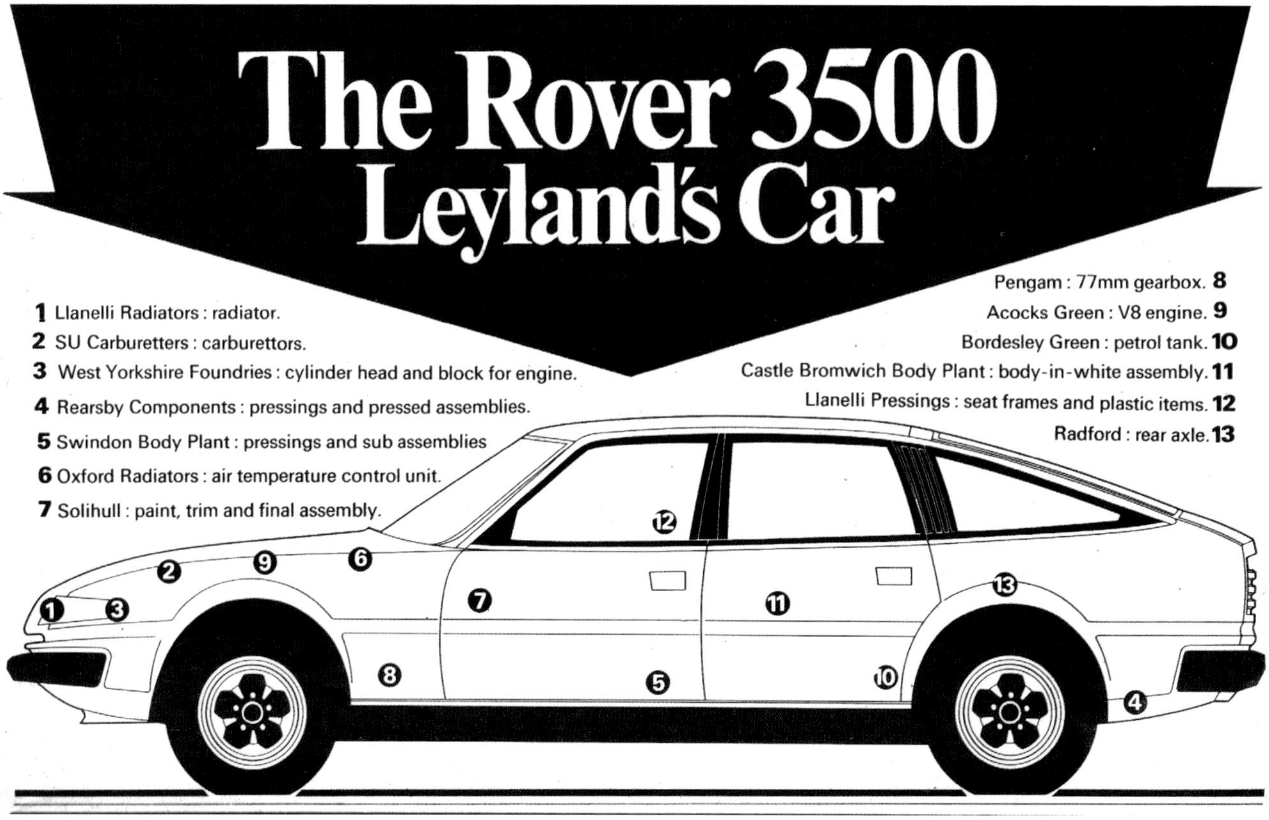

In this early illustration taken from the company's newspaper, the Leyland Mirror, the various suppliers and factories that contributed to the early cars are proudly listed. Note also the 'Leyland's Car' subheading, which reflects the time in the mid-1970s when marque identities were being suppressed in favour of a corporate Leyland image.

lems of the first sort. However, rust that has taken hold of the door inners at the bottom will be much more difficult to sort out.

Water leaks cause problems with the floor of the passenger cabin and the floor of the boot. Wet carpets are an obvious giveaway, but it is advisable to take a good look underneath apparently dry ones as well. In the passenger cabin, water typically gets in through leaky windscreens, and sometimes as a result of blockages in the drain tubes for the scuttle air intake. In the boot, water gets in through the big hatchback, but very commonly also through the apertures for the rear light units. These can easily be sealed more effectively with mastic. If water has been sitting in the spare wheel well for a long period of time, there is a good chance that this will have rotted through as well.

Both bonnet and tailgate can rust, too. The bonnet may rust at its leading edge, if paint damage from flying stones

Rust has accounted for large numbers of early SD1s. Even though this 1976 car was carefully maintained from new, paint problems surfaced in the most unlikely places and led to the type of rust seen here.

The SD1 made an excellent tow car, and in 1978 won a 'Tow Car of the Year' award. If a pre-facelift car is fitted with a towbar, it is wise not to remove it: it helps to protect the vulnerable rear bumper when reversing!

is not rectified, but it can also rust on the inside, where the outer skin meets the strengthening ribs. The tailgate is most likely to rust at its bottom edge, around the plastic air vents and the housings for the number-plate lights, caused by trapped water. The front panel below the bumper and between the headlights often rusts, and at the rear there may well be rust in the seams between the rear panel and the side panels.

On the upper bodywork, it is advisable to check for rust around the windscreen. Although this was bonded to the shell when manufactured, the bonding on replacement windscreens sometimes fails to seal the join completely, allowing water to sit between glass and metalwork and setting up rust in the windscreen frame. Cars with sunroofs deserve an extra careful examination, not just around the sunroof aperture itself but also lower down where rust caused by leaking or blocked sunroof drain tubes can occur. The drain holes in the sunroof frame should be checked for blockage, too. If the tubes are sound, they can usually be blown through with an airline.

On pre-facelift cars, it is worth checking the condition of the rear bumper. Poor visibility to the rear when reversing led to many people denting their rear bumpers when they could not see a post or other object low down behind the car. The almost total absence of this kind of damage on the facelifted cars is a clear illustration that their enlarged tailgate window did have a practical value.

Electrical System

Although an SD1 has a very simple electrical system by modern car standards, it was considerably more complicated than those that Rover (and Triumph) had used before. It is therefore wise to check that everything electrical works as it should when looking at a car for sale.

The first and most obvious check is to ensure that all the warning lights and gauges work. On the pre-1982 cars, for example, the handbrake warning light is notoriously fickle. Some post-1982 cars have the additional complication of a trip computer, which is not an essential element in enjoying the car but is certainly something else that can and does go wrong.

Central locking also gives trouble. The original Lucas type was replaced in early 1983 (at VIN 271981) by a Keikert system, which is generally more reliable. Some cars with the Keikert system have a habit of unlocking themselves more or less immediately after the locking mechanism has been activated; service literature identifies those affected as cars built up to VIN 298523 and puts the cause down to transient electrical pulses through the control unit. Electric windows are another common source of problems, although the cause of the trouble is more likely to be with the switch than with the motor itself. On those models with an electrically powered sunroof, it is advisable to check that the panel opens and closes fully and without jamming.

The V8-engined cars built before the 1982 facelift had a Lucas Opus electronic ignition; those letters stood for Oscillating Pick-Up System. This was bold new technology in the mid-1970s, dispensing with the traditional contact breaker, but it tended to break down over time. The problem was temperature-related, and as a result an engine that had stopped because of ignition failure would usually restart successfully later. The Opus system can be identified easily by an aluminium-cased ballast resistor pack located near the coil.

On 1983–84 cars, the Opus system was replaced by a Lucas Limb system, which can be recognized by an amplifier pack attached to the coil. This sometimes exhibits the same problems as the earlier Opus type. From 1985, a third system was used, an updated version of the Limb type, recognizable by its miniaturized amplifier (a small black box with two Lucar terminals) attached directly to the distributor.

Interior

Two problems in particular affect the interior. One is that component quality (especially on pre-facelift cars) was never great, and the other is water ingress. The fit and finish of the instrument panel on early cars, and of the associated fuse box, was frequently poor. Dark stains on the carpets mean that water has been allowed to get in and has stood for a long time, so even if it has now been banished, it may have caused deeper problems.

There are sometimes troubles with the adjustment mechanism of the front seats on pre-1980 cars, and also with the locking mechanism for the rear seat back. The post-1980 front seats are usually trouble-free, although it is always worth checking for seized reclining mechanisms. The quality of the early upholstery was not high, with the result that interiors can look quite worn; the materials used on post-1980 cars were very much better and seem to last longer. Remember that the Vitesse had special upholstery and that seats taken from other models will not be suitable as replacements.

Door trims on the pre-1982 cars can distort if they have become wet (as can happen if water has got past the window seals), and they generally feel quite flimsy and poorly made. The post-1982 type are very much better in every respect. Pre-1982 cars may also suffer from sagging headlinings, when the fabric facing material separates from the compressed fibre backing pad when the glue used to bond the two together fails. The only real solution is to replace the entire assembly. This problem is less common on post-1982 models.

A particular oddity on pre-1982 cars is that the pull-up choke lever on the centre console fails, so it is worth checking that the lever still does operate the choke correctly.

Suspension, Steering and Brakes

By modern standards, SDIs are no longer the outstanding cars they once were. The ride remains compliant but is harsher at low speeds than on newer designs; the steering is responsive but not as razor-sharp as many more recent types; and the handling is distinctly average, although still quite good for such a large car.

The SDI's suspension design was deliberately simple but was certainly not immune to wear. Problems commonly arise in the joints and linkages of the front suspension, and the rear dampers tend to have fairly short lives. If the rear end bounces a lot, the dampers need replacement. Many of the more expensive models had a Boge Nivomat self-levelling system on the rear suspension, and replacement dampers for this are considerably more expensive than standard dampers. Otherwise, the rear suspension is mostly trouble-free – but the axle itself can fail if oil leaks from the differential are ignored.

Second-hand parts from cars that have been broken for spares are not hard to find. This is the front subframe, with the lower suspension arms and anti-roll bar in place. There are seats and a dashboard in the background – but when looking for second-hand parts, bear in mind that there were many changes of specification over the years.

Most SD1s had power-assisted steering, so it is advisable to check the level of fluid in the PAS reservoir and to look for leaks. A certain amount of groaning from the system under lock is quite common, but there should be no knocking noises. A good test is to turn the steering from lock to lock when the car is stationary (bear in mind that this may put some strain on the system, so be gentle) and to listen carefully. It is not unknown for the steering column itself to be loose, so a good pull on the steering wheel at 9 o'clock, 12 o'clock, 3 o'clock and 6 o'clock will be a worthwhile test.

The brakes were another simple element in the SD1's design. There are discs at the front (with four-piston calipers on Vitesse, Vanden Plas EFi and some police models) and drums at the rear. Everything about the system is straightforward, but cars driven with enthusiasm get through front pads quite quickly, especially those cars with automatic gearboxes.

Engines

The character of an SD1 is largely defined by its engine (and, to a lesser extent, by its gearbox) and anyone whose sights are set on a V8-powered 3500 is likely to be disappointed with anything less. Performance is not outstanding by modern standards but all SD1s are more than capable of keeping up with everyday traffic. A comparison table showing acceleration, maximum speeds and typical fuel consumption figures is provided below.

The most powerful engines are of course the injected V8s in the Vitesse and Vanden Plas EFi models. When in good health, they give a smooth power delivery right through the rev range with a very satisfying thrust from quite low crankshaft speeds. The so-called 'twin plenum' engines fitted to many late-model Vitesses were never claimed by Rover to deliver more power than standard (the special injection system was fitted only to homologate it for racing) and acceleration in everyday conditions is not discernibly different. It is worth knowing, by the way, that many more Vitesse

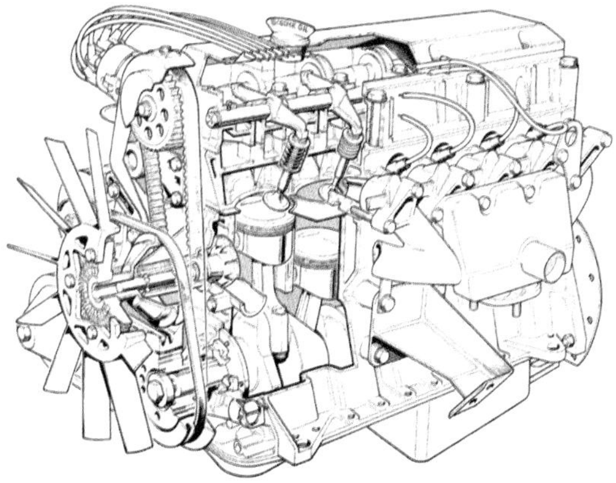

Understandably, perhaps, most SD1 enthusiasts want to own a V8-engined car. However, the 6-cylinder engines, especially the larger 2.6-litre type, give very satisfying performance as well as better fuel economy. The main thing is to make sure that sludge does not block the oilways in the cylinder head.

models now have twin plenums than were ever built with them when the cars were new. If a genuine twin-plenum model is the aim, make sure there is documentary evidence that a car is the real thing.

Most SDI enthusiasts are seduced by the idea of the V8 engine and there is no doubt that the engine (even in carburettor form) gives very satisfying performance together with a much-admired exhaust note. The engine itself is long-lived, as long as regular oil changes have been carried out. If not, camshaft wear and tappet rattle (when sludge causes the hydraulic lifters that take up clearances to seize) will result. Overheating is likely to cause head-gasket problems, as these are all-alloy engines, so check the coolant level on a car for sale. As the Rover V8 engine was used in many other cars, and nearly a million were built, spares are plentiful.

However, the 6-cylinder engines were also extremely good units, with a notably smooth power delivery. The 2600 in particular gives performance almost equal to that of a carburettor V8, although it does so in a less relaxed manner than the bigger engine. A 2600 engine will normally give noticeably better fuel economy than a V8. The smaller 2300 gives surprisingly good performance in view of the weight

SDI PERFORMANCE FIGURES

Note that these figures were for the cars when they were new. Wear and tear means that relatively few survivors will be quite this good.

Model	0–60mph	Max speed	Overall fuel consumption	Source
2000	12.4sec	104mph (167km/h)	22.8mpg (12.4ltr/100km)	*Autocar*, 20 March 1982
2000 automatic	14.1sec	101mph (162km/h)	32.1mpg (1) (8.8ltr/100km)	Austin Rover, March 1985
2300 manual (four-speed)		No figures available (2)		
2300 manual (five-speed)	11.9sec	109mph (175km/h)	24.0mpg (11.8ltr/100km) (average)	*Autocar*, 3 June 1978
2300 automatic	12.5sec	109mph (175km/h)	28.1mpg (1) (10.1ltr/100km)	Austin Rover, March 1985
2400SD Turbo	14.2sec	103.4mph (166km/h)	29.6mpg (9.6ltr/100km)	*Motor*, 30 October 1982
2600 manual	10.4sec	116.1mph (187km/h)	18.9mpg (15ltr/100km)	*Motor*, 4 July 1981
2600 automatic	13.8sec	110mph (177km/h)	23mpg (12.3ltr/100km)	*Autocar*, 14 July 1979
3500 manual	8.9sec	125mph (201km/h)	22.5mpg (12.6ltr/100km)	*Motor*, 31 July 1976
3500 automatic	9.8sec	119mph (191km/h)	20mpg (14.2ltr/100km)	*Autocar*, 20 August 1977
3500 manual (US specification)	10.0sec	116mph (187km/h)	20.5mpg (3) (13.8ltr/100km)	*Road & Track*, April 1980
Vitesse manual	7.1sec	135.4mph (218km/h)	22.3mpg (12.7ltr/100km)	*Motor*, 29 March 1986
Vitesse automatic	8.2sec	133mph (214km/h)	24.1mpg (1) (11.7ltr/100km)	Austin Rover, March 1985
Vanden Plas EFi	8.9sec	129.5mph (208km/h)	20.2mpg (14ltr/100km)	*Motor*, 15 December 1984

(1) Fuel figures quoted by the manufacturer were often very different from those obtained in independent road tests. For example, in March 1985 Austin Rover quoted 33.5mpg (8.4ltr/100km) as a composite average for the 2000 with manual gearbox; compare that with the 22.8mpg (12.4ltr/100km) obtained by *Autocar* on road test.

(2) The four-speed 2300 would have accelerated to 60mph as quickly as the five-speed model. Its top speed would probably have been slightly lower and its fuel consumption slightly worse.

(3) The fuel consumption figure for the US-specification 3500 appears to be shown in miles per Imperial gallon (the US gallon is about 0.8 of the Imperial gallon used in the UK). *Car and Driver* magazine for May 1980 quoted an estimated average fuel economy of 15mpg using US gallons and the EPA (Environmental Protection Agency) test criteria.

of car it has to haul around, but that weight counts against its fuel consumption and a 2300 – particularly if used hard – may struggle to better the economy of a 2600.

The two 6-cylinder engines depend on a toothed rubber belt to drive the camshaft, and this must be renewed at regular (but long) intervals. The biggest weakness of both engines is that the oil feed to the camshaft and valve rockers can become blocked with sludge and the consequent lack of lubrication leads very rapidly to component failure. The longer oil-change intervals recommended for the post-1982 cars (12,000 miles as against the earlier 6,000 miles) only made this situation worse. In the late 1980s and early 1990s, an aftermarket warning system was available. Made by Rosdilec, and with variants known as Rosdi, Rosdiwatch and Rosdiman, it illuminated a dashboard light if top-end oil pressure dropped below a certain level, which was an early indication of the sludge build-up that caused oil starvation and engine failure.

The 4-cylinder 2000 engine is rather ordinary, lacking both the smoothness and the power of the sixes. However, it is a durable engine and, as most parts are common to the O-series engines used in cars such as the Austin Ambassador, there is also a good supply of spares. Note that there are differences between the SDI and Ambassador versions of the engine, so it is important to check when ordering parts.

Finally, the turbocharged 2400 diesel engine deserves a better reputation than it has. It has plenty of bottom-end torque and is pleasantly economical. However, acceleration is only adequate, and the engine is much less refined than the petrol types used in the SDI. Spare parts and expertise are not hard to find, as an intercooled version of the engine was also used in Range Rovers between 1986 and 1989.

Gearboxes

All versions of the SDI except for the Vanden Plas EFi were available with the LT77 five-speed manual gearbox. This is a strong and long-lived unit that rarely gives trouble. However, any shortage of oil is likely to cause an unpleasant rattle that will probably be accompanied by vibration of the gear lever. If this is ignored, rapid wear will follow. When cold (and in cold weather), the synchromesh between first and second gear may cause upchanges to be difficult or even impossible. The best cure for this is to replace the gearbox oil with ATF automatic transmission fluid.

The only SDI model not available with an automatic gearbox was the 2400SD Turbo. Worth remembering is that SDI automatics are all three-speed types, and therefore

The SDI is recognized as an enthusiast's car outside the UK, too. This 1983 2600SE was photographed at a classic event in Switzerland in 2015. Note that the enthusiastic owner has fitted it with pre-facelift alloy wheels and has had to replace a damaged bumper bracket with large bolts.

less flexible, less responsive and sometimes rougher than modern automatics with a greater number of speeds. The automatics are best suited to the larger engines – V8s and 2600s – and do not allow the smaller 2300 and 2000 engines to give their best.

The first SDI automatics were all Borg Warner type 65 gearboxes. These were replaced by the newer type 66 in 1981 (at VIN 170576), which had some internal differences but did not affect the driving experience. From early 1983, a GM 180 gearbox (from the GM transmissions plant in Strasbourg) replaced the Borg Warner type, and some people argue that this is a smoother and more robust gearbox. The change to the GM 180 took place at VIN numbers 270276 (3500), 270325 (2600), 277453 (2300) and 281903 (2000). All automatic Vitesse and all Vanden Plas EFi models had the GM gearbox.

On all automatic gearboxes, check that drive and reverse both engage without a noticeable thump or kick (which could of course be caused by an engine idling speed that is too high). All these gearboxes have an inhibitor switch that prevents the engine from being started when a gear is selected (in other words, the starter will only operate when the selector is in N or P), but the switch can go out of adjustment and it is advisable to check that it is functioning properly. Changes should be smooth, both up and down the gears, although they will be more noticeable than in a modern automatic.

Individual Models

There is a wide variety of SDI models, but it is only human nature that enthusiasts tend to want the ones that offer the best performance or are for some reason rare. That tends to focus attention on the high-performance Vitesse and Vanden Plas EFi, and on the otherwise rare V8-S and 1980–81 3500 Vanden Plas. Other rarities include the Australian fuel-injected cars (although not in Australia itself, of course), the North American models and the South African-built cars. The automatic Vitesse is one of the rarest of all models, with just 363 cars built, although those who want the Vitesse for its high performance are often not keen on a version whose performance is slightly blunted by its transmission.

The Vanden Plas EFi probably offers the best of everything that the SDI range had to offer, but the cars are rare: only 1,113 were built. The V8-S is rarer still, as only

The V8 engine has attracted a number of enthusiasts whose interest lies in high performance and customizing. This custom-finished engine in a late-model car looks superb and no doubt delivers more power and torque than the standard type.

More customizing: this late-model V8-engined car was turned into a pick-up in the 1990s. However, SD1s are now rare enough for most owners to want to preserve them as they were.

As Chapter 3 explains, an estate derivative was on the cards. This one is a high-quality conversion made by an enthusiast, using the back body of a Volvo estate car.

1,040 cars were built and small numbers survive: these were among the last SD1s to be painted by the original method, so they have succumbed to rust, while problems with their additional equipment have often persuaded owners to give up on them.

Overall – and of course judgements like this can only be subjective – the best buys from the rest of the range are the 3500 and 2600 models, in each case probably with a manual gearbox. The higher the equipment level, the more the car feels like a 'proper' or traditional Rover, and that can be an important factor for some buyers. Some people prefer the purity of the original David Bache design as seen on the pre-1982 cars, but this has to be balanced against their generally inferior build quality. Others are quite content with the facelifted cars, which generally are likely to give far less trouble in use.

CAR AND MAJOR COMPONENT IDENTIFICATION

VIN

The VIN (Vehicle Identification Number) for all cars assembled in the UK conforms to an internationally standardized pattern. It consists of seventeen digits, of which the first eleven provide specification details and the final six are a sequential serial number. Note, however, that cars did not always come down the assembly lines in strict numerical order. Different prefix codes were used on the 1982 and later models; note that a hyphen between prefix and serial number is shown here only for clarity and is not present in the VIN stamped on the car.

The earliest cars did not have the initial SAR prefix.

An example on a first-series car might be SARRRWVF3AA-000803. This decodes as follows:

SAR	Rover, UK (manufacturer code)	
RR	SD1 (type code)	
W	5-door hatchback (body type code)	
V	3500 (engine size)	
		K = 2300
		M = 2600
F	3500 (model code)	
		A = 2300
		U = 2600
3	RHD, automatic (steering and transmission code)	
		1 = RHD, four-speed manual
		2 = LHD, four-speed manual
		4 = LHD, automatic
		7 = RHD, five-speed manual
		8 = LHD, five-speed manual
A		1976–1979 models (series code)
		B = 1980–1981 models
A	Solihull (place of manufacture)	
000803	Serial number	

A theoretical example of a second-series VIN might be SARRRAWB7CM-215001. This decodes as follows:

SAR	Rover, UK (manufacturer code)	
RR	SD1 (type code)	
A	Base (trim level)	
		E = Vitesse
		F = SE
		H = S
		M = Vanden Plas
		X = Police
W	5-door hatchback (body type code)	
B	2000 (engine type code)	
		E = 2400
		K = 2300
		M = 2600
		V = 3500 carburettor
		Z = 3500 EFi
3	RHD, automatic (steering and transmission code)	
		4 = LHD, automatic
		7 = RHD, five-speed manual
		8 = LHD, five-speed manual
M	Cowley (place of manufacture)	
		A = Solihull (found on very early cars only)
215001		Serial number

Serial Number

All Solihull-built SD1s were numbered in the same sequence. Rover production figures show the following first and last numbers for each calendar year of production. (Note that calendar year and model year are not the same thing.)

Year	Serial numbers
1975	000001 to 000093
1976	000094 to 008845
1977	008846 to 034556

1978	034459 to 084059
1979	083892 to 132124
1980	132121 to 151137
	155001 to 163945
1981	163946 to 192668
1982	200001 to 215736
	249999 to 274170
1983	274171 to 307398
1984	307099 to 327045
1985	326046 to 342094
	155001 to 163945
1986	342095 to 345831

Notes

1 The overlaps of some of these sequences illustrate the fact that cars were not completed in strict serial number order.

2 It is not clear why two separate sequences were used in 1980. The break may have occurred with the start of 1981 model-year production, but this is not proven.

3 It is not clear why two separate sequences were used in 1982. The quantities in the earlier sequence appear too high for the break to be associated with the change from Solihull to Cowley production.

Body Number

Body numbers have a five-figure prefix, a six-figure serial number and a single-letter suffix. The suffix letter was probably always L. A typical body number is 1SD1S002052L, which belongs to the car with serial number 000803.

1SD1S	standard body
2SD1S	body with sunroof

Engine Number

Engine numbers contain an engine type prefix code followed by a serial number. These are separated by a hyphen here for clarity, but the hyphen is not found in the numbers stamped on the engine. In each case, the initial number in the sequence is shown. Note that service exchange engines carry an S prefix (eg S10C-012345).

2000

20V/973/AHH-100101	manual gearbox
20V/974/AHH-100101	Borg Warner automatic gearbox
20C/A18/AHH-100101	GM automatic gearbox

2300

10C-00001	manual gearbox, Series 1
11C-00001	automatic gearbox, Series 1
10C-70000	manual gearbox, Series 2
11C-60000	automatic gearbox, Series 2
16C-00001	manual gearbox, S specification and air conditioning, Series 2 1982 model year
17C-00001	automatic gearbox, S specification and air conditioning, Series 2 1982 model year

2400 diesel

4HT-0000001	manual gearbox

2600

12C-00001	manual gearbox, Series 1
13C-00001	automatic gearbox, Series 1
12C-80000	manual gearbox and S specification, Series 2
13C-70000	automatic gearbox and S specification, Series 2
14C-00001	manual gearbox, Series 2; 2600SE and for Switzerland, 1983 model year 'A10 Spec'
15C-00001	automatic gearbox and air conditioning, Series 2; 1982 model year and for Switzerland, 1983 model year 'A10 Spec'
18C-00001	manual gearbox and S or Vanden Plas specification, Series 2
19C-00001	automatic gearbox and S or Vanden Plas specification, Series 2

3500 carburettor

10A-00001A	9.35:1 compression and SU carburettors; for manual gearbox
11A-00001A	9.35:1 compression and SU carburettors; for automatic gearbox
14A-00001A	8.13:1 compression, Zenith carburettors and air injection; Swedish specification; for automatic gearbox
15A-00001A	8.13:1 compression, Zenith carburettors and air injection; for air conditioning (Phase 1 and 1A types); Australian specification; for automatic gearbox
16A-00001A	8.13:1 compression, Zenith carburettors and air injection; for air conditioning (Phase 1 type); Japanese specification; for automatic gearbox
17A-00001A	9.35:1 compression, SU carburettors;

	for air conditioning; V8-S and 1981 model year Vanden Plas specifications; for manual gearbox
18A-00001A	9.35:1 compression, SU carburettors; for air conditioning; V8-S and 1981 model year Vanden Plas specifications; for automatic gearbox
19A-00001A	8.13:1 compression, Zenith carburettors and air injection; air conditioning (Phase 2 type); Australian specification; for manual gearbox
23A-00001A	8.13:1 compression, Zenith carburettors; air conditioning; 40ROW (see note 2) specification; for manual gearbox
24A-00001A	8.13:1 compression, Zenith carburettors; air conditioning; 40ROW specification; for automatic gearbox
25A-00001A	8.13:1 compression, Zenith carburettors; 40ROW specification; for manual gearbox
26A-00001A	8.13:1 compression, Zenith carburettors; 40ROW specification; for automatic gearbox
27A-00001A	8.13:1 compression, Zenith carburettors; 50ROW specification; for manual gearbox
28A-00001A	8.13:1 compression, Zenith carburettors; 50ROW specification; for automatic gearbox
34A-00001A	9.35:1 compression, Zenith carburettors and air injection; 1983 model-year Swiss specification; for manual gearbox
36A-00001A	9.35:1 compression, Zenith carburettors and air injection; 1983 model year Swiss specification; for automatic gearbox
38A-00001A	9.35:1 compression, factory reconditioned engine; for manual gearbox
39A-00001A	9.35:1 compression, factory reconditioned engine; for automatic gearbox

Notes

1 A 29A-prefix engine with 9.35:1 compression was prepared for a Nigerian Police order that was cancelled.

2 The 40-degree ('40ROW') specification denotes an engine tested to run satisfactorily at up to 40°C ambient temperature. The 50-degree ('50ROW') specification denotes an engine tested to run satisfactorily at up to 50°C ambient temperature. ROW stands for 'Rest of the World' and is used to denote a non-US specification.

3500 injection

12A-000001A	8.13:1 compression and air conditioning; USA specification; for manual gearbox
13A-000001A	8.13:1 compression and air conditioning; USA specification; for automatic gearbox
20A-00001A	8.13:1 compression and air conditioning; Australian specification (1982 model year onwards); for manual gearbox
21A-00001A	8.13:1 compression and air conditioning; Australian specification (1982 model year onwards); for automatic gearbox
22A-00001A	8.13:1 compression and air conditioning; Japanese specification, 1980–1981; for automatic gearbox
30A-000001A	9.75:1 compression; Vitesse specification; for manual gearbox
31A-000001A	9.75:1 compression; Vitesse specification; for automatic gearbox
32A-000001A	9.75:1 compression and air conditioning; Vitesse specification; for manual gearbox
33A-000001A	9.75:1 compression and air conditioning; Vitesse specification; for automatic gearbox
40A-00001A	air conditioning; 50-degree specification for Saudi Arabia, 1985 model year; for manual gearbox
41A-00001A	air conditioning; 50-degree specification for Saudi Arabia, 1985 model year; for automatic gearbox
42A-00001A	Finnish specification; for automatic gearbox

Gearbox Number

Manual gearboxes

The manual gearboxes have a three-digit prefix code which is followed by a five-digit serial number and a single-letter suffix code. The suffix code changed to indicate gearbox improvements, and is an A, B, C or D. A typical manual gearbox number might therefore be 16A12345B.

The prefix codes were as follows:

16A	Four-speed, for 2300; A, B and C suffixes only
17A	Five-speed, for 2300 and 2600; all suffixes
19A	Five-speed, for 3500; all suffixes
22A	Five-speed, for Police-specification 3500; all suffixes

23A	Five-speed, for Police-specification 2600; all suffixes
25A	Five-speed for CKD models; all suffixes
26A	Five-speed for 2400SD; C and D suffixes only
27A	Five-speed, for 2000; C and D suffixes only
28A	Five-speed, for Vitesse

A-suffix gearboxes were used only on very early cars. The B-suffix gearboxes (1977–1979 approximately) had larger bearings, and the C-suffix gearboxes (1979–1984 approximately) had further enlarged bearings.

The D-suffix gearbox was initially developed for the Vitesse. It featured needle roller bearings on the mainshaft instead of bronze bushes, a nut to hold the fifth gear to the layshaft instead of a circlip, and an oil catcher to improve lubrication of the input and front layshaft bearings.

Automatic gearboxes

The Borg Warner automatic gearboxes have a four-digit type identifier prefix, while the GM gearboxes have a two-letter prefix. In each case, this is followed by a serial number. The prefix codes were as follows:

021G	Borg Warner 65, for 3500
036T	Borg Warner 65, for 2300 and 2600
053G	Borg Warner 65, for Police-specification 3500
059M	Borg Warner 65, for 2600
061R	Borg Warner 65, for 3500
068E	Borg Warner 66, for 3500
070H	Borg Warner 66, for Police-specification 3500
079D	Borg Warner 66, for 2000
081G	Borg Warner 66, for 2300 and 2600
082D	Borg Warner 66, for Police-specification 2600

PG	GM 180, for Australian-specification 3500
PK	GM 180, for 2600
PL	GM 180, for 2300
TH	GM 180, for 3500
TK	GM 180, for 2600
TL	GM 180, for 2300
TM	GM 180, for 2000
TT	GM 180, for Vitesse and Vanden Plas EFi

Reconditioned automatic gearboxes initially had a number prefixed by AT or ATS. From 1979, a new serial numbering system was introduced. The number was stamped into the flange at the rear of the main case, using the following system:

V	Identifying prefix (RTC 144R) U = AEU 1142R
9	Year of manufacture (1979)
06	Month of manufacture (June)
001	Unit number

Axle Number

Rear axles are identified by a two-letter type prefix that is followed by a serial number. The prefixes are as follows:

RH	2.85:1 final drive, for Vanden Plas EFi and Vitesse automatic
RL	3.45:1 final drive, for 2000 manual, 2300 manual, 2300 automatic and 2600 automatic
RM	3.08:1 final drive, for 2600 automatic, 3500 manual and 3500 automatic
RP	3.08:1 final drive, for Police-specification 2600 manual
RS	3.45:1 final drive, for 3500 manual and 3500 automatic, and Police-specification 2600 automatic
RT	3.90:1, for 2000 manual
RY	3.90:1, for 2400SD

APPENDIX II

PRODUCTION FIGURES

These figures were provided by the British Motor Industry Heritage Trust in the 1990s on the basis of the records then available. They should not be treated as definitive, although they remained the best figures available at the time of writing.

	2000	*2300 and 2300S*	*2400SD Turbo*	*2600 (all models)*	*3500 (carb and injection)*	*V8-S*	*Vitesse*	*Vanden Plas EFi*	*CKD (all types)*	*Total*
1976					8,654				84	8,738
1977		1		2,611	23,797				128	26,537
1978		6,184		23,977	24,194				107	54,462
1979		5,498		20,994	18,565	1,040			502	46,599
1980		5,896		12,797	6,521				405	25,619
1981	1,050	6,753	25	15,803	8,393				3,861	35,885
1982	7,887	5,582	4,192	8,611	5,283		202		1,128	32,885
1983	5,881	5,453	3,770	10,448	5,937		1,437		529	33,455
1984	2,909	3,293	1,836	7,035	3,354		1,098	422	432	20,379
1985	2,827	3,037	258	5,216	3,139		748	691	N/A	15,916
1986		1,299		1,080	79		412		N/A	2,870
Total	**20,554**	**42,996**	**10,081**	**108,572**	**107,916**	**1,040**	**3,897**	**1,113**	**7,176**	**303,345**

Note that the 1976 total includes 93 cars built in 1975.

Production of V8-S models continued into 1980 but it is not currently possible to break the figures down by calendar year; the 1980 total is therefore included in 3500 figures for that year.

The 1985 and 1986 figures for CKD production are not available. They would presumably inflate the overall totals for each of those two years.

Of the 3,897 Vitesse models, just 363 had automatic gearboxes.

A small number of bodyshells were built up into competition cars (see Chapter 9) and these shells are not included in the totals for production cars shown above.

INDEX